STOP DRIFTING,
START
ROWING

ALSO BY ROZ SAVAGE

ROWING THE ATLANTIC:
Lessons Learned on the Open Ocean

Please visit:

Hay House USA: www.hayhouse.com®
Hay House Australia: www.hayhouse.com.au
Hay House UK: www.hayhouse.co.uk
Hay House South Africa: www.hayhouse.co.za
Hay House India: www.hayhouse.co.in

STOP DRIFTING,

START ROWING

One Woman's Search for
Happiness and Meaning
Alone on the Pacific

Roz Savage

HAY HOUSE, INC.
Carlsbad, California • New York City
London • Sydney • Johannesburg
Vancouver • Hong Kong • New Delhi

Published and distributed in the United States by: Hay House, Inc.: www.hayhouse .com® • *Published and distributed in Australia by:* Hay House Australia Pty. Ltd.: www .hayhouse.com.au • *Published and distributed in the United Kingdom by:* Hay House UK, Ltd.: www.hayhouse.co.uk • *Published and distributed in the Republic of South Africa by:* Hay House SA (Pty), Ltd.: www.hayhouse.co.za • *Distributed in Canada by:* Raincoast: www.raincoast.com • *Published in India by:* Hay House Publishers India: www.hayhouse.co.in

Cover design: Amy Rose Grigoriou • *Interior design:* Pamela Homan

Library of Congress Cataloging-in-Publication Data

Savage, Roz.
  Stop drifting, start rowing : one woman's search for happiness and meaning alone on the Pacific / Roz Savage.
    pages cm.
  ISBN 978-1-4019-4262-5 (pbk.)
  1. Savage, Roz--Travel. 2. Rowers--United States--Biography. 3. Women rowers--United States--Biography. 4. Rowing--Pacific Ocean. I. Title.
  GV790.92.S263 A3 2013
  797.12'3--dc23
  [B]
                          2013026755

Tradepaper ISBN: 978-1-4019-4262-5

16 15 14 13   4 3 2 1
1st edition, October 2013

Printed in the United States of America

"It is easier to sail many thousands of miles through cold and storms and savage cannibals . . . than it is to explore the private sea, the Atlantic and Pacific ocean of one's being alone."

— HENRY DAVID THOREAU

CONTENTS

INTRODUCTION
Dream Big, Change Your Life

"Perhaps it is better to wake up after all, even to suffer, rather than to remain a dupe to illusions all one's life."

— KATE CHOPIN, THE AWAKENING

If you rotate a globe until your view centres on Hawai'i, you will see a mostly blue view of our planet, a vast expanse of ocean barely besmirched by land. There is just a sliver of California visible in the top right corner, a glimpse of Australia in the bottom left, and a smattering of islands and atolls strewn like grain flung by a celestial farmer. The Pacific covers 65 million square miles, about a third of the world's surface. In places the water is nearly six miles deep, although mostly it's only about two miles deep. Not that it really matters to me. As soon as it's more than 5'4" deep, I'm out of my depth.

From 2007 to 2010, this water world was my home, as I inched my way, oar stroke by oar stroke, from California to Papua New Guinea to become officially the first woman to row solo across the Pacific. My stated goal was to use my adventure to wage a campaign of awareness and action on the most important environmental issues facing our world today, communicating my message through blog posts and podcasts from the ocean, and through speaking and writing once I was back on dry land.

Yet just a few years earlier, nothing could have been further from my mind than fighting the good green fight from the deck of a 23-foot rowboat. Crank the clock back to the year 2000, and you would find me age 32 and living in London, supposedly happy. I had a well-paid job, a big house, a successful husband, foreign holidays, and a little red sports car. In other words, I had the classic materialistic Western lifestyle.

My childhood had been austere as the elder daughter of two low-paid Methodist preachers. My father's quarterly stipend did not allow luxuries, so my mother grew fruit and vegetables to stretch her house-keeping allowance and made clothes for my sister and me with her sewing machine and knitting needles. As a teenager I had grown restless with this spartan lifestyle, and I yearned for a time when I would have money to spend, designer clothes to wear, and a big house to live in. After 11 years of chasing that dream in the City of London, I'd acquired everything that I had thought would make me happy.

But there was something wrong. The truth was that, despite all these material blessings, I wasn't happy—not happy at all. There was a persistent and ever-increasing feeling that there was a mismatch between the person I was and the person I was pretending to be. The tension between the two selves was becoming unbearable.

What brought it home to me was a self-help exercise I did one day. I sat down at the dining-room table and wrote two versions of my own obituary—the one I wanted, and the one I was heading for if I carried on as I was. They were very different, and I saw that I was moving in completely the wrong direction if I was going to be able to look back and be proud of my time on Earth. I realized then that I needed to make a major course correction if I was ever to find happiness and meaning in my life.

That exercise was the first, irrevocable step on a path that would take me away from all I had held dear—my husband, my house, and my sense of security. I would also have to let go of all the things that were cluttering my mind—the possessions that had come to own me instead of the other way round, the preoccupation with what other people thought of me rather than what I thought of myself, and the voices in my head that questioned whether I dared to be different.

This may sound like a painful process, but at each point of the transformation I was moved to undertake, something would happen to indicate to me that I was on the right track. What might have looked like sacrifices actually felt like liberations.

LEAVING MY HUSBAND WAS THE FIRST, and most difficult, part of the journey. I had married for love and for life, and even though the 11-year relationship was faltering, it took a long, hard struggle with my conscience before I reluctantly acknowledged that only one course of action felt right. In my heart I knew that for as long as I was with him, I could not truly flourish. I needed to escape my gilded cage to find out what lay outside—but that prospect terrified me.

Confused and indecisive, I took an old school friend into my confidence. I agonized over whether I should really leave him as my friend and I sat sipping wine at her house. She asked me repeatedly, "What do you *want?*" It was at once the simplest and the most difficult question I'd ever been asked. I had grown up to think in terms of what I *should* do, or what was expected, not what I wanted. I simply did not know the answer—or maybe did not want to admit that I knew, because that would require me to act on it.

While debating my options yet again with my ever-patient friend, I confided that I was afraid to be alone, particularly as I got older. What she said next changed my life.

She told me, "I can imagine you, me, and Steph [another old friend] sitting around the kitchen table when we're 60 years old, eating ice cream out of the tub and putting the world to rights."

With that one image she made me realize that there are many forms of companionship, that mutual support does not exist only in the context of a marriage, and that I no longer needed to fear being a single woman. I realized that what I actually wanted was to start over, to free myself from my existing boundaries to find out who I really was and what would make me happy—not what would make my parents or my friends or my husband happy, but *me.*

After long and tear-filled discussions, in 2002 my husband and I agreed that we had arrived at a parting of the ways, and I moved out. I didn't take much with me, and even those few possessions I soon sold. I had put my things into storage, and one day when I was there to retrieve something, I looked around the unit and realized that this stuff was no longer important to me. Outside the context of a home, these superfluous clothes, ornamental knick-knacks, and even my beloved books had become a hindrance.

I loaded up my camper van to the roof with these relics of my previous life, and drove to a car-boot sale (a kind of yard sale, where people show up and sell all manner of things out of the back of their cars). As I was parking, even before I opened the sliding door at the back of the van, people were pushing and elbowing, waiting to see what riches might lie within.

In all honesty, there was nothing of real value at all, but I rapidly discovered that one person's junk is another person's treasure, and that if you are willing to sell it cheaply enough, you can get rid of just about anything. A few hours later I had nothing left but a few books and garments that I donated to charity. I hadn't sold my things for financial gain—I only made a meagre £200 (about $300) for a vanload of stuff—but I felt so much lighter and freer without all the baggage.

I had let go of a lot—emotional attachments, material possessions, and most important, my fear of the unknown. I had launched myself into the abyss without looking before I leaped, and I found that rather than being a void, it was in fact a fascinating place, chock-full of potential.

I spent several months simply enjoying my newfound freedom. By not being too fussy about where I lived, I was able to keep my financial overheads to a minimum. I earned a trickle of money from photography and selling my home-baked cakes at a farmers' market, and this was enough to keep me afloat while I read books, met people, relished serendipitous conversations, and wrote in my journal. I was surfing on a wave of discovery, and every day I found new ways to be joyful.

But once again I became restless. Since my liberation, I had learned many new things about life and how to live it, but now I needed a purpose. I am a goal-driven person, and once my driving motivation was no longer to make money and acquire possessions, I needed some other objective to take its place. I had learned a lot about how to be happy, but I needed more. I needed meaning.

I tried to identify the root cause of this imperative to find some reason for my existence. I considered the possibility that it might be because both my parents had a vocation to preach the Christian gospel, so maybe I'd internalized at an early age the importance of having a purpose in life. But my hunch is that we all, deep down, desire meaning in our lives, irrespective of our parents or our circumstances. We don't want to accept that our time on this planet is ephemeral and pointless. We cringe away from Thomas Hobbes's dictum that life is solitary, poor, nasty, brutish, and short. We want to find intimacy, beauty, harmony, and inner peace, and to impart an enduring legacy, leaving this world a better place than we found it. This instinct may be buried deeper in some than in others, but I believe that it exists in all human beings if we search deeply enough. Whether or not life has objective meaning, subjectively we want to make it so.

I had figured out this much when I had my environmental epiphany.

I SHOULD FIRST OF ALL EXPLAIN MY PREVIOUS ATTITUDE towards the environment. As a child, I had some awareness that humankind was treading heavily upon the Earth, although of course I would not have phrased it in such precocious terms. Given their religious inclination, my parents saw nature as an expression of God's goodness, and they had instilled in me an appreciation of the natural world. My father was fascinated by the stars and planets, and devoured books on astronomy and physics. My mother's focus was rather more down-to-earth, in every sense. She took my younger sister and me on long walks and bicycle rides in the countryside, and taught us the names of birds, trees, and wildflowers. We were also taught never ever to drop litter. My parents would tut disapprovingly if we saw someone dropping a wrapper in the street, or came across a mess of fast-food containers and empty soda bottles littering the pavement. It was important to look after our environment, in the very local and immediate sense of the word, and they impressed upon me and my sister that to do otherwise was a crime most heinous.

Yet my sense of connection to nature seemed to come from somewhere deeper than my parents' obsession with litter. I can clearly recall as a child looking out from the back window of our boxy white 1966 Triumph 1200, admiring the neat patchwork of fields checkering the English countryside, and despising the incursion of the hideous electricity pylons that marched relentlessly across the landscape like enormous invaders from a hostile alien army. To my young mind, it just didn't seem right. We humans seemed to be making the world an uglier place, not a better one.

When I left home to go to university in 1986 and then to work in London in 1989, I lost touch with that appreciation of nature, which came to seem childish. I began worshipping at the altar of the new god called money. The other one, the God of my parents, became largely irrelevant to my fast-paced city lifestyle. My world was all about the pursuit of material possessions. Having lived in grimly functional church manses for my first 18 years, I now became an arch-materialist, the kind of woman who would rip out a perfectly adequate kitchen in order to install the latest fashionable units. I never even thought about where stuff went when I threw it "away." Household waste went into a black plastic sack, and the binmen took it. Building debris went into a skip, and that, too, went away. Rubbish disappeared from sight, never to be seen or thought of again. It vanished, conveniently and completely.

But that blinkered view of the world was about to change. I had taken advantage of a friend's offer to stay in her family's cottage in a hamlet outside Sligo on the west coast of Ireland. It was February 2004 when I arrived at the small, pebble-dashed cottage, and the day was cold and blustery. A wrought-iron gate bisected a low, whitewashed front wall, its balustrades the only ornamental flourish in an otherwise starkly plain façade. Three or four shrubs, wintry and leafless, dotted the lawn of the front garden. A narrow concrete path ran straight from the gate to the grey front door. Two small, square windows at the front of the house peered out like eyes from beneath the overhanging eaves of the tiled roof. A couple of irregularly placed chimneys marred the symmetry.

I stepped through the front door and into a time warp, straight back to the 1950s. The furniture in the living room was simple—a dining table with a patterned plastic tablecloth, four dining chairs, a long low sofa, three uncomfortable-looking chairs with wooden arms, and a sideboard with sliding frosted-glass doors, behind which I could see the hazy outlines of stacks of plates and bowls. An electric eternal flame flickered under the sacred heart decoration on the high mantelpiece above the stove, which also bore a small collection of ornaments arranged symmetrically: two artificial roses in crystal vases, two brass candlesticks, and two ceramic pots shaped like hens sitting on wicker baskets. The decor was basic and unpretentious. It was perfect for my purposes.

I was there for a self-imposed retreat. I intended to pay penance for the excesses of the Christmas season by eating simply and abstaining from alcohol and caffeine. My rucksack, presently sitting in the small hallway beneath the coat pegs, was half full of books, mostly lent to me by friends, on philosophy, spirituality, and religion. I planned to meditate, enjoy long walks, and take time to be with myself and see what ideas might emerge. Over the course of the coming month I did indeed lose weight, regain my fitness, improve my focus during meditation, and read prodigiously.

As it turned out, the fairly random selection of books in my rucksack would combine to change my life. Amongst them was *Ishmael*, by Daniel Quinn, which uses the literary device of a telepathic gorilla to describe humanity's behaviour from the perspective of an intelligent but nonhuman onlooker. It questions the wisdom of our shortsighted determination to eradicate our natural competitors for food, to the detriment of the planet and, ultimately, of ourselves.

I went on to read *Conversations with God*, by Neale Donald Walsch, which gave me permission to put behind me the modest, self-effacing spirituality of my parents and dare to be, as he put it, "the grandest version of the greatest vision you ever had of yourself," not as an act of selfishness, but as a duty and an obligation to contribute to the collective evolution of humankind.

It was into the fertile ground prepared by these books that the seed of *The Hopi Survival Kit* was sown. It described the prophecies of the Hopi tribe and their belief that these are now coming true. The predictions consist of a sequence of signs that the end of a civilization is approaching, and a new era is coming. The first sign is a "gourd of ashes" falling from the sky. The Hopi interpreted this occurring when the atom bomb fell on Hiroshima. Since then, they have regularly sent a delegation to the United Nations to issue an urgent call to action.

According to their philosophy, we have to look after the Earth if we want it to look after us. If we lose touch with our spirituality and forget that we are dependent on the planet for our survival, things are not going to go well. The people who will survive are those who know where to find their own food and water.

When I read this, it hit me between the eyes with all the force of a fundamental truth. On a finite Earth, it stood to reason that we can't continue to pull out all the good stuff—oil, coal, and minerals—and turn it into junk that we then throw into landfills. One day we would surely run out, of both the good stuff and the places to dump the debris when we've finished. This pattern of behaviour was clearly not sustainable.

Now that I was seeing the world holistically for the first time, I was horrified by how oblivious I had been. I'd never even considered these questions before, so preoccupied had I been with the pursuit of possessions. I'd never stopped to think about my home in the broader sense—the planet on which we live and the other inhabitants with whom we have to share it. What terrible damage had I already inflicted in my thoughtlessness, heedless of the consequences of my self-centred actions?

Not only had I been ignorant, but most of my peers also seemed to be completely unaware of our headlong rush towards self-destruction. I felt a powerful need to bring this to people's attention as a matter of the utmost urgency. With every passing year we were trashing the Earth still further.

I'd been looking for a life purpose, and I had found it. I was full of bumptious enthusiasm, overflowing with the zeal of the convert, and eager to do all I could to save the world. I had become a woman with a mission—but why would anybody listen to me? I was just a recovering management consultant. I needed a platform, a pulpit from which I could proclaim my message.

ABOUT FOUR MONTHS LATER, THE IDEA to row across oceans hit me in a blinding flash of inspiration, and I knew that I had found the perfect métier for my message. It would be unusual enough to catch people's eye and to provide fodder for public presentations, media interviews, films, and books, allowing me to spread the awareness. My voyages themselves would be environmentally low-impact, the boat powered only by my body, the electronics by solar panels.

It was an outrageously audacious plan, my relevant experience consisting of several years rowing on the River Thames, usually in a crew of eight. But when I started to wonder, *What if I'm actually going to do this?* and began to compile a grand to-do list of all the things I would need to read, learn, finance, buy, and otherwise do to prepare for an ocean row, it started to seem frighteningly achievable. I had broken the list down into such small steps that there was nothing on it that was too far outside my existing abilities. It felt as if everything that had happened so far in my life had been leading me to this point, preparing me for this task, and that I was uniquely equipped to pursue this quest. It was a perfect collision of personality, past experience, purpose, and timing.

So, with little going for me other than unstoppable eagerness, a sense of total commitment, and a stubborn refusal to give up on what felt like a divinely ordained scheme, I cast myself upon the waters of the world's oceans.

IN THE 8 YEARS AND 15,000 MILES that have now passed since I first dipped my oars in the turbulent waters of my first ocean, I have spent more than 500 days alone at sea, as I crossed the Atlantic (2005, described in my book *Rowing the Atlantic*), Pacific (2007–2010), and Indian (2011) Oceans. And yet I don't think I will ever feel truly at home on the ocean. It will always test me. I love it, fear it, hate it, respect it, resent it, cherish it, and frequently curse it. It brings out the best in me—and sometimes the worst.

Despite my uneasy relationship with the wet parts of our planet, I cannot think of any other activity that would have met my objectives so perfectly as ocean rowing. Besides my environmental mission, I wanted to find out who I am, what I'm capable of, and what life is all about. It was my quest for happiness that first got me out of the office and onto the water, and although happiness is an emotion in scarce supply while I'm at sea—my feelings usually ranging from resigned acceptance of my self-imposed travails, through low-grade stress, to moments of sheer terror—the resilience and life skills that the ocean has engendered in me have enhanced my existence on land beyond all measure. To embrace a cause, to feel passionate about what I do, to believe I am making a difference and leaving a legacy, to be part of a mission so much bigger than one small woman sitting in a rowboat—all these things have brought me enormous fulfillment. Truly, the sense of achievement is proportionate to the scale of the attempt, so to take on a challenge the size of the world and to patiently chip away at it, one oar stroke at a time, has been a tremendously rewarding experience.

The ocean has been a harsh but effective teacher. She has taught me the value of simplicity—without all the distracting noise of life on land, I've found myself clear and focused on the things that really matter. She has reminded me that we humans are not separate from the environment, but are completely interconnected with it, and any notions we may have that we're above or beyond nature are dangerous delusions. And she has shown me how an ordinary human being can achieve the extraordinary, by presenting me with challenge after challenge, pushing me to what I thought were my limits, only for me to find out that when I have no choice, I can go beyond those boundaries and achieve more than I would ever have dreamed possible.

I hope that the story of my Pacific voyages will leave you feeling inspired and invigorated, eager to face the future with courage and positivity. I wish you enjoyment of this book, and of the rest of your glorious, unique, important journey. You have one life. Live it.

Roz Savage
London, England
June 2013

CHAPTER ONE

FACING AND EMBRACING FAILURE

"Success is not final, failure is not fatal: it is the courage to continue that counts."

— WINSTON CHURCHILL

The ordeal began on 21 August 2007. My boat capsized twice that night. The first time, the *Brocade* rolled right over until she was upside down in the water. I landed sprawled across the cabin roof, while all around me in the darkness I could hear belongings escaping from their straps and sliding around the curved walls like clothes being tumbled in a dryer. The tiny sleeping cabin was only about three feet high, so I hadn't fallen far from floor to ceiling, but the shock of the capsize and collisions with solid objects battered me emotionally and physically.

For several seconds the *Brocade* remained inverted. I held my breath, willing her to turn the right way up again. She was designed to self-right, the air trapped in the two cabins fore and aft making her unstable in the upside-down position. Having already crossed the Atlantic in this same boat, I had faith that she would turn, but she was taking her sweet time about it. At last she slowly started to roll back to an upright position, and my belongings and I returned to the floor in a jumbled mess.

I pushed aside the bags of food, clothes, electronics, and instruction manuals, and wriggled reluctantly out of my warm sleeping bag to check the status on the darkened deck. As I opened the hatch, I was hit by a cruel blast of wind and cold, salty, sea spray. I clipped a neoprene waist strap around my middle and secured its carabiner onto a D-ring bolted firmly to the boat so that if another destructive wave came along, I wouldn't be swept away.

Things didn't look too bad out here, considering that the boat had just rolled a full 360 degrees. Spending 103 days at sea on the stormy Atlantic had trained me to keep everything securely attached to the vessel or else expect to lose it overboard. I quickly unfastened the cockpit bags from their fixings and threw them into a locker in case a second capsize might prove too much for them, and hastily slammed the hatch cover back in place. A wave crashed over the side of the boat, drenching me in cold seawater. I swore.

Soaked, I returned to the cabin and, turning on the light, restored some order. Once everything was as shipshape as possible under the circumstances, I wriggled back into my sleeping bag and tried to get warm again. The bag was designed specifically for ocean usage, comprising two inner bags of thick, woolly fleece inside a waterproof outer shell. It retained the last vestiges of my body heat, but it took a long while before the fleece wicked away the dampness from my skin and my hands and feet lost their chill. I strapped myself to the bunk using two seat belts secured to the cabin floor, fastening them across my chest and thighs so that I would not end up on the ceiling if the boat should flip again.

I didn't feel particularly afraid as I lay there in the darkened cabin, despite the violent pitching and rolling. For the first two weeks of my maiden voyage, nearly two years previously, I had been petrified. The carbon-fibre hull had amplified the noise of the Atlantic waves so that they sounded terrifyingly huge. I had lain awake night after night, quaking in my cabin, convinced that the boat was going to be smashed in two, or at the very least have her rudder torn off. I'd listen to the pounding and thumping of the waves, berating myself for having taken on such a foolhardy challenge and wondering if I would even live to see the morning, let alone the other side of the ocean.

But after enduring two weeks of terror on that voyage, I eventually grew tired of being scared. My boat had withstood the tempestuous conditions thus far, and so I reasoned—fallaciously, but it cheered me to believe it—that she would continue to hold together. I, too, had withstood a fortnight at the mercy of the ocean, so maybe I would continue to hold together as well. I quickly adapted to my new circumstances, and the fear ebbed away. Now, on the Pacific, I quickly tapped back into the strange serenity that comes from being able to greet fear as an old friend.

Two hours later, the second capsize came. As my body weight met the resistance of the restraints, the belts held for only a moment before they ripped their bolts out of the cabin floor and once again I found myself on the ceiling. I waited for a long moment before gravity asserted itself and the *Brocade* laboriously rolled right side up.

This time when I crawled out on deck, the beam of my head torch picked out the bundled-up sea anchor escaping from its ties. *Ah, the sea anchor—that will help.* I got the nylon fabric back under control, and deployed the anchor—a 12-foot parachute on a 250-foot rope—over the side of the boat and beneath the waves. As the red-and-yellow dome filled with water, its rope pulled on a ring on the bow of the boat, pulling the bow around until it pointed into the wind and waves. Now, instead of sideswiping the *Brocade*, the waves pushed past her sides so that she pitched forward and back rather than rolling side to side. *This should reduce the risk of capsize.*

Satisfied that I had done all I could to ensure my safety, I returned to my bunk. It was the least dangerous place to be. At least I couldn't be swept overboard while I was inside the enclosed capsule of my cabin. Although I felt relatively safe, the hectic pitching of the boat and the crashing of the waves made for a poor night's rest, and I slept little, alternating between disturbed dreams and unhappy wakefulness.

The next day was rough, but nothing worse than I had seen on the Atlantic. I spent most of the day in the cabin, trying to stay as warm and dry as I could while the waves raged around the *Brocade*. Both hatches, fore and aft, had leaked slightly while they were submerged, so everything was damp, making it difficult to stay warm. The only times I emerged from my cocoon were to answer the call of nature, cursing the necessity and wishing that I were a man and able to relieve myself into a convenient vessel without having to go outdoors. The traditional sailors' description for the most basic of sanitary facilities is "bucket and chuck it," but in fact I use a bedpan, finding it less precarious than trying to hover over a bucket. As I squatted, however, the waves drenched me, so despite my best efforts I invariably brought a trail of saltwater back inside.

Between trips to the deck I hunkered indoors, gazing out of the round hatch and watching the waves foaming and frothing against the clear Perspex. It was mesmerising, like watching the laundry inside a front-loading washing machine, except that I was inside the machine and the foaming water was on the outside.

I had little choice but to bide my time. I knew that the storm would pass—eventually—and that in the meantime, I just had to stay safe and sane. I imagined how my boat must look from the outside, a seemingly fragile little silver craft being buffeted this way and that, pounded by the foaming waves, a tiny speck on an angry sea. When I'd seen her being hoisted out of the water at the end of the Atlantic crossing, I had cried with emotion. She had looked so small. She was a big boat to row, but a tiny boat in which to cross an ocean.

At intervals throughout the day, I spoke via satellite phone to my weatherman, Rick, in Hawai'i, an experienced yachtsman and former U.S. Navy meteorologist and oceanographer. He had been recommended to me by one of the world's foremost forecasters, Stan Honey. I had not yet met Rick in person, our communication having been conducted by telephone and e-mail only. Now Rick told me that at least another 60 hours of rough conditions were forecast, with gale-force winds and seas of 8 to 11 feet. That may not sound like much, but to a 23-foot boat, an 11-foot wave is plenty big enough. Another 60 hours of this sounded like a long time, but I was determined that I could tough it out.

The second night of the gale arrived. Around 10 P.M., a powerful wave rear-ended the *Brocade*. I shot down my bunk, my sleeping bag tobogganing over the slippery vinyl of the mattress. I came to an abrupt halt when my skull collided with the wall at the end of the cabin.

Ouch.

I sat up, and felt blood trickling across my scalp. I explored the damage with my fingers. It didn't seem too bad. I dabbed the blood away with a flannel and lay back down on the bunk to try and sleep, but every time I heard another big wave coming, my arms automatically shot out to brace myself against the cabin walls so that I wouldn't be flung across the cabin. Sleep was impossible.

A little later the boat capsized again, the third time in 24 hours. My head cracked against the cabin ceiling, and again I felt the trickle of blood.

Something was amiss. Since I'd put the sea anchor out, the *Brocade* should be pointing into the waves and therefore be much more stable, the waves running along the sides of the boat rather than catching her beam-on. Unappealing though the prospect was, I knew I'd better go outside to investigate. I pulled on a waterproof jacket and a head torch, mustered my courage, and exited the cabin to the watery cauldron of the deck. The boat rocked violently from side to side, and I crouched low and hung on firmly to the guardrails as I staggered to the front of the boat, the beam of the head torch casting a circle of cold, white light onto the seething surf.

Sitting backwards on the rowing seat, I pulled on the main line to the sea anchor. There was a suspicious lack of resistance as I drew it in. After a couple of seconds, I reached the rope's frayed end. It had broken just six feet from the point where it attached to the boat. I turned my attention to the trip line, a second line to the sea anchor that assists in retrieval by collapsing the chute, dumping the water out of it and making it easier to draw it back in. But that, too, came to a premature end, at the first of its two flotation buoys. My sea anchor had escaped its lines and gone to a watery grave.

This was bad news. Now I had no defence against further capsizes. I deployed a pair of drogues, mini versions of the sea anchor, but they were too small to make any difference. There wasn't anything I could do other than retreat to the safety of the cabin, where I lay in my bunk, feeling vulnerable and alone. I was in an increasingly unseaworthy boat, about 80 miles from shore on a dark, dangerous ocean, with another two and a half days of storms and high seas ahead of me. This was not the ideal start to my voyage.

I HAD SET OUT NINE DAYS EARLIER, on a foggy but bright Sunday morning, from the small town of Crescent City in Northern California. Aiming to become the first woman to row solo across the Pacific Ocean, I had hoped to launch my 8,000-mile quest from the iconic Golden Gate Bridge in San Francisco. But on that part of the California coast, the prevailing winds blow onshore, and although I waited for many weeks for a letup in the strong sea breezes, Rick could find no window of opportunity long enough for me to make a clean getaway from the coast. If I left it too late in the year to depart, I faced the risk of running into winter gales in the latter stages of my journey as I neared Hawai'i. Eventually, Rick suggested that I could leave from the Golden Gate Bridge, or I could leave in 2007, but I couldn't do both. He advised me to head north to the calmer conditions near the border between California and Oregon.

So I had hitched the boat trailer to the tow bar of my little yellow pickup truck and driven eight hours north to Crescent City. With me was my title sponsor's public-relations agent, Nicole Bilodeau. A lively brunette in her late 20s, Nicole had been working closely with me during the media blitz in the run-up to my row as she supervised photo shoots, arranged interviews, and wrote press releases, and we had become good friends. When I stated my intention to head north to Crescent City, Nicole offered to come along to see me off, on her own time and at her own expense, and then drive my truck and empty boat trailer back to San Francisco afterwards. I had gratefully accepted.

My boat was named after my title sponsors, Brocade, a Silicon Valley company specializing in data and storage networking products. I had met their CEO at the time, Mike Klayko, when I was exhibiting my boat (formerly known as *Sedna*, named after the Inuit goddess of the ocean) at a special one-day event for schools at the Tech Museum of Innovation in San Jose. Mike had listened with interest to my story and invited me to submit a sponsorship proposal, which I did with alacrity. This kind of request does not come along every day in the world of adventure sponsorship. Within days we had a deal, and I can honestly say that Brocade were an absolute pleasure to work with.

Nicole and I arrived in Crescent City a couple of days before my projected launch date and checked into the Light House Inn. A life-size fibreglass Blues Brother greeted us in the entrance, and other kitschy items adorned the reception area. As we explored the town that evening, we saw a plaque on the wall of the harbour master's office showing the 20-foot maximum height of the tsunami that had devastated the town in 1964—a reminder, as if I needed one, of the phenomenal power of the ocean.

The following day, Nicole backed the trailer down a ramp to launch the boat. Neither of us enjoyed trying to manoeuvre the thing in reverse, but on this occasion I had to be in the boat, ready to man the oars as the boat floated up off its trailer, so I had a cast-iron excuse for delegating to Nicole. Once afloat, I rowed around the corner and moored the *Brocade* to the fuel dock in readiness for the launch, which was scheduled first thing the next morning.

The following day I was awake early, roused by a mixture of anticipation and anxiety, both eager and reluctant to get started. Conditions were perfect: the air still, the water like a mirror. Nicole and I carried a few bags of fresh provisions down to the boat, the more durable rations such as snack bars and dehydrated meals having been stowed on board long before.

A small group of people had gathered on the dock to see me off, including a news crew from Eugene, Oregon. They had been none too keen to come, as it was a considerable drive from Eugene and they would have to set out around 3 A.M. to get there in time. But Nicole had coaxed and cajoled in her most winsome way until they had finally relented and agreed to come and report on my departure. We'd hoped for much more media coverage, and if I'd been leaving from San Francisco we would have had it, but Crescent City was an obscure outpost of humanity, far from big urban centres and media outlets.

There were a few other well-wishers. A father had brought his little girl, no more than a toddler, to present me with several bars of imported Lindt chocolate for my voyage. Several men from the local boatyard had come to see me off, too, but generally it was a low-key affair. Although more media attention would have been welcome, I decided that a quiet departure suited me just fine. Celebrations were for arrivals, not departures.

After a few words to the TV camera, I got into my boat and Nicole pushed against the oar to propel me away from the floating dock. I looked at my watch and noted the time to be recorded later in my logbook: 6:49 A.M., 12 August 2007. A smattering of applause accompanied the first few strokes of the several million that lay ahead.

The day was beautiful, and I was in a relaxed mood as I paddled out of the harbour. That didn't last for long. No sooner had I cleared the harbour wall than there was a gentle crunching sound, and my boat stopped dead. I swore. I had run aground. It was low tide, I knew that, but I'd had no idea that the water would be this shallow. Embarrassed, I scanned the harbour wall. I didn't see anybody. I gave a sigh of relief that apparently my humiliation had not been observed.

I tried to push the boat off the sandbank with the oars, but to no avail. Sighing with irritation this time, I took my feet out of the rowing shoes, rolled up my black leggings to my knees, and gingerly swung my legs over the side of the boat into the chilly water. It barely covered my ankles. I pushed the boat off the sandbank, clambered back on board, and quickly resumed rowing as if nothing had happened.

Unfortunately, you can always count on a photographer to be around when you least want them to be. The following day *The Daily Telegraph* in Britain published an article under the headline: "Roz Savage runs aground minutes into journey," with a photograph of me standing in the water, bending over slightly with my hands on my knees as I survey the situation. If it had been a caption competition, my facial expression suggested that anything I had to say at that moment would most likely be unprintable.

Afloat once more in golden morning sunlight, I rowed past the historic lighthouse at Battery Point, a pretty whitewashed cottage with a large maritime light sticking out of the middle of its red-tiled roof like a preposterously overgrown chimney. As I paddled out to the open Pacific, the mist thickened while the sun continued to shine, creating a glowing, ethereal haze. Small groups of sea lions swam alongside my boat, their heads popping up like periscopes from the waves to check me out. They were playful, rolling their black, water-sleek bodies around and over each other like roughhousing teenagers, bringing a smile to my face.

Rick had predicted a clear run for the first four or five days out from the coast, which we hoped would be long enough for me to put a safe distance between myself and the rocky shoreline before the prevailing westerly winds kicked back in. I quickly fell back into the routine of ocean rowing, which will be familiar to readers of my first book, *Rowing the Atlantic*. . . .

AFTER A NIGHT THAT MAY OR MAY NOT INVOLVE much sleeping, depending on how rough the sea is, I wake up as the first rays of daylight seep into my sleeping cabin. The space is about the size of a queen bed at its widest, tapering down to a little over a foot wide at the stern of the boat. I have just enough headroom to sit up at its highest point, which is also the widest, again tapering down towards the stern. The walls and ceiling form a continuous arch, so it's rather uncomfortable sitting against the wall of the cabin as the curve forces me to hunch over. Lying down is by far the most comfortable position on the boat, and it's one I adopt with great gratitude, my favourite moment being when the day's rowing is done, my blog has been updated, and my head hits the pillow for some well-earned rest and recuperation.

The bunk runs down the middle of the cabin, so my body weight doesn't tip the boat off balance, and on either side of the bed there is a lee cloth, a strip of canvas the same length as my bunk and about a foot wide, fixed to the cabin floor and suspended by cords from the ceiling. The purpose of the lee cloths is to stop me being tipped off the bunk if a big wave knocks the boat onto her side.

Depending on the temperature inside the cabin, I lie either in or on a sleeping bag, which in turn rests on a foam mattress, thin enough that I can fold it back to get to the storage lockers beneath. My luxury is a proper pillow, which usually goes mouldy while at sea, but is essential to any hope of sleep.

I lie in the bunk with my feet towards the stern and my head towards the entrance hatch that leads out to the rowing deck. This makes it easier for me to check my marine instruments during the night. They are mounted in a panel to one side of the entrance hatch.

My first thought on waking is always, *Where am I?* I want to know where the boat has drifted overnight. Unlike rowers, winds and currents don't sleep, so I never wake up in the same place where I stopped rowing the night before. I plan my route to work with the prevailing winds and currents, rather than fighting them, which means that about 90 percent of the time I will wake up a bit closer to where I want to be. Sometimes I wake up a lot closer—my best ever night has been 22 nautical miles to the good—but more often it's just a handful of miles, and sometimes I wake up farther away, which is not a good start to the day.

So my first act upon waking is to turn on the GPS to allow it to get a fix on the satellites while I'm extricating myself from my sleeping bag and grabbing a Lärabar (a whole-food bar made of nuts and dried fruit) for my breakfast. By the time I have my logbook and pencil at the ready, the GPS has identified my position. At this point it is my tradition to utter, "Hurrah," or "Boo," as appropriate.

Then I pop my head out of the hatch to take a look at my red ensign, the British maritime flag, which also makes a good weathervane, its direction and demeanour revealing the angle and strength of the wind. Making a mental note of my estimates, I close the hatch and note down in my logbook the wind speed and direction. Consulting various instruments, I add the amount of charge in my two solar-powered ship's batteries, the distance and bearing to my final destination, the number of hours I have spent sleeping and rowing since my last entry, and a one-line comment on how I feel about life at this particular moment. This varies from the poetic to the profane, depending on circumstances.

As I finish the last bite of my Lärabar, I pick up my iPod from where it has been charging overnight and roll it up with my sun hat, rowing gloves, and a few spare Lärabars. I pick up my seat pad and a clean(ish) cover made out of lightweight and superabsorbent fabric (actually a pack towel, intended for use on camping trips), wrapping the cover around the pad, fixing it with Velcro. Placing the sun hat and its contents on the seat pad, I push the bundle out onto the deck, with me following close behind, closing and securing the cabin hatch firmly behind me. As well as providing dry space for sleeping and storage, the two cabins also act as buoyancy chambers, the air trapped inside making the boat unstable when upside down so that eventually it returns to the upright position. Keeping the hatches closed at all times apart from the barest moments required to enter and exit a cabin is the first rule of ocean-rowboat safety.

I attach the seat pad to the rowing seat with two press studs. I release the oars from their overnight stowage position, still in the oarlocks but swiveled around so that the oars are flush with the sides of the boat, with the spoon ends each secured in a clip on either side of the sleeping cabin. I sit on the seat and pull on my sun hat and rowing gloves. I secure the iPod to a hook on the deck using a carabiner, put in the earbuds, and hit the play button on whatever audiobook I'm currently enjoying. Time to row.

I usually row four shifts a day, of two to three hours each, depending on motivation, energy levels, and conditions both present and forecast. Between shifts I update my logbook, eat, have a siesta if required, and do various chores around the boat. I try to keep these to a minimum, as I don't enjoy tinkering for its own sake. I'd rather be pushing on towards my destination. Daily tasks include tending to the pot of bean sprouts that supplement my onboard diet, retrieving more raw-food crackers or freeze-dried meals from their respective storage hatches and moving them to my designated galley locker, writing the daily blog post, phoning my mother, and occasionally scrubbing gooseneck barnacles off the bottom of the boat—by far my least favourite task. I don't enjoy having to work underneath the boat, as it makes me feel rather vulnerable, and it also makes me feel guilty to prise the barnacles off their happy home on the hull, sending them to certain death in the depths.

Around sunset I take my dinner break, boiling water on a Jetboil camping stove in order to rehydrate my freeze-dried dinner. I don't mix it in the bag, which would leave a residue that would quickly start to smell bad (I keep all trash on board until I reach port). Instead, I decant the freeze-dried rubble into my trusty thermos mug, wide mouthed with a screw-top lid, and add any extras that might make it more palatable, such as powdered coconut milk, herbs, spices, or other seasoning. This task is a lot easier said than done. Trying to transfer powdered foods from packet to mug in a brisk sea breeze is a messy business, and as often as not I end up with my skin liberally coated in various ingredients, which get stuck in the sweat and sun cream, but it's worth it to sit back and enjoy a well-earned meal while watching the sun set.

I row for a few more hours after dinner, and then bathe using a bucket, a sponge, and my favourite tea tree and mint shower gel, which makes my skin tingle with cool freshness. Finally, I retire to the cabin for the night.

DURING THOSE FIRST FEW DAYS OUT from Crescent City, I spent long hours at the oars, but there were some light headwinds that slowed my progress, sometimes to a paltry one knot or even less. I would usually expect to make at least two knots—still not exactly a phenomenal speed, but twice as fast as one knot nonetheless. (One knot is one nautical mile per hour.

A nautical mile is about 1.15 statute, or land, miles. This is equivalent to 1/60th of 1 degree of longitude at the equator, there being 360 degrees of longitude making up the circumference of the Earth.)

I kept plugging away, doing what I could to get as far from land as soon as possible, but it was like trying to run the wrong way up an escalator. After six days I had made some progress south, but was still only 20 nautical miles from land.

On the eighth day, the headwinds abated. The instruction from my weatherman was to "row like hell." I did. But on the ninth day I rowed not like hell, but into hell. My logbook entries for 21 August record the rising wind speed. At seven o'clock in the morning, it was a rower-friendly 15 knots. Two and a half hours later it was 23. Then 34, 39, 43, 47 . . .

Initially it was exhilarating. After the frustration of the headwinds, I was delighted to at last be heading in the right direction. I recorded a video of myself plying the oars, singing the theme tune from *Hawaii Five-O* as I surfed down the waves. It all seemed great fun, and I was in high spirits.

But as the wind speed rose beyond 40 knots, the exhilaration gave way to anxiety. The waves were now growing quite large, higher than forecast, and I clipped myself to the boat to avoid being swept overboard. Later, when the waves grew higher still, to around 20 feet, I retired to the sleeping cabin, which was by far the safest place to be. It was uncomfortable, noisy, and scary, but nothing too bad could happen to me while I was in there.

Conditions that night became worse. My last logbook entry of the voyage, on the morning of 22 August, records, "2 capsizes in night. GPS and wind monitor no longer working."

Despite these problems, it never crossed my mind to abandon the attempt. When American Tori Murden was attempting to become the first woman to row solo across the Atlantic, her boat capsized 11 times in one night. That was my benchmark, and the situation was far from being as serious as that. I was determined to keep going. I spent the morning of the 22nd inside the cabin, riding out the storm as best I could. I would just have to hold out until the storm abated, which Rick now told me would be within 24 hours. It would no doubt be a very long 24 hours, but on the Atlantic I had spent longer than that cooped up inside during periods of strong headwinds. I knew I could do it without succumbing to cabin fever. It wasn't hard to reconcile myself to prolonged spells indoors when I considered the alternative of spending time on a wave-drenched deck.

But that afternoon, control of the situation started to slip away from me. Unbeknownst to me, somebody had contacted the Coast Guard, thereby setting in motion a chain of events that rapidly acquired its own momentum.

A small plane appeared overhead. For a while I tried to ignore it, hoping it would go away. I told myself that it must be there for somebody else. The trouble was that there wasn't anybody else. Eventually I had to admit to myself that: (a) they were there, (b) they were there for me, and (c) they weren't going away.

Reluctantly, I picked up the VHF radio handset and established contact. A disembodied voice from the plane announced itself to be the U.S. Coast Guard (USCG). They told me that they'd received a report that I was in difficulty. I berated myself. In my last blog post, I had mentioned the capsizes, the knock to my head, and the loss of my sea anchor. It had never occurred to me that this might provoke a call to the authorities.

The voice on the radio went on to tell me that a 660-foot tanker, the *MV Overseas Long Beach*, was going to bring me a replacement for the missing sea anchor, and that a U.S. Coast Guard ship, the *Dorado*, was on its way. They also said that the USCG Control in Humboldt Bay wanted to talk with me immediately "to discuss the viability of your voyage." I felt like I was being called into the headmaster's office. Sulkily, I took my satellite phone from its waterproof case and turned it on. The marine radio worked only as far as line of sight, to ships or planes in my vicinity. To call the shore, I would need the more powerful technology of the satellite phone.

The station commander in Humboldt Bay interrogated me at length about my onboard safety equipment. I found it difficult to conceal my irritation. Before my departure I had repeatedly invited the Coast Guard in San Francisco to come and inspect the *Brocade*. After being referred from department to department and ultimately to the Coast Guard Auxiliary, I was informed that they did not inspect leisure craft (as they categorized the *Brocade*, with no apparent irony), and so my boat did not fall within their remit. I had tried as hard as I could to be proactive in getting their approval, but they had not seemed interested. I knew that my safety provisions were of the highest standard, and that this satellite phone call was a waste of expensive airtime.

In my mind, the voyage was still viable. I had my oars and my rowing seat, as far as I knew my watermaker was still working, and apart from a couple of minor knocks to the head I was fine—no symptoms of concussion or any other serious problems. After crossing the Atlantic with her, I trusted the seaworthiness of the *Brocade,* and I knew that the risk of death was extremely small provided that I stayed with her.

To be unambiguous about this, I have the utmost respect for the U.S. Coast Guard. Its members are brave people, putting their lives on the line to ensure the safety of all seafarers within their jurisdiction. They have to go out in the worst conditions, no doubt often to help people who with a little more foresight and preparation would not have got into trouble in the first place.

But I did not feel that I was that kind of person, nor was I in the kind of dire straits that warranted their intervention. My situation was not ideal, to be sure, but it was not life threatening. Furthermore, I'm not American, so I felt I had no right to call on the U.S. Coast Guard for help. For that very reason, I had taken out private insurance with a medical-evacuation company called Global Rescue that claimed to be able to rescue their clients from anywhere in the world. Given just how extremely remote I was likely to be, I hadn't wanted to take them at their word, so my team had spent a lot of time with them discussing my plans and devising a set of emergency procedures. We had a flowchart detailing who would do what in every potential scenario we could think of, from a minor communications failure to a full-on Mayday situation. Everyone in my team had a copy of it, and knew what their roles and responsibilities were. If I had wanted assistance, and if I had asked for it, our procedures would have swung into action.

But in my view, a couple of very minor cuts to the head did not constitute a medical emergency, and I hadn't even considered calling on Global Rescue.

However, somebody had deemed otherwise and had taken it upon him- or herself to call the Coast Guard. I was livid. I didn't know who it was, but I was outraged that somebody would have the arrogance, the *presumption*, to deem themselves a better judge than I of what was good for me. *How dare they?*

But whoever had done it, and however little I liked it, the Coast Guard was here, and they were determined that there would be no casualties on their watch. The best way they could be sure of that was to bring me in.

"Are you in distress?" they asked me. On the ocean, as I recalled from my VHF radio course, *distress* is a technical term, meaning that the crew of the boat perceive that they are "threatened by grave and imminent danger, and require immediate assistance." I'd had better days, I told them, but I was not "in distress" in the technical sense. I did not require assistance or rescue.

According to the Coast Guard, however, the weather was going to get even worse over the next 48 hours. I phoned Rick to double-check, and he reiterated his earlier prediction: that if I could just hang in there for another 24 hours, the conditions would ease and the waves subside. It was difficult to know whom to believe.

Over the next six hours the Coast Guard's calls became more persistent, increasing the pressure on me to accept rescue. We debated the issue backwards and forwards on the radio. They would push, and I would resist, in a verbal tug-of-war.

As the pressure grew, I became less and less certain of myself, and doubt over the viability of my voyage took root. I was concerned about the state of my boat. I had lost the use of a number of instruments, as well as my sea anchor. I was experimenting with an autopilot for the first time, having used a simple foot-steering mechanism on the Atlantic, but the device had taken a knock during one of the capsizes. The O-ring that formed a waterproof seal around the seam in its middle had slipped out of place, giving the black plastic case the appearance of having been disembowelled, the translucent white O-ring hanging out like a loop of intestine. Water would now be getting inside, and like most electronic devices, it would not take kindly to a soaking. But this was no big deal. It would be easy enough to switch to the backup plan: rudder strings that could be adjusted by hand and then secured through cleats on either side of the rowing position.

Marginally more serious was the problem that the GPS chartplotter had stopped working. Again, there was a backup plan—a second GPS in my emergency "grab bag"—but the unit was a small and basic model that didn't show nautical charts of the coastline. And again, it wasn't a big deal. Once I got away from the California coast there was nothing for me to bump into. All I needed was my latitude and longitude and that would be enough to get me to Hawai'i.

By far the most serious problem was the loss of the sea anchor. This was an important safety device in rough conditions, and could also help in mitigating backwards drift in a headwind. I wasn't wildly keen on the idea of continuing my voyage without a sea anchor. If I ran into big seas again later on, I would have no defence.

None of these issues in themselves would have been enough to make me abandon my attempt, but in combination they added up to a situation that was decidedly less than optimal. I sat in my cabin, swaying as the waves pummeled the boat, weighing up the pros and cons of the situation. As I did so, I became less certain about resisting rescue. One minute I would be marginally in favour of continuing despite the equipment losses and breakages, the next minute my mental seesaw would tip and I would be marginally in favour of returning to shore while I still had the opportunity to repair the boat. Sleep deprivation had interfered with my decision-making abilities, and I couldn't make up my mind.

In mid-afternoon, the arrival of the *MV Overseas Long Beach* temporarily interrupted my deliberations. The merchant vessel was answering the Coast Guard's summons to bring me a replacement sea anchor. The huge ship throttled back as she approached, wallowing in the heavy seas. I was amazed, and a little awed, to notice how even a ship of her size was affected by the conditions. Waves crashed around the enormous bows that loomed like cliffs from the water.

The captain brought his ship as close as he dared without swamping me, and hailed me on the radio.

"Thank you so much for coming to help," I said, somewhat insincerely. I didn't want help. I wanted everybody to go away and leave me alone. "But please make sure that you do not put your crew at risk. I repeat, do not put your crew at risk. I am not in distress. It would be helpful to have a sea anchor, but it is not important enough to risk anybody's safety for."

"I understand," he reassured me. "I will not put my crew at risk. We are going to try to shoot a line across to you, which we will then use to send over a sea anchor from one of our lifeboats. Do you have a boathook?"

"Yes, I have a boathook," I replied. Ever since I had needed to use a boathook to repair my oars when all four of them broke during the Atlantic crossing, I had vowed never to set to sea without one again. They're designed primarily to hook a mooring buoy in order to tie up a boat for the night, and are therefore theoretically useless in mid-ocean, but you never know when a long, telescopic pole might come in useful.

"Good, so we'll get the line as close to you as possible, and if it lands in the water, you might be able to use the boathook to reach it," the captain said.

"I'll certainly give it a try," I promised.

And try I did, but despite repeated attempts, they were unable to shoot the line within range of my boat. After each attempt they had to steer around in another huge circle in order to approach me again from upwind, as there was no point trying to shoot the line into the teeth of the gale. Each circuit took about half an hour. I stayed out on deck, getting progressively colder and wetter as the waves soaked me, waiting for them to come around to try yet again.

At last, on the seventh attempt, I managed to reach the line as it trailed in the water and hauled about 500 feet of thin orange line on board. This thin orange line was tied to a thicker line, which in turn was tied to a still thicker line. At last, when the entire deck of my boat was covered in a tangle of ropes, I reached the end, to which was attached a lifebelt, a buoy, and a small conical sea anchor made out of thick yellow canvas. It wasn't as large as the 12-foot parachute-shaped anchor I had lost, but maybe it would work. I wasn't sure why they had sent me the buoy and the lifebelt. Maybe they were just there for flotation. I pushed them into a corner of the deck.

It took about an hour for me to disentangle the lines, but eventually I was able to deploy the anchor off the bows of my boat. I watched anxiously to see if it would succeed in making the *Brocade* pivot around to lie with her bows into the waves. At first I thought it had worked—the boat turned through 90 degrees—but then she carried on turning until she had done a full 180, so I was still sideways to the waves, but facing the opposite way. Sideways was not where I wanted to be. This was where the boat was most liable to capsize.

My spirits plummeted, and I suddenly felt exhausted. I had barely slept for two nights, and I hadn't eaten much, my appetite affected by the nauseating movement of the boat. I'd spent hours on deck trying to get hold of this sea anchor, another hour sorting out the tangle of ropes, and ultimately it had made no difference whatsoever. The prospect of another dark night of capsizes loomed.

Just then the Coast Guard called back. "We need a decision, right now," they said. "We can't get a boat out to you—the *Dorado* had to turn back because the waves were too big."

This made me pause for thought. Too rough for a Coast Guard cutter? This really was quite a storm.

"You're drifting away from the coast," they went on, "so by tomorrow you'll be out of range of a helicopter rescue. It's about to get dark. If we're going to send out the helicopter for you, it needs to be now. The weather is going to deteriorate. We're very concerned about you." *Accept our help before it's too late*, was the subtext. *Just say yes.*

Just say no! screamed my heart. *Don't give up on your dream!*

I asked for five minutes to consider my options and hung up. I tried calling my weatherman, but got his voicemail. It looked like I was on my own. The choice would be mine, and mine alone.

It was one of the toughest decisions of my life. I had spent well over a year preparing for this voyage—raising money, renovating and improving the boat, training, reprovisioning. It wasn't easy to let all that hard work go to waste. I was ten days out from shore, and in the last 48 hours had actually been making impressive progress in the right direction. I believed I'd done the most difficult work—getting clear of the coast—and I didn't want to have to go back and do that part again. Like so many enterprises, the hardest part of an ocean row is the beginning—those early, nervous, vulnerable days when there is still the option to turn back. But as the saying goes, a job begun is a job half done, and since I had left harbour, got the first few miles over and done with, and settled into my routine, I was keen to maintain the forward momentum.

Additionally, it would be embarrassing to turn back. Thanks to Nicole's hard work there had been quite an avalanche of media coverage. For it all to end prematurely in failure would be humiliating.

And what of my self-respect as an adventurer? I prided myself on being fiercely independent, on not quitting when the going gets tough, and on not getting myself into situations that I wasn't willing to get myself out of. To accept rescue went against my stubborn grain.

But on the other hand, my safety was now compromised by the loss of my sea anchor, the load of broken electronics, and my cabin being a mess of uselessly dangling lee cloths and untethered seat belts. I still had at least two more months out on the ocean and wanted to be ready for whatever the weather might have in store for me. I was being offered an opportunity to restore my boat to a shipshape state before continuing. *Safety has to be paramount,* I reminded myself.

It went against my instincts, but accepting rescue seemed to be the sensible thing to do. *Argh*—I hated this feeling of caving in to the pressure.

I rang them back. "Okay, let's do it," I said. "Come and get me."

I hung up the VHF handset and burst into angry tears. I had long dreamed of this row ending with a triumphant arrival in Hawai'i—not an airlift into a Coast Guard helicopter.

It would be a half-hour wait before the helicopter arrived. So many times during those 30 minutes I reached out involuntarily towards the VHF handset. Was it too late to change my mind? Could I still call off the rescue?

But each time my hand fell back to my side. The die was cast. I pictured the helicopter on its way, lifting off from the Coast Guard base, tilting and turning towards the ocean, and speeding across the waves into the gathering twilight. I had made my decision, and now I would have to stand by it. When the time came, I would meekly obey their order to abandon ship. The prospect appalled me. This felt wrong, so wrong.

The radio crackled. It was the helicopter pilot. "Vessel Roz, vessel Roz, vessel Roz," he called. That was funny. They thought Roz was the name of my boat, not the rower. I almost smiled, desperate to find some humour in this awful situation.

I picked up the handset. "This is Roz."

"We are going to lower the swimmer into the water. When you see the swimmer is ready, you are going to jump into the water and swim over to him. Do you understand?"

"Yes," I said sounding calm enough, but inside I was thinking, *You've got to be kidding me! You expect me to jump out of my boat—my nice, safe boat—into 20-foot waves?* Suddenly staying on board seemed much more attractive than the alternative. But I had made my decision, and I had to follow through.

It suddenly occurred to me that I should take my laptop and mobile phone. I would need them to communicate with my team and my mother once I reached shore. And if I was to never see my boat again, I wasn't willing to leave them behind.

"Can I bring a bag with me?"

"No. You can't."

"It's a very small bag," I eyed the grey Pelican case that housed my MacBook. It wasn't exactly small. But it wasn't too big, either. It depended on what you were comparing it with, really.

"Okay then," the voice on the radio conceded.

"Just give me a couple of minutes," I said, and hung up before the voice could change its mind.

I wriggled awkwardly into my survival suit, a red, rubber-lined, all-in-one garment like an overgrown baby's romper. It had got damp during the Atlantic crossing, and despite my best attempts to dry it out, the rubber lining had started to rot. I hadn't expected to need it, though, so I hadn't replaced it. As I pulled it on over my shorts and T-shirt, the material clung clammily to my bare arms and legs. *Yuck.*

I swiftly looped a strap through the handle of the grey Pelican case that held my electronics and slung it diagonally around my body. Pushing it out on deck ahead of me, I groped my way along on all fours, staying low to avoid toppling or being swept overboard. I retrieved the *MV Long Beach* lifebelt from the corner of the deck where I had flung it earlier and put it around my middle. I didn't want the weight of the Pelican case dragging me down to the bottom of the ocean, and the lifebelt would keep me afloat.

Leaning back into the sleeping cabin, I picked up the radio. "I'm ready."

I watched as the hovering helicopter opened its door, and a small orange figure was lowered on a line into the water, like a spider abseiling down a strand of gossamer.

"Okay, *go!*" I heard the command from the radio inside the cabin.

I latched the cabin door behind me and, taking a deep breath, steeled myself for the plunge. Was there even the slightest chance I could still change my mind? No.

Go, go, GO!

I jumped.

Saltwater spray stung my eyes and the Pacific sucked at the legs of my survival suit as I half-swam, half-wallowed through the towering waves to the orange-suited Coast Guard swimmer. The helicopter's blades thumped deafeningly into the 50-mph winds overhead. The swimmer helped me into a harness and hitched me to the winch line. At his signal, the helicopter started to gain altitude and we rose from the water in tandem, much too intimately entwined for two people who had met only a moment before.

As we were hoisted aloft, I looked down at my trusty rowboat, labouring in the foaming swells. She had looked after me throughout 103 days of storms, struggles, and solitude on the Atlantic crossing the previous year. On that voyage she had witnessed my gradual transformation from a nervous novice, a 30-something former management consultant hopelessly out of her depth on the high seas, into a self-sufficient, capable adventurer. She had been my prison cell, but also my life-support capsule. I owed my life to her. But now I was abandoning her. I felt a harsh pang of guilt and an overwhelming sense that I was making a bad mistake.

As we reached the threshold of the helicopter door, helping hands came out to haul me in. As the helicopter bore me swiftly towards land through a rapidly darkening sky, I huddled disconsolately on the floor in the back, my survival suit peeled down to my waist and a thick, standard-issue grey blanket wrapped around my shoulders over my T-shirt. A puddle accumulated around me as I sat in my soaking clothes, alone with my thoughts. All I could see of the helicopter crew was the back of their heads, and the headphones clamped over their ears made conversation impossible. I was in my own little world of misery.

I replayed the events of the last few hours again and again in my mind. I had set out to complete an ocean row to draw attention to environmental issues facing the ocean. Now, ironically and unwillingly, I had contributed to ocean pollution by losing my sea anchor, I was riding in a chopper that was burning fossil fuel at a phenomenal rate, and I had abandoned my precious boat—my only possession in this world apart from my old yellow pickup truck. What a mess.

Yet, I reminded myself, this is what I signed up for. When I had written those two versions of my obituary several years before, I had thought of the obituaries I enjoyed reading in the newspaper—the colourful characters who seemed to have packed several lifetimes into one, who followed their passions, who might succeed or fail equally spectacularly, and who, if they failed, would pick themselves up and dust themselves off and try again. They had been my inspiration, and now I had to draw on their example and find the strength to persevere.

I had wanted to push my limits, to get outside my comfort zone—and of course that would, by definition, be uncomfortable. On the Atlantic, I had thought many times that I was about to hit my limits—of pain, frustration, anger, boredom—only to find that my limits were far beyond where I thought they were. I had time and again gone past the imagined point of impossibility, only to look back on it from the other side and wonder why I'd held such a small view of my capabilities.

When setting out across the Pacific, I'd known that I was pushing myself even farther—5,000 miles farther. The more I pushed, the more likely it became that I would fail. There was only one way to find out how far I could go, and that was to go there. At the outer limits, there's a fine line between courage and stupidity. On this occasion, at least, I had stayed on the right side of the line.

Although to some extent the choice had been taken away from me, I nonetheless held myself responsible for my decision. I had committed to being the captain of my own ship. Setting out across the Atlantic soon after my divorce, I'd been determined to demonstrate my self-reliance, to myself as much as to others. I wanted to prove that I didn't need a husband—or anybody, in fact—to take care of me. This didn't just mean the physical self-reliance of being alone on a rowboat; it also meant the psychological self-reliance of making my own decisions and standing by them. There was nothing to be gained by blaming the informant or the Coast Guard. Ultimately, the choice had been mine, and there was no benefit to regretting it or revisiting it and wondering if I'd done the right thing. I would never know what might have happened had I taken the other option and steadfastly refused the rescue. The decision had been made, and my job now was to figure out what to do to make the best of a bad situation.

In fact, my mind was already racing with what to do next. I was compiling a mental list of all the items that needed to be replaced, repaired, or added to my boat to make her seaworthy again; and I was determined to resume my quest as soon as possible. Abandoning my bid felt very wrong, and I wanted to right the wrong at the earliest opportunity.

I made a vow. "Stay safe, *Brocade*. I'll be back soon."

CHAPTER TWO

THE KINDNESS
OF STRANGERS

"No act of kindness, no matter how small, is ever wasted."

— AESOP

Having been saved from the tumult of the storm, I could have died on the way back to shore. Usually U.S. Coast Guard helicopters operate on a maximum range of 120 nautical miles, allowing 20 minutes to hover while they conduct the rescue, followed by an immediate return to land. I would later find out that when the helicopter set out for the *Brocade*, my reported position was 132 nautical miles from their base. So we were running on fumes by the time we reached the California coast—or, to use the euphemistic Coast Guard terminology, we were "fuel critical."

But reaching the coast did not mean we were safe. We needed to land where there was fuel, and the closest option, at Point Arena, became socked in with fog as we approached. The next refueling point, Ukiah, was another 15 minutes away, and we were now whatever comes beyond "fuel critical." Possibly official terminology fails at this point and something more salty becomes appropriate.

However, as you can deduce from the fact that I am alive to write this book, we survived. With the last few drops of fuel, we made it to Ukiah and safety. When I later found out what a close-run thing it had been, I was relieved for all our sakes that I hadn't abandoned the relative safety of my boat only for us to stall and plummet into the California redwoods. That would have been a tragic waste of the lives of four courageous men: Lieutenant Stephen Baxter, Lieutenant Kevin Winters, Flight Mechanic Jason Bauer, and Rescue Swimmer Chuck Wolfe. And it would have spoiled my day, too.

It was completely dark by the time the big bird touched down in Ukiah. Following the crew through the cool Northern California night, I wobbled barefoot across the gravelly tarmac to the single-story military building, the ground lurching beneath my feet as my confused brain tried to adjust to being unexpectedly back on dry land after the rocking and rolling of my boat. The hour was late, and the building was locked. A call was made. While we waited for the key holder to arrive, I asked where I would stay and what would happen next. The crew didn't answer my questions directly, but they assured me that everything would be all right.

How could everything possibly be all right? I had no clothes, no money, and no ID. I realized that it would have been a good idea to put my passport in the case with my laptop and mobile phone, but the thought had not even crossed my mind. I couldn't have brought money because I had none on board the boat. I hadn't planned to need any until I reached Hawai'i, there not being too many shopping opportunities in mid-ocean.

After a few minutes, some Coast Guard personnel appeared and unlocked the buildings to let us in. We stepped through the door and into a room that to me seemed surreal in its normality. A small kitchenette on the far side of the room contained a kettle, microwave, refrigerator, jars of coffee, and boxes of teabags. The furniture was simple and utilitarian. It was exactly as you would imagine a military lounge to be—functional, minimal, overly bright, and yet drab. I blinked in the harsh fluorescent light, feeling very much the odd one out as the Coasties chatted and bantered.

I suddenly felt very lonely. It may seem bizarre that I had just spent ten days completely alone apart from the company of whales and sea lions, yet now that I was surrounded by people I was uncomfortably aware of my very solitary status. They were military; I was civilian. They were simply spending another day at work. I had just had my long-held dreams turned upside down—literally. They were in familiar surroundings, while I'd been plucked from the sea and transplanted to this strange place. They would go back to their families and homes at the end of this shift. I had no way to get back to my floating home, or anywhere else for that matter.

I missed the *Brocade*. I felt like a part of me had been wrenched away in a traumatic amputation. Despite my attempts to face failure with equanimity, I wanted nothing more than to return to her and to carry on. To use the phrase ironically, I felt all at sea. I stood uncertainly by the door, pulling the grey blanket more closely around me in an attempt to comfort myself both emotionally and physically.

When there seemed to be an opportune moment, I coughed slightly to remind them of my presence and said, "I'm getting cold. Do you have any dry clothes?"

I had assumed that they probably plucked distressed sailors from the sea every day of the week, and therefore had a wardrobe full of spare clothes for precisely this eventuality. But it turned out that I was mistaken. The helicopter crew rifled through their own duffle bags to try and find something that would fit me. I was embarrassed by this and tried to backtrack, insisting that I was fine, but they wouldn't hear of it. I was touched by their kindness and compassion towards a stranger in need.

A female Coastie offered me the use of their shower and I gratefully accepted, glad to have something to do and an opportunity to be alone again. Supplied with an odd assortment of men's garments, I was ushered towards a locker room and a hot shower, and told to help myself to whatever shampoo and shower gel I could find in there.

I shut myself into the locker room and peeled off the immersion suit. Hundreds of little flecks of white rubber from the rotting lining stuck to my legs. It's strange what the mind focuses on in a crisis. I had noticed this phenomenon before, on the Atlantic. When a knockdown on that ocean had nearly tipped me overboard, my most immediate concern was that I had lost my thermos mug containing the last portion of my favourite freeze-dried meal, chilli con carne. Now, my attention fixed on these unsightly patches of white rubber lining.

I looked in the small mirror on the wall of the locker room. A strange face stared back at me. My eyes were red from saltwater and shadowed by dark circles of tiredness. My skin was sunburned and salt encrusted. My hair was plaited into pigtails, as it usually is when at sea to stop it getting irretrievably tangled, but most of it had escaped from the pigtails and was sticking out in a messy, matted halo around my face. A few clots of dried blood were visible on my scalp. I looked exactly like someone who had been tumbled around in a capsizing boat, dunked in seawater, blown around by helicopter rotors, and baked until crisp. I was a complete mess. The sight made me think of murdered Banquo's ghost in Shakespeare's *Macbeth*, dragged back from the dead.

I turned away from the disturbing sight in the mirror and stepped into the shower. The hot water felt wonderful on my cold, salty skin, and I stayed in the shower until I was warmed to my core, then emerged into the steamy air. Getting clean had done wonders to restore my circulation and my spirits and, to an extent, my looks—although it had no impact whatsoever on the pieces of white rubber. They were still stuck to my skin like superglue. I would spend the next few days trying to scratch them off with a fingernail until my skin was red and raw.

Chuck, the Coast Guard swimmer, had loaned me his navy shorts and a grey T-shirt. He was a big guy and they were a poor fit, but better than my own soaking clothes. I returned to the lounge looking marginally more presentable, but feeling self-conscious about my lack of underwear and the blobs of white rubber stuck to my legs. I am quite used to being completely naked when alone on the ocean, but going commando in the company of others was a different thing entirely. It all added to my general feeling of strangeness and displacement.

The female Coastie made me a mug of hot chocolate, and one of her colleagues had ordered pizza. While we waited for the food to arrive, I asked for paper and pen, and sat jotting down the list that I had been mentally compiling during the helicopter ride of things that needed repairing on the boat before I could set out to sea again. I had no idea at this stage how I was going to recover my boat, but I would worry about that later. My situation was rather overwhelming, and I could only focus on one problem at a time. I wanted to get these things down on paper before I started to forget.

It also gave me another excuse to keep myself to myself. I fielded a few questions about my boat and my expedition, but I wasn't feeling particularly conversational. I didn't bear a grudge against these guys—I knew they had only been doing their job. But under the circumstances, I just didn't feel much like talking, despite their sympathy.

The pizzas arrived, as big as coffee tables. Normally pizza is not the kind of food I would eat, but for the first time in two days I no longer felt seasick, and I was suddenly ravenous. This was no time to obsess about nutritional standards and trans fats. I ate two enormous slices, while secretly wishing to be sitting on my boat with a freeze-dried meal while serenely watching the sunset, as I had done during the calm days before the storm. The Coasties ate and chatted socially amongst themselves while the TV blared.

Once we had eaten our fill, we returned to the helicopter for the final leg of our journey. It was after midnight by the time we reached the base in Humboldt Bay. I was tired, but before I was allowed to go to bed I had to be examined by a medic. He checked my blood pressure, listened to my heart and lungs through a stethoscope, shone lights in my eyes, and made me watch the tip of his finger while he moved it back and forth.

By now my personal fuel tank was as empty as the helicopter's had been, but I was reminded that I had to make some phone calls to reassure various people that I was safe. I picked absently at the white rubber flecks on my legs while I made the calls—to my mother, the weatherman, Nicole the PR agent, and Brooke Glidden, the member of my team who had been the primary liaison with Global Rescue. I was warm now and starting to enter a post-traumatic euphoria at having survived the stress of the storm. The people on the other end of the phone line probably would have said that I sounded in good spirits, although the truth was that I was too tired to know how I felt.

My calls completed, a friendly young Coastie called Gino showed me to the room in the barracks where I would be staying for the night. The cheap wooden door swung back to reveal a large, rather bleak room with a stained brown carpet, a queen bed with a pile of folded sheets and blankets placed on its bare mattress, two large recliners in front of a TV, a microwave, and a bright green fridge—a bizarre splash of colour. The bathroom was institutional looking, with stainless-steel sinks and white tiles. A mop, bucket, and bottles of cleaning fluids stood in the corner.

It was late—nearly one in the morning—and it had been a long day. I had barely slept in the last 64 hours, and I was exhausted. I put the linens on the bed, took off the borrowed clothes, and swung my weary body in between the sheets. There was a lot to worry about, not least being the fact that my precious boat was drifting abandoned 100 miles offshore, but there was nothing I could do about it until tomorrow. I fell asleep almost immediately.

I woke the next morning with a jolt and a profound sense of being in the wrong place. I had been dreaming about the rescue as my subconscious replayed the previous day's events and tried to make sense of them. In my dream I had still been on my boat, and it was a shock to find myself on dry land. Wrong, wrong, wrong. This was not where I was supposed to be. I thought about my boat and wondered how she was doing. Was it still rough out there? Had she capsized again? Whose version of the weather forecast had proved to be true?

A loud, military rap at the door came again. I looked at my watch: 7 A.M. I'd had six hours of sleep—nowhere near enough to make up for the deficit. I sighed and swung my legs out of bed. Pulling on the oversize T-shirt, I swayed over to the door.

It was Gino. "Good morning!" he greeted me, as cheery as he had been the night before, although he must have had even less sleep than I had. "What would you like for breakfast?"

He handed me a laminated sheet of breakfast options, none of which complied with my usual nutritional rules. For both health and environmental reasons, I generally choose unprocessed foods from the lower end of the food chain. I have even managed to incorporate these principles into most of my expedition meals, depending heavily on organic whole foods such as raw-food crackers, raw snack bars, bean sprouts, porridge, nuts, nut butters, powdered coconut milk, and dried fruit. Everything on this menu looked very processed and desperately unhealthy.

"Umm, breakfast roll, please." I picked the least of the evils.

"The base commander would like to see you," Gino went on. "When you're ready."

"Okay. Can I have a bit of time to get myself together?" I asked, blearily.

"You betcha!" said Gino. "Just give me a call when you're ready. I've got some clothes for you, too." He handed me a pile of folded dark-blue garments with a pair of black military boots on top and departed.

I closed the door and assessed my outfit for the day: a pair of navy Coast Guard pants, a navy Coast Guard shirt, and a pair of black Coast Guard boots, size 10. Still no underwear. I guessed that was not included in military issue kit. I quickly showered and got dressed. The boots were three sizes too big for me, but if I laced them up tightly, they didn't flap around too much.

I was very much aware of my impending appointment with the base commander, but there was a task I wanted to complete as a matter of urgency. I took my laptop out of its case and typed out an account of the events of the previous day as accurately as I could remember them. There had been so many conversations with so many people, passing by in a haze of fatigue, and already I was having difficulty placing events in logical sequence. I needed to try and chronicle what had happened and identify the pivotal moments that had led me from the wilds of the open ocean to this brown barrack room with its crème de menthe green fridge.

An hour or so later I had finished, my typing interrupted only by the arrival of my breakfast, an unappetizing, microwaved roll containing cheap fatty ham, a flat disc of reconstituted egg, and a soggy layer of processed cheese. I thought longingly of the tasty and healthy Lärabars that I ate for breakfast on board the *Brocade*. I ate a few mouthfuls of my breakfast and put the rest in the bin. I have a near-pathological hatred of wasting food, but something as synthetic as this didn't count.

The contrast between what I preferred and the food on offer here only served to reinforce my sense of disempowerment. I had gone from being totally in control of my world, captain of my ship, to being utterly dependent on others. I'd had all the freedom of the ocean, but now that freedom had been abruptly stripped away. I imagined it must feel a little like this to be institutionalized, in a hospital or a prison. I had been sucked unwillingly into a system, and all decision-making power had been taken away from me. And I couldn't see my way out of the situation.

It was time to meet the base commander. I knew that this interview could be important; the previous year the Coast Guard in the Canary Islands had forcibly towed back four solo ocean rowers and forbidden them to depart again from Canarian waters. I did not want to end up in a similar deadlock with the U.S. authorities, so it was vital to convince them that my project was safe and viable.

Gino took me to meet Paul, a short, friendly faced man, and my fears of censure turned out to be needless. There were only a few moments when I felt I was being called to account—at one point Paul said he wanted to make sure that I would not be a "repeat offender," as he put it, and I hastened to assure him that I had all necessary safety equipment, skills, and procedures. I emphasized that it was only due to an unfortunate sequence of events that I had run into trouble this time, and that it would be a relatively straightforward matter to avoid those things happening next time. Provided I had adequate water ballast and two sea anchors, I should not need to trouble the U.S. Coast Guard again.

The interview over, I prepared to meet the press, who had been summoned by the Coast Guard. I understood that I owed them this PR opportunity, and that it was a chance to express my gratitude, but the words of appreciation stuck in my throat. I smiled and attempted to act normal, but inside I was mortified. They had bagged a trophy with my rescue, and I was being paraded before the public as an example to others. With every fibre of my being, I yearned to be back on my little boat.

THE PRESS CALL OVER, I RETURNED TO MY ROOM to consider what to do next. I was determined to continue my Pacific row within a matter of days, but a few significant logistical challenges stood in my way.

I was now in Eureka, five hours north of San Francisco, with nothing but the clothes I stood up in. I couldn't get anywhere with no ID and no money. I didn't know anybody within a radius of several hundred miles. I had a mobile phone and a laptop, but who to call? What to do?

Luckily, help was at hand. Brooke Glidden, my Global Rescue liaison, texted me the phone number of some friends who lived in Eureka. I knew nothing about Rich Ames other than that he had known Brooke's family for a long time, but when I called him from my mobile, he came to pick me up from the Coast Guard base. He turned out to be a white-bearded, blue-eyed man, with a mischievous sense of humour, deriving great entertainment from my big black "kinky boots," U.S. Coast Guard military issue. He and his wife, Marilyn, took me in and fed and clothed me for the next two days while I tried to figure out how to get back to San Francisco. A small support group sprang up around my cause, with various friends of the Ameses helping out by providing Internet access, clothes, a duffle bag, and a much-appreciated dinner party, where I gratefully anaesthetized myself with good red wine and began to relax for the first time since before the storm.

But still only half my mind was in Eureka. The other half was out on the ocean, reaching out towards *Brocade*, wondering how she was faring without me. It was a source of bitter humour to me that "Eureka!" was uttered by Archimedes when he stepped into a full bath and discovered the principle of displacement as it overflowed; in Greek, the word means, "I've found it!" By contrast, my abiding memory of Eureka was that far from finding something, I had lost just about everything—my dignity, my autonomy, and my boat.

My good Samaritans managed to persuade an airline to let me on board without a passport, and loaned me enough money for a ticket. At last I was on my way back to San Francisco and, I hoped, a chance to redeem my interrupted voyage.

ON BALANCE, I WOULD HAVE PREFERRED not to have had this unscheduled pit stop in Eureka, yet I was touched once again, as I have been hundreds of times since I started ocean rowing, by the heartwarming gift of human kindness. Time after time I have been moved and amazed by the willingness of people to reach out and embrace a stranger, opening up their homes and their hearts, and often their wallets, to help me achieve my dreams.

My interpretation of this phenomenon is that strong need, whether generated by a mission or a crisis, creates an energy vortex that draws people in and allows them to express their love and affection for a fellow human in a way that is rare within the boundaries of ordinary life. An adventurer or a victim is a rogue variable thrown into the mix, and draws forth the goodness inherent in most people. One of the biggest perks of my work is that I get to see this wonderful, kind, generous, life-affirming side of human nature, which I rarely witnessed in my office-bound days.

At first I had struggled with embarrassment at asking for favours or living on charity, but then I read about St. Francis of Assisi, who encouraged his followers not to be too proud to beg, and I was inspired to overcome my embarrassment. I was, I believed, doing a good thing arising from good motives, so I reasoned that I would have to get comfortable with being on the receiving end of altruism. People seemed to derive genuine joy from expressing their generosity, so who was I to deny them that pleasure? I learned to receive and to be grateful, and to try through my endeavours to give as much back to them as they were giving me.

My blog was one way that I could reciprocate. I understood that many of my supporters would love to have an adventure of their own, but due to circumstances, family obligations, or time constraints, they were unable to do so. The least I could do was to allow them to vicariously enjoy my adventure by taking the trouble to craft an interesting and thoughtful blog post every day. It was often difficult for me to embrace this task with enthusiasm. After a long day at the oars, I was impatient to reach the relative comfort of my bunk, and it could take well over an hour to unpack laptop, phone, and cables from their waterproof case, type out a blog post, add a photo, upload it via the satellite phone over a tenuous connection that would often drop many times during the transmission, and then pack everything away again. It was a labour of love, and it reaped huge dividends in the form of appreciative online comments and messages of support. I wasn't able to view the comments, having only e-mail capabilities, but my mother would send me the best of them, and so blog posts and comments would develop into a mutually satisfying dialogue as my readers and I exchanged ideas and opinions on a wide variety of topics.

The blog also allowed me to gently push out my environmental messages, although I made an effort to keep these to no more than about one in five of my blog posts, not wanting it to turn off potential readers who did not regard themselves as environmentally inclined. I reckon that you can't win converts if they've stopped reading.

Over and above the blog posts, I felt that the best way I could reward my faithful supporters was to succeed in my mission. There were many, many days at sea when the only thing that kept me going was the knowledge that there were people around the world who were watching and waiting and caring about my fate. If the goal had just been about getting to the other side of the ocean, there would have been numerous times when it would have seemed hardly worthwhile. But the blog comments were regular reminders that my adventures mattered to many people besides myself, so even if my motivation was waning, I told myself that I owed it to others to keep going.

So it was also for them, the supporters both known and unknown, that I was determined to continue my voyage, to put behind me the humiliation of this disaster.

CHAPTER THREE

ULTIMATE FLEXIBILITY

"Be infinitely flexible and constantly amazed."

— ATTRIBUTED TO JASON KRAVITZ

It was midnight, and a full orange moon was rising over San Francisco when the *RV White Holly* set sail from Sausalito. The moon cast an eerie shadow on the clouds that rested lightly on the tops of the pylons of the Golden Gate Bridge. As we motored under the bridge and looked back, the shadows shifted. At first the shadow pylons had been in alignment with the real ones; but with our changing perspective, the shadow pylons appeared to tilt and topple into San Francisco Bay as if the bridge were collapsing in slow motion, a disturbingly apocalyptic sight. We all stood on deck, mesmerized, until the bridge and its phantom pylons disappeared into the darkness.

The *White Holly* was a 133-foot research vessel, usually carrying a team of scientists intent on deepening human knowledge of the oceans. A shark cage resting on the ship's deck bore silent witness to the risks that the researchers faced in pursuit of their mission. The Farallon Islands, about 20 miles west of the Golden Gate Bridge, are famous for their seasonal population of great white sharks and form part of the Red Triangle, an area of the ocean notorious for shark attacks. The crew now on board were no less intent on their mission than the scientists, but it was a mission of a very different nature. We were setting out to intercept my rowboat as she drifted down the California coast.

There was no time to lose. We needed to salvage the *Brocade* before anybody else got to her. Under the law of the sea, she was now technically abandoned and would legally become the property of any-body who took her into their possession. They could then do with her as they wished, including charging me full market value if I wanted her back. Some of the crews who had been forced to abandon their boats during the 2005–2006 Atlantic Rowing Race had fallen prey to this law when local fishermen found the capsized vessels and demanded full pay-ment, so the risk seemed real enough.

Even assuming we managed to find the *Brocade*, we would then face another challenge. We would need to bring her on board the *White Holly*. It is difficult enough to locate a tiny rowboat in the vastness of the ocean, but the most important part of the task is also the hardest: physically re-connoitering one boat with another without inflicting damage on either.

I hoped to continue almost immediately with my row to Hawai'i, but we would need to make running repairs first, and we needed a relatively stable platform to do this. That was why I had chartered this particu-lar vessel. Equipped for marine buoy maintenance, she had a powerful crane that we could use to lift my boat out of the water and onto the deck. The *Brocade's* boat trailer, last seen in Crescent City and then driven by Nicole back to San Francisco, had been retrieved from storage and brought on board, lashed securely to eyebolts embedded in the deck of the *White Holly*, ready to serve as a makeshift cradle to hold the boat safe and steady while we worked to restore her to seaworthiness.

To get the *Brocade* safely on board, we needed calm conditions. Ac-cording to Rick, we had just a small window of opportunity, early on Wednesday afternoon. Any earlier or later than that and the waves would be too big, and we would run the risk of pounding the fragile carbon-fibre shell of the *Brocade* against the unforgiving steel hull of the *White Holly*, destroying her rather than rescuing her.

IT WAS NOW JUST TWO DAYS SINCE I HAD RETURNED to San Francisco from Eureka. During those two days I had been working flat out to find a suitable sal-vage vessel; launch the mission; and source every last nut, bolt, and screw that I might possibly need to repair the *Brocade*. I'd been helped immea-surably by Aenor and Melinda, a couple of 50-ish friends whom I had met only a couple of months previously when I gave a presentation to a small group of women at a home in the Oakland hills. Melinda was a corporate lawyer and an Australian by birth, although her family had moved to the United States when she was young. Aenor was an orthpaedic surgeon and a survivor of colon cancer. She had volunteered to be expedition doctor, pledging to be available by phone 24/7 in case of emergency and filling a large case full of pills, potions, bandages, and needles for me to take on my boat to cover every possible medical eventuality.

But now she and Melinda were about to become an even bigger part of my story. They had made it their mission to find and buy every item on my considerable shopping list, and many more things besides, "just in case." They had scoured every West Marine chandlery store in the Bay Area, and we had duffle bags full of marine miscellanea—stainless-steel hardware, flares, hand tools, safety equipment, survival suits, and so on.

It was also thanks to Aenor and Google that we had found the *White Holly*, possibly the only vessel in the Bay Area that met my requirements. The charter would cost a small fortune, but to reconstruct my boat from scratch would cost even more. I had invested my life's savings in buying and fitting out the *Brocade*, and to leave that huge investment of time, money, and effort drifting around the Pacific as a large and potentially hazardous piece of flotsam went against all my principles.

As I was using my row to raise awareness of environmental issues, including the impact of climate change on the small island states scattered across the South Pacific, it made me wince that the airlift and salvage operation combined would produce more than 16 metric tons of carbon dioxide. In the space of a week I would have doubled my emissions for the year, taking me slightly over the American average and 100 percent over the British average. It was difficult for me to incur these massive costs financially and environmentally, but ultimately I had little choice if I was ever going to row again—and that was never in doubt. Quitting simply was not an option.

BY GOOD LUCK—IF THERE IS SUCH A THING—the *White Holly* was available at the time when we needed her. With my permission, Aenor had arranged the charter with the skipper, Captain Vince Backen, a tall, craggily handsome man who reminded me of George Clooney and most definitely had a way with the ladies. The first time we met, he took my hand to help me aboard and, looking deep into my eyes, said, "You're younger than I expected." It is lucky I am not susceptible to such obvious charms, I told myself sternly, as I stepped onto the deck of his ship.

The afternoon before we set out, I received a phone call from Aenor as she and Melinda conducted yet another chandlery raid on the West Marine store in Alameda.

"Roz, we were wondering. . . . We really don't want to get in the way, so please say if this doesn't work for you, but we wondered if we could possibly come along?"

"Could you? Wow, yes, absolutely! I would *love* it if you could come along!"

I had cleared it with Captain Vince, who agreed on condition that they buy the food for the expedition. So Aenor and Melinda hit the shops yet again, the supermarket this time, and arrived with enough food to feed a small army—or navy.

Also on board was Eric Sanford, my boyfriend, who was from White Salmon, Washington. It would be his birthday in a couple of days, and he had been due to go to the Burning Man festival in Nevada, but he'd sacrificed both birthday and the Burn to come and lend a hand. Since the airlift, he had been tracking my boat's progress as she drifted south, taking the reported GPS coordinates from her Marinetrack beacon and plotting them on his laptop. He had extrapolated her current trajectory to predict the position where we were most likely to intercept her course. As our resident geek/navigator, his role would prove to be crucial.

Also on board were Vince's crew: Caitlin, his whippet-thin girlfriend; Chris, a blond, good-looking young deckhand; and Mike, a salty old fisherman complete with moustache. So there were eight of us in all. We had loaded our gear onto the boat that afternoon and made up our beds in the communal bunk room. The interior of the boat was spartan. It was definitely a working vessel, not a luxury liner.

After watching the Golden Gate Bridge retreat into the darkness, we went belowdecks. Melinda took up her post in the galley, the industrial-style ship's kitchen constructed entirely of stainless steel, from where she would produce a steady procession of generously proportioned and delicious meals over the coming three days. After dinner, Eric showed me the chart he had plotted on his laptop, tracking the progress of my errant vessel since her abandonment.

LITERARY CONVENTION WOULD HAVE ME SAY a few words about Eric at this point. I will buck convention and start with his demeanour rather than his looks, for it was his ebullient personality that first attracted me to him.

When, about nine years earlier, I had sat down and written two versions of my own obituary—the one I wanted and the one I was heading for if I carried on with the salary-slave existence I was living at the time—I had thought about the people I admired, whose obituaries I enjoyed reading in the newspapers. They seemed to have lived many different lifetimes in one, constantly reinventing themselves as circumstances changed or as they realized that their existing incarnation was no longer challenging them to grow. They tried many things, lived large, and had a gusto and a zest for life that lesser mortals seemed to lack. Whatever life force is, they must have been at the front of the queue when it was handed out. They were *joie de vivre* personified.

Eric was such a person. So although he's 18 years older than I am, about the same height, and would never be considered Hollywood handsome, I'd fallen for him. Within the first few weeks of our relationship, Eric had taken me kayaking, cross-country skiing, mountain biking, and windsurfing. I dismally failed to display an aptitude for any of them, but Eric was endlessly encouraging. It may have been wishful thinking on his part, hoping that he had found his ideal adventure playmate—too bad that I was a complete klutz at anything apart from rowing. How rarely are we able to see someone as they truly are, rather than as we wish them to be.

The first crack in our relationship had appeared the previous year while we were sailing in Mexico. We had four friends staying on board, and I welcomed the opportunity to spend some time working on my book about the Atlantic crossing while Eric had so many other hands on deck. But one day he took me aside and expressed his disappointment that I wasn't participating more in the sailing activities.

I had been proud of my progress with the book—it was proving difficult to find time for writing amongst all the adventures that were such a feature of our life together—and I was deeply wounded by his criticism. I saw the book as an essential step in my mission to show that there are ways to be happy other than having a steady salary and a large house in the suburbs, and had hoped that Eric would be more supportive of my goals. We had talked about them at length, and I knew that he understood. So I was upset that he didn't seem to understand that I needed to devote time to fulfilling my purpose.

Matters deteriorated further during our trip to Africa to climb Mount Kilimanjaro, after which I was due to spend some time back in Britain. I was quietly relieved to have this opportunity to take some time away and to focus on what I felt was important. I realized that relief was probably not an appropriate emotion if I was really committed to making the relationship work, and that for the time being I was probably better off being single. That had been the state of play when I had set out across the Pacific.

So we were a crew befitting the standard formula for a Hollywood disaster movie: the dishy captain, the glamorous girlfriend, the hot deckhand, the crusty old sea dog, two staunch female friends, and a couple whose relationship was on the rocks.

No matter what the state of our romance, I was very pleased to have Eric on board. An experienced mountain-rescue expert, he had that confidence-inspiring mix of common sense and emotional wisdom often found in people who have had to guide others through adversity and misadventure. These were trying and traumatic times for me, and I welcomed his reassuring presence.

ACCORDING TO ERIC'S CHART, WE WOULD INTERCEPT the *Brocade* around noon the next day, so after discussing our plans with Captain Vince, we retired to our respective bunks to get some sleep in preparation for a busy day ahead. The *White Holly* motored on into the moonlit night, the drone of the engines lulling us to sleep.

We were up bright and early the next morning, and I was anxious. *In what state will we find my boat?* I wondered. *Has she capsized again since I involuntarily abandoned her nearly a week ago? Will we have everything that we need to make the necessary running repairs?*

But first and foremost we needed to find her. Despite Eric's careful plotting of the *Brocade's* position, this was a big ocean and she was a small boat. Rick had predicted calm conditions, and the flat water would help. I knew from past experience that it could be very difficult to spot her in rougher seas. During the Atlantic crossing, the Royal Navy's *HMS*

Southampton had wanted to make a rendezvous with me on Valentine's Day during their passage from Grenada back to Great Britain. Despite knowing my last recorded position and having a boat bristling with radar equipment, they hadn't been able to find me. It had been a rough day and my boat was hidden from sight down amongst the waves, which also caused enough interference on the radar to conceal me. Ultimately I spotted them before they spotted me.

So unless the conditions were dead calm, we might not see the *Brocade* until we were almost on top of her—if, indeed, we managed to get that close. What would we do if she weren't where we expected her to be? The position reports from the onboard transponder were coming back irregularly, sometimes hours without an update. What if the signals became even more intermittent or stopped altogether? We would have to resort to crisscrossing the ocean in a grid pattern or circling outwards in an expanding spiral from our best guess at her last position.

Captain Vince had offered to undertake this mission almost at cost, just covering his crew's wages and the cost of fuel, but even those came to $4,000 a day. Time was of the essence. The longer we were out, the more fuel—and the more money—we would burn.

Fortunately Rick's prediction proved to be correct. During the morning the waves, already slight, subsided further, and by late morning conditions were flat calm. All hands were on deck, scanning the horizon for a first glimpse of the *Brocade*. Aenor took up position in the crow's nest near the top of the mast. After finishing her breakfast duties in the galley, Melinda came up on deck to keep a lookout. Eric stood next to Captain Vince on the captain's bridge, alternately gazing out to sea and peering down through his half-moon glasses to check and double-check the tracking positions on his laptop.

I installed myself at the guardrail just in front of the bridge, my hair blowing in the wind, my eyes straining into the distance until they ached. I regularly checked the satellite phone to see if we had received another position update, which would be relayed to me by Rick, who was monitoring the website. We'd taken the site out of the public domain so that only the core members of the team had authority to access it. We didn't want any unauthorized salvage missions to get to the *Brocade* before we did.

"I see her!" Aenor's shout from the crow's nest came loud and clear.

"Where, where?" I couldn't see anything.

"Over there, almost dead ahead!"

At first I still couldn't see anything, but gradually a small silver speck came into view, occasionally glinting in the bright sunlight.

Eric's dead reckoning of her position had been almost perfect: We had to make an adjustment of only two degrees to aim straight for the *Brocade.* Given the number of variables involved, and that we were coming at the boat almost from right angles, this was a quite magnificent feat of chart plotting. The tiny speck gradually resolved itself into the familiar outline of my boat, bobbing gently in the swell.

There's something strange, I thought. *There's something missing.* Ah yes, that was it. There was no rower at the oars. I was so unused to seeing my boat from the outside that the only mental images I had of her in the water were the photographs taken during the Atlantic Rowing Race, and in all of them I am at the oars, rowing purposefully. It seemed very odd to see her in the water, un(wo)manned.

It was also clear that she had not capsized again since I had left. Everything on deck appeared exactly as it had been when I abandoned ship. So much for the Coast Guard's dire predictions that the conditions were going to get worse before they got better.

As we approached the rowboat, Eric and I donned wet suits. The plan was that we would jump into the water and swim over to the *Brocade.* Once on board, we would take out a rope harness from its stowage hatch and attach it to the four D-rings that were firmly bolted to the bulkheads in the four corners of the cockpit. I'd had these D-rings fitted at a boatyard in Richmond Point, California, just in case the boat ever needed to be winched aloft. I'd managed to get part of the considerable cost met by the *New York Times,* which had wanted to do a photo shoot of the boat suspended vertically with me standing alongside, as a parody of the traditional shots of sports fishermen standing triumphantly alongside enormous marlins. (As it turned out, they eventually decided on a dramatic nighttime shot that had involved a near-hypothermic experience on a windy, rain-soaked evening, necessitating some considerable time to be spent afterwards in a bar with a medicinal scotch or several.)

Now I was extremely glad of the harness and D-rings. Before they had been installed, the only way to hoist the boat was to place canvas slings beneath the hull, which would have been extremely difficult while she was in the water.

As it turned out, the water was so millpond-calm that Captain Vince was able to steer the *White Holly* right alongside the *Brocade,* close enough that Eric and I were able to climb down a rope ladder and step directly onto her deck. We swiftly found the harness and attached it to the D-rings using strong shackles. Operating the derrick arm from a control panel in front of the bridge, Captain Vince lowered a hook, and we looped it through the harness. So far, so good.

Now Eric and I were supposed to get off the *Brocade* to reduce her weight, and get back on the deck of the *White Holly* to help hold the bow and stern ropes. These had been attached to the *Brocade* to stop her swinging once she was out of the water. But due to some miscommunication, Captain Vince started to lift the boat before we had a chance to disembark.

As we rose free of the water, a wave struck the side of the *White Holly*. It was only a tiny wave, but it was enough to set the *Brocade* swinging like a pendulum on the end of the crane arm. Mike and Chris had hold of the bow and stern ropes, and Eric yelled at them to hang on tight. Mike, unprepared for the sudden jerk on the rope in his hands, let go. Chris clung on for dear life and was dragged bodily across the deck as his feet failed to find purchase on its slippery metal surface. The rope burned the skin of his hands—we would later see the painful evidence—but alone he was unable to regain control over 2,000 pounds of swinging rowboat.

As Captain Vince swung the derrick arm across the deck of the *White Holly*, my precious *Brocade* collided with the shark cage once, twice, three times. Eric was shouting and swearing from the deck of the rowboat, frustrated by being in the wrong place and unable to do anything to help. I had my head in my hands, unable to watch. I couldn't believe that we had come all this way and successfully found my boat, only to beat the living daylights out of her just as our mission was on the verge of success. Aenor weighed in to help man the ropes, but not before *Brocade* had suffered several dents to her hull and some damage to her rudder.

At last she was brought under control and lowered to rest on the trailer. I slowly uncovered my eyes and clambered down to the deck to survey the damage. Chris ruefully examined his skinned palms. Eric berated Mike.

"Don't worry, we'll get that all fixed up for you," Captain Vince reassured me, as I looked doubtfully at the splayed wood along the damaged bottom edge of the rudder.

THERE WAS NO TIME TO WASTE on regrets and recriminations. It had already been late in the season when I set out from Crescent City, and I wanted to get the boat repaired while still at sea so I could relaunch my bid without delay. The team set to work. The main tasks were to slot in a new autopilot, the previous one having been destroyed in one of the capsizes; to reinstall the lee cloths and safety belts in the sleeping cabin, ensuring that they were securely bolted right through the floor; and to replace the sea anchor. I supervised, Eric and Aenor worked, Melinda kept everybody fed and watered, and Chris and Mike tended to the damaged rudder.

Throughout the day I was on the satellite phone to my weatherman and the Ocean Rowing Society (ORS), discussing strategy. The ORS is the governing body of ocean-rowing feats, as recognized by the Guinness book of records. It was founded by Kenneth Crutchlow who, although he has never rowed an ocean himself, has been involved in ocean rowing since the 1980s. He famously took a resupply of food to the late, great Peter Bird when he was running out of rations in mid-Pacific, thousands of miles from the nearest landfall. Kenneth chartered a catamaran and set out with a boatful of supplies to rendezvous with Peter. Thus was born the Ocean Rowing Society. My main question for the ORS was whether it would count as a valid ocean crossing if I put my boat back in the water in the place where I had been airlifted and resumed my row from there.

Ken was now considerably older than in his heyday, with a walrus moustache and white hair. He lived in North London with his elegant Russian wife, Tatiana, in a large crumbling town house near Camden Lock Market. I had stayed there once, on the ground floor, and had been disconcerted to find assorted Russian ocean rowers secreted in various cupboard-like bunks beneath staircases, and my sleep that night had been disturbed by the sound of mice rustling through the society's archives.

"Ken," I said into the bulky handset of the satphone, "I'm planning to resume my row just as soon as we get the boat fixed up. The record isn't really all that important to me—you know I'm really out here as an environmental campaigner—but I don't want to exclude the possibility of an official record from the outset. Would it be valid if I relaunched from the point where I was picked up?"

He harrumphed. "No, no, that wouldn't do. It would be an interrupted row. That wouldn't count. You'll have to go back to the mainland and start again."

My heart sank. I felt that I'd already done the hardest part of the row, the first hundred miles from the coast, and it was getting awfully late in the year to start over again. I thanked Ken for his advice and hung up.

I shared my problem with Captain Vince. "How about if we go back as far as the Farallons?" he suggested. "Officially, they are part of the city of San Francisco. Surely that would be valid."

I got back on the phone to Ken. "What about the Farallons?" I asked. "They're 20 miles out from San Francisco, and officially a part of the city."

"Well, you've still got the same problem, haven't you?" he said, and I could picture his moustache bristling in displeasure. "An interrupted row."

I was thinking on my feet. I wasn't ready to give up that easily. "But Ken, when we do the Atlantic Rowing Race, we set out from the Canaries and end up in Antigua. It's island to island. This would be no different. Island to island."

"Hmph!" he snorted. There was a pause on the end of the line. "Yeesss. That's a very good point, Roz. Let me think. Hmm, yes, Tatiana's nodding. Yes, I think we would have to allow that."

I reported back to Captain Vince, and we changed course. We'd been heading north towards the point where I had been picked up. Now we turned to the east, and headed back in the direction of San Francisco, a route that would take us past the Farallons. Because the islands are a U.S. National Wildlife Refuge and a special permit is required to set foot there, we did not plan to go ashore but to tie up at a buoy just offshore. Captain Vince had made many trips to the Farallons delivering supplies, and there seemed a fair chance that we might be able to come to some arrangement with the biologists stationed there.

But there was another variable to take into consideration: the weather. In the run-up to my departure from California, Rick and I had created a traffic light system to indicate acceptable levels of risk. Taking into account wind speed, wind direction, tides, and current, one-hour time slots would be designated as green, amber, or red, signifying respectively *go, maybe,* and *definitely not.* I was now calling him to get forecasts relevant to my proposed launch locations and times as they evolved. He was dubious.

"These conditions are what you previously defined as amber-slash-red," he said. "You're moving the goalposts. And it's late in the year. I can't promise you won't run into winter storms as you approach Hawai'i."

This was not what I wanted to hear. I wanted to eradicate the whole unfortunate episode that had ensued after the Coast Guard turned up, as if to pretend it had never happened, and to restart this year seemed to be the best way to achieve that end. I was still stubbornly clinging to my dream, tattered though it was. I thanked him and pensively pressed the Off button on the satellite phone.

I was also checking in with Nicole to ask her advice on how best to handle this from the PR point of view.

"There is a lot of negative comment going on," she told me. "The reporting has been pretty fair, but a lot of people aren't getting the full facts of the case. They don't know that you had private medevac insurance. They don't know that you didn't call for the Coast Guard. The story on the *San Francisco Chronicle* website had hundreds of comments, and most of them were bad."

This was sobering. I was upset and indignant. I'd thought that I no longer cared what people might think of me, but evidently I wasn't as immune to public opinion as I liked to believe.

"What do the folks at Brocade think I should do?" I asked quietly, referring to my corporate sponsors.

"They will support whatever decision you make," she said. "But it would probably be a good idea for you to come back to shore. Be seen to be safety conscious. Fix the boat up. Take your time before you set out again."

"But I don't have any time," I whined. "It's already late in the year. If I don't get going again now, I'll have to wait until next year."

Her silence said everything.

I SLEPT LITTLE THAT NIGHT AS WE VOYAGED towards the Farallons. The day's conversations buzzed around and around in my head. To go or not to go, that was the question. I was reluctant to surrender my plan to set out across the Pacific this year. And everybody had put so much work into getting the *Brocade* shipshape for the relaunch.

But on the other hand I didn't want to run into winter storms. I'd had enough of capsizing for one year. And maybe Nicole was right—I was aware that as well as being conscious of my own safety, there might be aspiring ocean rowers who would look to my example, good or bad, so it would be better to be seen to be prudent. Thinking more broadly about my objectives, including the environmental goals, I realized that I was supposed to embody values such as prioritizing long-term over short-term interests, and maturity and responsibility over hotheaded arrogance. Seen through this lens, my decision became clear.

I WAS WOKEN FROM A LIGHT DOZE by the sudden cessation of the ship's engine. A pale dawn light was filtering in through the portholes. I rubbed my bleary eyes and swung my legs out of the bunk. After pulling on a few garments, I made my way to the communal bathrooms. Aenor was already in there.

"So, this is it," she said. "Launch day."

I shook my head. "No, Aenor," I told her. "I'm really sorry, but it just doesn't feel right. Rick says it's too late in the year, and the conditions are marginal. I'm not going to do it." She nodded in understanding and hugged me.

I went out on deck to find a grey, foggy daybreak. The crew were mooring the *White Holly* to a large buoy. The buoy's bell clanged dolefully, as if mourning my ruined hopes. The Farallons were almost invisible, just a darker shade of grey in the bleak morning mist. I invited the crew to join me and the others in the galley. We sat on two bench seats, facing each other across the table.

"I'm sorry, guys," I began. "I've been thinking about it all night, and I'm not launching today. I really appreciate everything you've done to get the boat ready, but on balance it's just not safe. The weather forecast is poor, and it's likely to get worse rather than better. Let's go back to San

Francisco, and I'll get the boat properly fixed up and try again next year. I know you've worked really hard, so I'm sorry for letting you down."

"You're not letting us down," Aenor insisted. "Not at all. We did this because we wanted to give you the option to set out again this year. We didn't want you to lose that option because the boat wasn't ready. We made the boat ready, but we know that there are lots of other variables involved, like the weather. We couldn't do anything about those. But this was something we could do for you. We wanted to give you the flexibility to go, if everything else aligned."

"Ultimate flexibility," Melinda chimed in. "Keeping open as many options as possible for as long as possible, until enough facts emerge to make clear which option is best. If your boat's ready, but if it's not right for some other reason, no worries."

I understood. They genuinely didn't mind, because their objective in coming on the rescue mission had not been to see me relaunch, but to do what they could to grant me the flexibility to launch or not launch, as I saw fit.

A few days earlier I had barely known these wonderful women, but now I felt incredibly lucky to have them as friends. I choked up a bit.

"Thanks," I croaked. "Let's get going."

As we headed back to San Francisco, Eric found me in the bunk room and gave me a hug. "You're doing the right thing, sweetie," he said, and then stood back. "Is it really over between us?" he asked.

I looked at him wearily. I had had to make so many tough decisions in the last few days. Yes to the Coast Guard. Yes to spending a significant proportion of my sponsorship money on chartering the *White Holly*. No to relaunching. Was he really asking me to make yet another decision? He'd done so much for me, not just on this final voyage but throughout our relationship, but I knew in my heart of hearts that we had run our course, that I didn't feel the way about him the way that a girlfriend should. He deserved happiness, but he wasn't going to find it with me.

"Yes, it is over," I said. And then I remembered. "Oh, and, er, happy birthday."

FRIENDS ALLOWED ME TO STAY at their lovely cliff-top house in a small beach town just north of San Francisco. I drove north over the Golden Gate

Bridge, turned left onto Highway 1, and followed the spectacular coast road across the San Andreas Fault and onto the Point Reyes peninsula. You won't find the town unless you know it is there. There used to be a signpost, but the locals didn't want anybody to find them, so they took it down. The authorities put it up again. The locals took it down again. Eventually the authorities tired of this game and gave up. I will respect the town culture and not disclose its name nor its exact location, but suffice it to say that it is a very special place, consisting of an old-fashioned saloon, two restaurants, a coffee kiosk, a few small stores including a surf shop, and a couple hundred houses. If you know the town, you will know where I mean.

It was the perfect place for me to retreat to lick my wounds. The cuts on my head were healing, but it had been a hurtful experience in more ways than the physical. My personal disappointment was compounded by the public criticism. The fact that most of it was based on an incomplete knowledge of the facts did little to assuage my feelings of distress and indignation.

I had an irresistible urge to set the record straight. Nicole restrained me from responding individually to the Internet trolls, and instead suggested I publish a blog post called "Setting the Record Straight," which I did. I don't know how many of the armchair critics saw it, but it made me feel marginally better to know that I'd done what I could to argue my case.

I was still finding it hard to reconcile myself to what had happened. I kept asking what I had done to deserve this. *Could I have been more rigorous in my preparations? Should I have been firmer in my conversations with the Coast Guard? Should I have refused to leave my boat? They surely couldn't have removed me by force.*

Even though I tried to rationalize it away, there was a sense that in some way this disaster had been a moral judgment. *Had I been too proud? Too arrogant? Had I tempted fate?* I questioned my motives—had they been pure enough? Had the greater good of people and planet really been my primary goal, or had there been too much ego in the mix?

One night I was browsing through my hosts' extensive DVD collection. I found a documentary about the Dixie Chicks and put it on the player. *Shut Up and Sing* tells the story of the outcry that ensued when

Natalie Maines, the lead singer of the Texas band, made a political re-mark during a concert in London just days before the U.S. invasion of Iraq. "Just so you know, we're on the good side with y'all," she said. "We do not want this war, this violence, and we're ashamed that the President of the United States is from Texas."

Republicans were outraged. Dixie Chicks CDs were burned in the streets. Natalie Maines received hate mail and death threats. She could easily have caved in and done what so many in her position would have done—backtracked on her comments, claiming they had been taken out of context. But she didn't. While she made a brief statement a few days after the concert, saying that the office of the President deserved respect, she had meant what she said at the time, and she still meant it afterwards. She was not going to back down. She stood tall, strong, and defiant, and took it like a woman. In fact, she said it again. Her only regret was that the two other women in the band were also affected, emotionally and financially. But they stayed loyal and stood by her side throughout.

I was moved and impressed by her courage. I thought of the huge amount of public criticism that she had taken and survived, and my own recent troubles paled into insignificance. It's true that the higher you climb, the harder you fall. But that's no reason not to try and climb in the first place. When you finally got there, the view from the top would be amazing. I reminded myself of the Chinese saying, "Fall down nine times, get up ten." I had only fallen down once so far. It didn't matter whether I fell down once, or 9 times, or 99. The most important thing was to keep getting up again.

And so, eventually, I did. The pain of disappointment started to pass, and I began to look again to the future instead of dwelling on the past. I put the 2007 episode down to experience, that invaluable thing that you get just after you need it. I have ever since retained the notion of ultimate flexibility as a guiding principle in my life, acknowledging that we rarely have access to all the necessary information when we have to make a decision. It pays to keep the options open for as long as possible.

In a heartwarming postscript to my encounter with the Coast Guard, I later exchanged messages with the base commander, the pilot of the aeroplane, and the pilot of the helicopter.

This message was posted using the contact form on my website:

Hello everyone.

I am Paul, who was the person leading the rescue and assistance effort at CG Group Humboldt Bay. I was also the person who spoke with Roz on the satellite phone, suggesting to her that a decision was needed because of deteriorating factors.

My concern, and those of my Command and the Coast Guard, is and was the safety, health, and well-being of this lady. We all have nothing but praise and admiration for her and her efforts. I am quite honored to have been able to speak with Roz, even considering the situation. I wish her best of luck and health. She can certainly call or write me any time she wishes.

Regards,

Paul Hofbauer, GS-11,

USCG Search and Rescue Specialist

From: Kenny Crall

I was on the Coast Guard C-130 airplane that went out to help Roz today . . . We're glad you made it ashore safely and I hope your next attempt is successful. I will continue to watch the website for news. You gained another supporter in me. What you are doing is amazing and I have the utmost respect for you. I hope we don't meet again under the same circumstances on the mighty Pacific. As we say in the Coast Guard, Roz, Fair Winds and Following Seas.

Ken Crall

From the pilot of the U.S. Coast Guard helicopter:

> Roz–
> You are very welcome.
> I have been tracking your website now and probably will until you get to [the other side of the Pacific]. You have touched many people here in the Northern California area. What you are doing sounds absolutely crazy at first, but once I met you it seemed more than worth it as your true being is embellished with every word you speak.
> Good Luck on the journey to come and we will keep you in our prayers!
> Stephen
> LT Stephen T. Baxter
> Asst. Aviation Operations
> Public Affairs Officer
> Group/Air Station Humboldt Bay

I took their respect and good wishes with me as I once again prepared to embark upon the Pacific. The next time there would be no false start. My credibility depended on it.

~~~

CHAPTER FOUR

THE UNIVERSE
WILL PROVIDE

"Everything works out in the end.
If it hasn't worked out yet, then it's not the end."

— UNKNOWN

There was never any doubt in my mind that I would carry on with my bid to row the Pacific Ocean. But first of all there was that awkward little problem—that my boat seemed unable to stay the right way up—and it had to be addressed.

The *Brocade* was now back in San Francisco, considerably the worse for wear. It wouldn't be too difficult to replace the broken electronics and the sea anchor, but I needed to come up with a strategy for preventing future capsizes. I found myself discussing this vexing question with the skipper and first mate of the *Cheyenne*, a record-breaking catamaran belonging to the late Steve Fossett, the legendary American adventurer. Except at that stage nobody knew yet if he was indeed late, or just . . . late. He had been on a solo flight in Nevada when he and his plane had failed to return. Nobody knew what had happened to him, and a huge search operation was underway.

Before his fateful flight, and while my boat was still drifting abandoned offshore, my shore team had been investigating options for retrieving the *Brocade*. The *Cheyenne* had been one of the few vessels traversing that part of the ocean between San Francisco and Hawai'i, so my team had made contact. Steve Fossett had given permission for the

Cheyenne to divert from her course to pick up my rowboat. However, at that point I still hoped to resume my row from the spot at which I'd been airlifted, so I had overruled the suggestion. Very shortly after that, Steve Fossett had gone missing.

NOW THAT THE *CHEYENNE* CREW AND I both found ourselves in San Francisco with unexpected amounts of time on our hands, we met up for a drink. The skipper was a Brit called Mark Featherstone, originally from the Wirral in Cheshire, my home county, but more recently of Salcombe, Devon. With him was Nancy Scurka, a pretty and robust young woman with long blonde hair, whom Mark introduced as one of the best fibreglass craftspeople in the business.

We brainstormed ideas on how we could stabilize the *Brocade*. My theory was that I had inadvertently made her top-heavy by adding too much equipment up high. I'd been keen to gather all kinds of data that might be of interest to the at-home adventurer, and to this end I had cluttered the superstructure with an array of data-gathering devices—a Davis weather station, two anemometers, a video camera, and a digital SLR stills camera in a large metal drum. This had all joined the existing barrage of technology: a Sea-me radar target enhancer, the GPS antenna, the Iridium satphone antenna, the VHF radio mast, a navigation light, and a rail light from Eric's solar gadget company, Simply Brilliant. Also stowed up high were my new oars. After all four of my carbon-fibre oars had broken on the Atlantic, I had chosen solid ash oars made in Oregon, which weighed 13 pounds apiece versus the 3 pounds of their predecessors. I had four of them on board, adding another 50-plus pounds above the boat's centre of gravity.

All this weight alone, I was able to see, could have been enough to make my boat turn turtle. In fact, it now seemed a miracle that it had been able to self-right with all the extra poundage. No single item seemed excessive, but in combination they had been enough to disastrously alter the *Brocade*'s equilibrium in high seas.

I was more than happy to strip away a lot of this superfluous weight. The oars would stay, but much of the rest could go. I wanted to take no chances, so I would also increase the weight down low, just to make sure. I knew that it would slow me down, but reasoned that I would rather lose a fraction of a knot from my average speed in favour of staying the right way up.

We mooted various possibilities, including the addition of a daggerboard, a removable fin that would protrude from the bottom of the hull to provide extra weight and improve the boat's directional stability. But this would have required major reconstruction of the hull, and I didn't have the budget for such extensive work.

Phil Morrison, the British designer of my boat, became an invaluable part of this process over the weeks that followed, as Mark, Nancy, and I consulted him on our proposed changes. E-mails, sketches, and photographs flew back and forth across the Atlantic as we discussed options.

Eventually we settled on a workable and relatively low-budget solution. We would install 200 pounds of lead shot in the bottom of the hull, creating false floors in the footwell and one of the lockers and using resin to seal the small lead balls in place. We would also add an extra five inches of depth to the chine, the rib that runs longitudinally along the lowest point of the hull, again to add extra weight but also to mimic the stabilizing effect that a daggerboard would have given.

It was a strange time for Mark and Nancy. Their boss was missing in action, and until he was either found or declared officially dead by the authorities, their future was uncertain. Pending an outcome, they pushed on with business as usual. That beautiful speed machine, the *Cheyenne*, was to be dismasted and reincarnated as a submersible launch vessel, and this work took up most of their day. Nancy would then stay after hours, working long into the evening to make the modifications to my boat. I dropped in from time to time at the boatyard in Alameda, and I was profoundly grateful for, and impressed by, the high standard of her work.

One day I turned up to find the *Brocade* slung from *Cheyenne*'s underbelly, beneath the vast netting trampoline that stretched between the two bladelike racing hulls of the giant catamaran.

"We needed a hoist to get your boat off her trailer while we fitted the new chine," Nancy explained, "and *Cheyenne* was the nearest convenient thing. And your boat is about the same size and weight as the submersible, so this doubles up as a test for the modifications we've made to *Cheyenne*."

The contrast between the two vessels could not have been greater. My little *Brocade*, top speed about 5 knots for a few seconds while surfing down a wave, swinging beneath the *Cheyenne*, top speed about 40 knots. The only things they had in common were that they both floated, and both would appear in the Guinness book of records.

AFTER A COUPLE OF MONTHS OF WORK, my boat was ready, and I bided my time waiting for spring to bring more clement weather and the opportunity to try again. Over those months, I often thought back to the events of that fateful day and wondered how it might have played out differently. I considered the various points in time at which I could have taken a different path. What would have happened if I had been less attached to leaving from San Francisco, and so could have gone earlier in the year from a different location? What if I hadn't mentioned my predicament in a blog post, if I had decided not to make contact with the Coast Guard plane, if my weatherman had picked up his phone, or if I had continued in my refusal to accept a rescue?

A friend tried to console me by telling me, "Everything happens for a reason." I pondered this. I was not convinced, although I could see why it would be a comforting belief. Many people may find it disquieting to imagine that the world could be a random place in which bad things can happen to good people while the unscrupulous prosper. There is a desire, either innate or engendered by myths and fairy tales and Hollywood, for justice and harmony to prevail. We want to believe that our immediate tribulations will eventually lead to some reward, or that we have subconsciously invited this adversity into our lives because it will teach us a valuable lesson.

After long reflection, I found that I could not believe that there is any guiding force, either external or internal, that puts these obstacles in our way. We don't "deserve" it, or subconsciously "want" it—some stuff simply happens, be it good, bad, or indifferent.

I had first considered this possibility on the Atlantic. For much of that crossing, I took it terribly personally that the ocean was being so mean to me. Winds blew me backwards. Waves tipped my boat this way and that, and occasionally right over. Currents whisked me off course. These things happened so often that I couldn't believe it was just bad luck;

there seemed to be a malevolent will at work. A wave would come along at precisely the wrong moment and slosh into my dinner mug, swamping my meal in cold, salty water, or one would soak me just as I was about to retire to my cabin for the night.

I tried to figure out what the ocean was trying to teach me. According to the traditional hero's tale, the hero is made to suffer so that he can learn an important lesson. When he has this breakthrough, he is rewarded with the removal of obstacles and unimpeded progress towards his goal. For a long time I thought that if only I could work out what lesson I was supposed to draw from my sufferings, the ocean would relent and let me pass.

Eventually I realized that the ocean was not rearranging the laws of physics purely for my edification. It is not a sentient being. The ocean was completely and utterly indifferent. It wasn't trying to teach me anything. It was simply doing what oceans do.

Instead, it's how we respond to adversity that makes it meaningful. The trouble itself doesn't mean anything, but it does present us with an opportunity for growth and learning, if that's how we choose to receive it. It doesn't "happen for a reason" in the sense that the reason arrives externally, conveniently packaged up in the adverse event. But we can choose to find positives in the hardship, to glean something productive from a tough experience. We don't control what happens to us, but we can control how we choose to respond to it. This is where our true power lies.

How, I asked myself, *will I respond to this?* As I moved forward, I learned that some people love to carp and criticize, and that it says more about them and their inadequacies than it does about me. I would learn to keep problems to myself and my core team until they were resolved. And most of all, I would continue. The best way that I could answer my critics was to go out again the next year, wiser, better prepared, and do it right this time.

And so, eventually, I stopped reliving the past. I decided that while it is good to analyse mistakes in order to learn from them and not repeat them, beyond a certain point there is nothing more to be gained. I would accept what had happened and move on. With the passage of time, the pain and humiliation subsided. Everything passes, eventually.

I HADN'T HAD A PERMANENT HOME since 2002, when I moved out of the one I had shared with my ex-husband in London, so while I waited for spring 2008 to come round, I travelled to a variety of places, governed by whim, inclination, and free rent. By the time I returned to the UK to hike the West Highland Way in Scotland with my younger sister in late September 2007, hopes of finding Steve Fossett alive were fading. By late November I had visited New York, Hawai'i, San Francisco, Seattle, and Montana, and Fossett's wife was petitioning to have her husband declared dead. By February 2008, I had been dogsledding in Minnesota, spent time with friends in Oregon, done a speaking tour of New Zealand, and settled into a guest cottage back in the Bay Area, and only then was Steve Fossett finally declared dead by a Chicago court. I was sad the world had lost such a great adventurer, but quietly appreciated that those tied to him could begin to seek closure and move on. By spring 2008 Mark, Nancy, and I were all free to pursue our respective paths.

IN MAY, MY DREAM CAME TRUE, and I was able to leave from San Francisco's Golden Gate Bridge, as I had hoped to do in 2007. All the media attention of the previous year had backfired when my bid ended prematurely, so this time around, my sponsors and I decided to take a low-key approach. It helped that circumstances dictated a midnight departure, which might have looked like I was skulking out under cover of darkness, but in fact was timed to coincide with the slack water at high tide. These conditions would put me in the right place at the right time to derive maximum benefit from the outgoing tide, which can rip through the narrow channel under the Golden Gate Bridge at a rate of up to five knots, a helpful slingshot out into the Pacific.

I had been offered use of the ramp and facilities at the Presidio Yacht Club, on the Marin side of the Golden Gate Bridge. Just a couple of hundred yards away from the yacht club is Coast Guard Station Golden Gate. In an ironic twist to the previous year's tale, the Coasties came over, uninvited, to inspect my boat just a couple of hours before I departed. The previous year I had tried every avenue to obtain an inspection, and this time, here they were without my even having to ask. As far as I could ascertain, they were unaware of 2007's drama, and I didn't want to revive the subject. Their inspection could have been due to concern for my safety, while a cynic might suggest that it was inspired by the presence of a TV camera crew making a documentary about them—but out of respect, I would say no such thing.

In the pool of brightness cast into the night by the camera spotlights, they inspected my Emergency Position Indicating Radio Beacon (EPIRB), my "ejector button" in case of dire emergency; VHF radio; satphone; and fire extinguisher. My boat and safety equipment having been deemed seaworthy, I put the oars in the oarlocks, and to a smattering of applause and cries of "Good luck, Roz!" from my small group of supporters, I once again set forth across the Pacific.

I rowed carefully out of Horseshoe Cove, emerging from the sheltered bay into the main harbour. The orange lights of the Golden Gate Bridge glittered on the ruffled water. I tried to paddle out under the bridge, but it felt as if the tide were still coming in, preventing me from making headway. Tides couldn't run late, as far as I knew, so this shouldn't be happening, but the undeniable fact was that I had to row hard just to stay in one place.

A film crew was on board a sailboat alongside me, shining a light on my boat so that the camera could pick me out in the darkness. Another camera crew was on the bridge above. I became increasingly embarrassed by my lack of progress and was grateful we hadn't invited the media. It was like one of those nightmares where the dreamer is running and running but going nowhere. For half an hour I battled the current. Every time I looked across at the pylon of the bridge, I was still exactly level with it, despite my increasingly strenuous efforts.

At last, either because I redirected my attack to a point closer to the shore, or because the tide had finally turned, I managed to break free and emerge to the ocean side of the Golden Gate. I paused from my rowing to punch the air, and whoop and cheer as if I had just crossed the finish line, rather than merely the start line of my row. *Surely it has to get easier from here on,* I fervently hoped.

It was around 3 A.M. when the camera crews bade a belated farewell and left to go home and get some sleep. But there would be no sleep for me. I rowed away from the bright lights of the city, past the dark silhouettes of the headlands that guard the entrance to San Francisco Bay. I was surprised by how quickly I found myself surrounded by inky darkness, the

Golden Gate Bridge a dividing line between the safe shelter of the bay and the wild ocean outside.

I navigated a succession of three buoys, their lights tiny pinpricks in the blackness of the night. Despite the close proximity of the great city of San Francisco, already I felt very alone. It was deeply counterintuitive to row away from friends and familiar surroundings, out into the unknown. I had no way of knowing what adventures might await me between here and Hawai'i. I just hoped that this voyage would redeem me from the humiliating failure and the at times still-raw fury of the previous year.

I ROWED THROUGH THE NIGHT. I saw no maritime traffic, but I was keenly aware that I was in a major shipping lane, so it could be dangerous to go off watch. By seven o'clock the next morning, the sun had risen and I was getting tired, the long night being the culmination of several days of frantic activity and little sleep. Technically I had been on standby to depart for several days before I actually left, but when the call came from Rick, I found that all the tiny little last-minute tasks added up to a considerable amount of time. The night before I set out had been spent mostly in a fitful doze as my restless mind interrogated itself to find out if I had forgotten anything vital. Part of my brain tried to convince me that my packing list was reliable and everything had been checked off, but that little voice of worry that besieges the small hours of the night refused to accept the reassurance and continued to nag at me. Now, as dawn broke on my first day at sea and my eyelids drooped, I decided that surely I could take a half-hour power nap without disaster.

My head had barely hit the pillow when a Klaxon sounded outside my cabin. I wearily returned to the deck. A pilot boat bobbed nearby, and a voice came over their loudspeaker. "You can't stop here, you'll have to keep moving," it boomed. I sighed, and put out my oars once more. No rest for me yet.

Later in that interminable day, I was rowing past the Farallon Islands. When the *White Holly* had stopped there on that early morning in 2007 and moored up to the buoy, the islands had been fogbound. Now it was a clear and sunny day, and I paused to take a few photos of myself against the backdrop of the craggy skyline that had earned the islands the nickname of the Devil's Teeth.

A little later, I was concerned to see a small rigid inflatable boat (RIB) bouncing across the waves towards me. Trepidation knifed through my tired mind. This was a marine protected area, and I wondered if I had strayed somewhere I shouldn't, and was about to receive a rebuke from the authorities.

The RIB's engine cut off and it drifted towards me until we were within earshot. "Ahoy!" one of the two men on board called out. "Where are you going?"

"Australia," I replied, still wondering if I was in trouble.

"No kidding!" came the reply.

It turned out that I was not in trouble—far from it. Pete and Russ were two marine biologists stationed on the Farallons to study the local wildlife. They had spotted me through their binoculars and been intrigued by this bizarre craft passing their remote and lonely outpost, so they'd come to investigate.

"You're the most interesting thing we've seen all year," they told me. "Do you mind if we bring out our interns to meet you?"

"Sure," I answered slightly uncertainly.

They offered to bring me a beer, which I declined, as I run a dry ship, mostly for safety reasons, but also because rowing is the perfect opportunity for a detox, far from the temptations of land. They also offered to bring bananas and some chocolate, which I accepted. I knew that this would nullify my unsupported status, but that was of no importance to me. I had already proved on the Atlantic that I could complete an unsupported row, even turning down the offer of replacement oars when all of mine broke, so I felt no need to make the point again.

Russ and Pete went to fetch supplies and interns, peeling away in the direction of their wind-blasted island home, leaving a trail of foaming wake.

A half hour later they were back, with a gaggle of young women on board. We chatted for a while, and I traded them a business card for the food. It may seem strange to have business cards on board a boat bound for the high seas, but you never want to miss a chance to make a friend.

They asked me about my trip and seemed to find the scale of the challenge almost incomprehensible. I found their reaction amusing—I never fail to get a kick from the look of slack-mouthed amazement that usually greets my description of what I do—but it was also sobering to hear the words coming out of my own mouth. It's so easy to get caught up in all the busy-ness of departure, and it is only after I have cast off that the daunting scale of my endeavour becomes all too real.

After a while, I had to get going. Once again I only had a limited window of opportunity to get away from dry land before the onshore winds strengthened, so every moment was precious. Exchanging final farewells, we parted company. The marine biologists and their interns would be the last humans I would see for a while.

ON THE SECOND DAY OUT from land, the GPS chartplotter stopped working. This was the same one I'd had the year before, which had seemed to temporarily malfunction during the capsizes, but once back on land it had dried out and appeared to work perfectly. Its early demise was, to put it mildly, disappointing.

I didn't want to borrow the backup GPS out of my grab bag. The point of the grab bag was that if I needed to abandon ship and get into the life raft, there would be just one thing to grab, rather than having to run around the boat collecting everything I needed. So it was best if I left its contents fully intact. Looking around my cabin, I spotted the TomTom satellite navigation unit from my truck. A friend was going to sell the truck on my behalf, and as I was leaving, I realized I had nowhere else to put the satnav unit so I had thrown it into the sleeping cabin. Now I turned it on and tried a few options on the touch screen. Aha! On a little-used menu, I found the option to display latitude and longitude. This was all I needed. There were no islands between San Francisco and Hawai'i, apart from the Farallons, so I could simply navigate using my GPS coordinates.

FOR THE FIRST FEW DAYS AFTER setting out from the Presidio Yacht Club, conditions were calm and pleasant as promised by my weatherman. But then the winds rose, as did the seas. The *Brocade* was once again battered by high waves, and I wondered if this row would end as prematurely as the previous year's. Before I set out, a veteran ocean rower had told me I had "no chance" of a successful departure from San Francisco, and I started to wonder if he was right. I didn't quite dare to believe that I would succeed, so I adopted an attitude of feigned indifference—or as I preferred to describe it to myself, pseudo-Buddhist nonattachment. I would focus on doing everything that I could on a day-to-day basis to ensure success, but I would not tempt fate by speculating as to the actual outcome.

I had learned this motivational technique on the Atlantic, after driving myself nearly insane by looking too far into the future and trying to control things that were inherently uncontrollable, such as the weather. When I had eventually found the mental space to step back and analyse why life felt like such a struggle, I realized I was setting myself up for mental meltdown if I carried on as I was. I learned to keep a strong vision of my goal constantly in my mind and surrender to the uncertainties of my situation, while always doing everything in my power to inch a little closer to my objective. This technique now proved its worth.

The period of rough seas and headwinds dragged on—for about a week I could neither row nor make progress. I passed the time by listening to audiobooks on my iPod, a welcome innovation since the Atlantic, when I had endured the journey accompanied by nothing but my own thoughts and the sounds of nature after my boat's stereo rusted to death early in the voyage.

I put out the sea anchor to mitigate my backwards drift, but that created yet more problems. The trip line kept getting tangled up with the main chute, so I had to use brute strength to pull the sea anchor back in while it was still full of seawater. As I was battling with it one day, a wave caught the sea anchor and jerked it away from me, walloping my finger painfully against a fitting on the boat. The finger swelled to almost twice its normal size, probably broken, and I cut up an old pair of rowing gloves, as my injured finger was now too fat for me to force it into gloves that were still intact. It hurt, but not too badly.

One night the sea anchor tore itself clean off its rope. Where the long splice ended, the rope had twisted as the chute rotated in the waves. Eventually the twist became a weak point, and my sea anchor disappeared forever. I was made abruptly aware of this fact when the boat capsized just before 2 A.M. My memory flashed back to the fiasco of the year before, and I wondered if yet again my voyage would end in failure, but the boat self-righted as it should and stayed upright for the rest of the night. The cause became apparent when day broke to reveal the frayed end of the line. Not wanting a reenactment of the 2007 airlift, I took the precaution of not mentioning this in my blog.

But meanwhile, I had a more immediate concern. The piece of equipment most essential to my continued survival was the watermaker, a small desalination plant that uses reverse osmosis to transform saltwater into freshwater, powered by the solar panels attached to the roofs of both fore and aft cabins. Electronics and seawater are not a good combination. Water plus salt plus electricity equals corrosion. Even exposure to sea air, let alone seawater, is enough to cause problems. Immersing the entire apparatus in saltwater for about 24 hours guarantees complete destruction. Trust me on this—I've proved it. I recorded the following notes in the ship's logbook.

3rd June: WORRIED: watermaker hatch flooded. Bailed and tested—seems okay for now.

4th June: Put Bag Balm [a skin remedy that I use as a waterproofing gel] around watermaker hatch to try and waterproof it.

5th June: Put WD-40 on watermaker. Seems to be working but sounds rather feeble.

8th June: Watermaker not working—hums but no water from output pipe.

9th June: Watermaker worked. Almost pleasant on deck today—fewer crashing waves.

14th June: Watermaker didn't work. Better luck tomorrow?

15th June: Watermaker worked! Sounded healthy.

18th June: Ran watermaker.

20th June: Ran watermaker for about an hour.

21st June: Watermaker sputtered to a stop after a minute.

22nd June: Tried directing all solar panels to one battery to boost power, but watermaker only ran 1 min.

23rd June: Can't get watermaker to run off either battery. Spent 2½ hours trying to fix watermaker. Rang Darren [at Spectra Watermakers] twice. No luck. PUR 06 [backup watermaker, operated manually], here I come.

Later: A trying day—watermaker problems, rough water, _Good Morning America_ cancelled interview. Tomorrow has to be better.

26th June: PUR 06 test: 45 mins to produce 600 mLs [equivalent to little more than a Starbucks grande latte]. Pathetically slow and laborious.

27th June: Spoke to Kyle at Spectra. Faintly hopeful.

Later: Spoke to Rich Crow. He promises we will get watermaker going. More hopeful.

28th June: Opened up watermaker feed pump. Totally f---ed.

1st July: PUR 06 backup watermaker now also kaput. Sprung leak, won't work. Note to self: don't buy vital survival equipment off eBay.

The PUR 06 was unused when I bought it and had been tested before I set out. For it to fail at this inopportune moment was most extraordinarily bad luck. I prided myself on being professional and thorough in my preparations, so while concern over my survival should have been uppermost in my mind, my immediate emotion was indignation at the unfairness of it all.

More out of a sense of due diligence rather than in realistic expectation of a repair, I called the manufacturers of the manual watermaker, Katadyn. They told me that I would need specialist tools and parts, which I had not brought with me because their unit was only ever intended as a backup for use in emergencies. To borrow a line from Oscar Wilde, to lose one watermaker may be regarded as unfortunate; to lose two was starting to look like carelessness. The customer-service representative offered to fix the manual watermaker if I could send it in. I didn't go into detail, but simply stated that this might be logistically challenging.

LOOKING BACK ON THAT STAGE OF THE ROW from the comfort of dry land, I wonder that my logbook is not even more full of expletives. A steady accretion of problems was threatening every aspect of my expedition. But there was never a single moment when everything was bad all at once. One day I would be worried about the water situation, another day my broken finger would be aching, the next day I might be concerned about the effect of the headwinds on my course, and on yet another day it would be the sea anchor that was uppermost in my mind. Yet it never reached crisis point, and I just kept doggedly hanging in there.

You might imagine that this would be a tremendously stressful situation, particularly for somebody who, in her land-bound office life, had been accustomed to being very much in control. But the events of the Atlantic crossing and of the previous year had taught me a new humility about my ability to control circumstances. I had come to expect and accept difficulty as the normal mode of life at sea. I was resigned to the fact that there would always be problems—it was just a question of how many and how serious.

The Atlantic had given me confidence in my ability to cope with stress. It had forced me to develop formidable resilience to suffering, and I felt certain that no matter how hard this Pacific row might be, it surely could not be as difficult as my maiden voyage, when I had been relatively unformed as a person and as a seafarer.

I have a pet theory about the nature of stress: that we all have a set point of stress with which we feel comfortable. If we don't have enough in our lives, we subconsciously engineer additional tension to bring us closer to our set point. See the film stars, rock musicians, and supermodels who appear to have supremely privileged lives, yet somehow contrive to introduce trouble in the form of illicit affairs, family conflicts, drug problems, and criminal convictions. At the opposite end of the spectrum are those enduring enormous amounts of all-too-real stress, such as war, financial duress, homelessness, illness, or bereavement. Yet somehow most of them find the strength to keep going without succumbing to breakdown or suicide. They adapt to this as the new norm. Human beings are remarkable in their ability to adapt and cope.

It is the people who endure the everyday hardships not of their own making that truly inspire me when I am unhappy at sea. I have, at least, chosen my challenge, while they had their challenges thrust upon them. I had no right to complain—which, of course, is not to say that I never did. But out of deference to those with real and valid problems, I tried to confine my whining to the pages of my logbook rather than going public on my blog.

I confess that there were moments when I succumbed to anxiety. When I contemplated what consequences could ensue from my situation, I sometimes felt a rising panic and had to deliberately quell it, pushing it back down to the dark place from whence it came. I knew that panicking would only cloud my judgment and blur my thinking. I had to stay calm and rational if I were going to survive.

ALTHOUGH I HAD CHOSEN NOT TO POST about the watermaker on my blog, I'd shared the bad news with my mother. Mum was keen to put the word out that the device had broken and that I needed a resupply of water, but I was considerably less eager. There were two aspects of my unfortunate experience the previous year that made me hold back. First, I didn't want anybody to know that there was a problem, in case another would-be hero decided to intervene. Second, I knew from my encounter with the *MV Overseas Long Beach* just how difficult it was to transfer anything from a very large vessel to a very small one. I couldn't see how we could get a resupply of water over to me without running the risk of losing it in the ocean, nor what kind of containers they could put it into that could then be stowed securely on my boat. Ideally, heavy items such as water supplies are stowed in hatches below the level of the deck, to keep the centre of gravity low and ensure that the boat can self-right in the event of a capsize. If the water was in containers too large to go into the hatches or that could not be at least secured to the deck, then if the boat started to go over, the containers would start to slide and add to the momentum of the capsize.

In fact, the only obvious way that I could see for any resupply to succeed was to use bottled water—and that ran counter to the very point I was trying to make on this leg of my voyage, that single-use plastic objects are environmentally disastrous. I would be rowing around the outskirts of the Great Pacific Garbage Patch, a concentrated area of trash reported to be around twice the size of Texas, and containing around 3.5 million tons of rubbish.

I had done some research into the problem of plastic pollution before I left dry land so that I would have the facts and figures on hand when writing blog posts on this huge environmental problem. All research had to be done in advance, as the unreliable, slow modem of my satellite phone would only allow me to send and receive e-mail. It didn't have the bandwidth for me to browse the Internet.

I had found out that the floating debris accounts for only about one third of the total; the rest has sunk to the ocean floor, where it interferes with the natural gaseous exchange between the ocean bed and the water. Although roughly 20 percent of this pollution comes from ships, the other 80 percent comes from land. The plastic photodegrades in sunlight, breaking into smaller and smaller fragments. Although less visible, these are in a way more insidious than larger pieces because they can be eaten by smaller fish, so they enter the food chain lower down. The associated toxins accumulate to higher levels as they move up the food chain, until they end up on the dinner plate of the apex predator of the oceans—us.

The more I found out about the problem, the more horrifying it seemed, so the last thing I wanted on my boat was dozens of plastic water bottles, which by now had become complete anathema to me. Ever since I had my environmental epiphany and started to perceive the Earth as the ultimate closed-loop system, I'd been unable to acquire or dispose of anything without considering where it had come from and where it was going to end up. Being in expedition mode did not in any way assuage my green guilt. My principles applied no less on the ocean than they did on dry land. Nature would not care whether I had an excuse. The end result would be the same—yet more unnecessary plastic, and I couldn't square that with my conscience.

I HAD A STRANGE INTUITION that a suitable solution would present itself, so I played for time, pointing out to my mother that I still had plenty of water reserves stashed in rubberized canvas Dromedary bags in hatches under my bunk and beneath the forward cabin. For now, these would keep me alive.

I had to take these storage bags, one at a time as required, and carefully decant the contents into the red jerrycan that resided in the footwell, being careful not to spill a single precious drop. While my watermaker was still functioning, I went through most of the jerrycan's two and a half gallons in a single day, using the water for drinking, rehydrating freeze-dried meals, watering the bean sprouts in the sprouting pot, and taking sponge baths. Now, each time I unscrewed the lid and inserted the tube of the small hand pump to get water for one of these purposes, I would count each squeeze of the pump's bulb and use the absolute bare minimum, aware that this water had become a scarce and finite resource. There is nothing quite like life on a small rowboat with a broken watermaker to make you aware of the vital necessity of water—except for maybe living in places where water has to be carried home from a well in heavy pitchers. I felt great sympathy with the women of the world for whom this is a necessary part of everyday life.

Now that every drop was sacred, certain luxuries had to go, such as bathing in freshwater. From now on it would be saltwater baths only. Usually the whole point was to wash the salt off my skin, from both sweat and the sea, so although a saltwater sponge bath was better than nothing, it left me still rimed with a thin layer of stickiness and was rather unsatisfactory.

At least I didn't need to worry about water for laundry. As has become traditional in ocean-rowing circles, I normally row naked once out of sight of land, as it reduces chafing and is generally more hygienic. I am not at all given to exhibitionism and cannot imagine many prospects more unattractive than a nudist colony, but when alone and safely away from prying eyes, it actually feels rather pleasant to row as nature intended—if, indeed, nature ever intended us to row, naked or otherwise.

I considered whether it made sense to continue growing bean sprouts, my only source of fresh vegetables. I decided that, on balance, it did. If I was really careful it took only a tiny amount of water to rinse and water them twice a day, and the benefits to my nutrition and morale more than justified the extravagance.

The container that had once supplied water for a day I now eked out to last half a week. It occurred to me one day as I rowed along, my eyes resting idly on the jerrycan in the footwell in front of me, that it was roughly the same size as a toilet cistern. How many times in my life had I flushed the loo, never considering once the extravagant waste of precious fresh water? How many people on dry land still did so, with not a thought for where the water came from—or where the waste went to? This experience was certainly making me uncomfortably aware of my bodily inputs and outputs in a way that I never had been before. Even on the Atlantic, I hadn't needed to be so careful, as my watermaker had chugged away reliably, the only major piece of equipment that had not broken on that crossing.

The one thing that I didn't intentionally stint on was drinking water. And yet, no matter how much I tried to follow the needs of my body, I couldn't help it—I was instinctively drinking less than usual, aware that I now had a finite water supply. I have never been a naturally thirsty person and always find it a chore to drink as much water as doctors recommend. If I had felt in any danger of dehydration, I would have stepped up my intake, but I just didn't feel the need.

My expedition doctor, Aenor, became the self-appointed "pee police." I would get e-mails from her asking rather personal questions about my water intake and excretion: How much pee? What colour? Probably not since I had been potty trained had my bodily functions come under such scrutiny, and I felt it rather an intrusion on my privacy. It seemed to me that this was strictly a matter between myself and my bedpan, and I fobbed Aenor off with answers that were engineered more to stop her worrying than to provide accurate information. *Does anybody actually tell their doctor the truth?* I wondered, to reassure myself.

At the back of my mind lurked the ocean rowers' horror story of Don Allum having to drink his own urine when he ran out of drinkable water after the water tanks on his boat became contaminated with seawater. This had been in the days before watermakers were invented, so he had had to take all his water with him at the start of the voyage. As his urine was recycled at ever more concentrated levels, it had taken its toll on his health, and in later life his kidneys failed several times, eventually leading to a fatal heart attack. Although I knew at least one health fanatic who believed in the benefits of drinking a glass a day of one's own urine, my general philosophy was that it was better out than in. If my body had chosen to get rid of it, I wasn't going to override that decision. I would stick with unrecycled water for as long as I could.

Besides, I had a feeling that a solution was going to turn up. And sure enough, it did.

ONE DAY DURING OUR CONVERSATION on the satphone, my mother told me that one of my online followers had posted a comment on my blog to say that the *Junk* raft was slowly converging on my position.

I had heard of the *Junk* raft. Two men from the California-based Algalita Marine Research Foundation had wanted to stage a stunt to raise awareness of the Great Pacific Garbage Patch. They had hit on the idea of making a raft entirely from trash and sailing it from Long Beach, California, to Hawai'i. Some months earlier, someone had suggested that I should make contact with them, given that our goals were virtually identical, to figure out how we could collaborate. I had managed to get Dr. Marcus Eriksen on the phone one day, and he had seemed open to the possibility of collaboration, but in the final hectic preparations for our respective expeditions we had never quite got around to figuring out just what form that collaboration might take. Now it looked like circumstances were conspiring to make that collaboration happen, in a way so perfect that we couldn't have come up with anything better if we had tried.

A loyal follower of my blog, John Herrick from Florida, had been tracking the progress of both our voyages and realized we were on a similar latitude and that the *Junk* was gaining on me. Not knowing just how vital a mid-ocean rendezvous might be in my present circumstances, he suggested that we try to meet. My prayers were answered. This was much better than trying to arrange a resupply from a passing container ship.

My mother made contact with the *Junk* raft's support team by sending a message via their website, and she received an e-mail reply from their shore manager, Anna Cummins. Having established contact, she obtained a satphone number for the *Junk* and passed it along to me. But the number didn't work. I tried several times over the next couple of days, wondering if it was due to lack of a satellite connection or if their phone was temporarily out of order, but I had no success.

Mum went back to the shore team to check the number. It transpired that they had never needed to call this number, as the crew (or the Hunks on the *Junk,* as they had been dubbed by the press) had always called to shore rather than vice versa. We then had to wait for the *Junk* to check in again, so it was a couple more days before I finally obtained the correct number, and the raft was given due warning to expect an incoming call at a particular time.

At last, in the late afternoon on 8 August and about six weeks after my watermaker had broken, I made contact and spoke to both Marcus Eriksen and Joel Paschal, the *Junk*'s navigator. By this point I had less than 30 litres of water left, equivalent to about ten days' supply on short rations. While still not confiding why this rendezvous was so important, my blog post for that day records:

> Today we compared latitudes, longitudes, courses and daily average mileage, and it appears that we are on converging routes. The JUNK is gaining on me steadily. We are going to try to rendezvous—most likely in three or four days time—but this is going to be VERY tricky. We are two small, not very manoeuvrable craft, trying to meet up amidst towering waves on a very large ocean.
>
> If we succeed, theirs will be the first human faces I have seen since I passed the Farallon Islands on 26th May. I am now rather thinner, browner, and considerably saltier than I was back then. Time to dig out some clothes and try and make myself presentable!

IT WAS, AS PREDICTED, CHALLENGING to rendezvous with another slow-moving vessel in mid-ocean. We checked in with each other on a regular basis over the next few days to find out how the other boat was progressing. They told me that their voyage was taking much longer than they had expected. This was at least partly due to the design of their raft. Made from 15,000 empty water bottles, lashed together into pontoons with cargo netting, they had not got very far from Long Beach when the lids of the bottles started to unscrew and the raft started to sink. They had had to make an unscheduled stop-off at Catalina Island just a few days into the voyage to tighten the lids before setting off again. But even with everything securely in place, they were not going much faster than I was. Ultimately their crossing would take 88 days compared with my 99—exceptionally slow for a sailboat, but maybe not so surprising for a sailboat made out of rubbish.

The upshot of this slow progress was that they were running out of food, and although they were not in imminent danger of starvation, they were extremely bored of surviving on peanut butter and granola. They had been supplementing their diet with fish, but this was an unreliable source of nourishment, as days would sometimes pass with no catch. So I was delighted to be in a position to offer them a resupply of food. I had plenty, and it would be better for my self-respect as an adventurer that we would be able to make an exchange of goodies rather than accepting a one-way donation from them to me.

After I spoke to them on 9 August and heard of their predicament, I spent a while rummaging around in lockers to put together a care package and turned up a few buried treasures. It has never ceased to amaze me how things can disappear on such a small boat, to be found later hiding away in far corners of lockers. I found a solitary remaining boil-in-the-bag MRE (meal ready to eat) and had it for my dinner. It was a real treat to have proper satisfying chunks of food to chew on rather than the little pieces of freeze-dried rubble that make up a typical dehydrated expedition meal.

I also found some more tamari sunflower seeds. I mix them in with bean sprouts, tamari almonds, nama shoyu sauce, and tahini to make a delicious and nutritious lunch. And there were some dried apple slices—very welcome variations to my larder.

I put together a generous stack of expedition meals, Lärabars, and jerky to give to the *Junk* crew. I would have been happy to give them some of my dehydrated flax crackers, too, but I suspected that no matter how short on variety they were, they might not share my more extreme whole-food tastes.

I put it all into biodegradable trash bags, ready to hand over when we finally met. The bags were ideal for this purpose, although I had found out the hard way that they biodegraded in less than three months when mixed with seawater, and my small trash stash in the locker beneath the rowing seat now consisted of a mess of food wrappers and sun-lotion tubes surrounded by a few pointless shreds of disintegrating green plastic.

10 August came and went. So did 11 August. We were speaking every day and adjusting our respective courses to stay on track for a rendezvous. I was continuing to row, expecting that they would soon catch up with me, but the winds had subsided, and even with a sail the *Junk* was barely gaining ground. I was starting to get impatient. The scheduled phone calls were interfering with my usual routine, but there was also a more pressing motivation for wanting to meet sooner rather than later, and it was nothing to do with my waning water supplies.

Each time we spoke, Joel would promise me a fresh fish supper when we finally got together, and I was really looking forward to it. I don't fish when I'm at sea. I am rather squeamish about having to bash a fish's brains out, and the process of gutting and cleaning would make a horrible mess of my deck. But I was more than happy for someone else to do the hard work, and I was almost salivating at the idea of a nice fresh catch for dinner.

12 AUGUST WAS A CLEAR, CALM, SUNNY DAY, the ocean still and glossy. It was very beautiful, but not conducive to fast progress in a sailboat. After an early afternoon conversation with Joel, we agreed that I would have to stop rowing if they were going to catch up with me. So I stowed my oars and made the most of my idle time by posting early on my blog:

> It would be amusing to watch the progress of our two vessels from above. Their top speed is about 2.8 kts [knots], mine about 2 kts. We are two very slow-moving objects converging on each other ever so slowly, like two garden snails about to mate (do snails mate?).

After hanging around for an hour waiting for them to catch up, I spoke again to Joel on the *Junk,* who came up with a highly pertinent point. He had been tracking their progress relative to mine, watching the small blip on their radar that represented my boat. Over the last few days, he'd found that the wind tended to die down during the afternoon, and they would lose ground relative to my position. The wind would then pick up again overnight, and they would regain the lost ground and more. According to his calculations, they were unlikely to catch up with me before nightfall, and if the wind followed the usual pattern, they would probably overtake me during the hours of darkness. We would be, quite literally, two ships passing in the night, and my chance of a fresh fish supper—not to mention life-saving water supplies—would pass me by.

That did it. There was only one thing for it. I would have to turn around and row back towards them.

This caused me some considerable discombobulation. After nearly three months of heading west, west, always west, and rowing in the same direction across the Atlantic a couple of years previously, it felt totally unnatural to turn the *Brocade*'s bows deliberately to point east, watching the compass needle swing through 180 degrees, and to deliberately undo precious progress made. But the prospect of our upcoming dinner party helped me overcome my momentary sense of disorientation and any slight resentment at the loss of miles.

East I rowed, towards their last reported position. I had to keep craning to glance over my shoulder. Usually it was no problem that rowers face towards the stern of the boat, as for the last few months there had been nothing but sea and sky no matter which way I looked, but on this occasion it was rather inconvenient. Luckily it was a calm day, and I was relieved to finally see a bright dot on the horizon, which gradually resolved itself into a square white sail. Supper was in sight.

I got on the satphone again. "I can see you!" I called. "I'm over here. Look to the west!"

Joel had been watching my boat on the radar and now clambered up the mast to assume a lookout position. Even though he was about 20 feet above the water, he couldn't see me until I was about 200 yards away. When he told me this later, it really brought it home how invisible I was on this vast ocean, even to someone who knew exactly where to look.

At last we were within a few dozen yards of each other, but actually docking my boat against theirs proved to be more difficult than anticipated. They tried to throw a line to me, but it fell short. My boat drifted farther away again. The problem was that I couldn't row to keep my boat on course and be ready to catch a line at the same time. I simply didn't have enough hands.

Eventually Marcus jumped into the water and swam over with a thin line so that we could connect the two vessels. After so many months of no human contact, it was a most welcome sight to see a face pop up over the gunwale of my boat—especially as it was an exceptionally good-looking, suntanned face pierced with striking blue eyes. *Hello, Sailor!* I thought, and the moniker "Hunks on the *Junk*" suddenly made sense.

Marcus handed me the line, and I tied it to a makeshift cleat that I had fashioned to help pull in the sea anchor, then used the line to bring the *Brocade* close enough for me to jump aboard their vessel.

And what a vessel she was. A raft supported by thousands of plastic bottles lashed together with cargo nets, a deck made out of an open grid of yacht masts, the fuselage of a Cessna aircraft as a cabin, and a plush-pile bucket seat from a car as a captain's chair. The *Junk* was very homemade and looked like she should never have been allowed out of port, but no doubt stranger ships have made it across oceans.

At last I met Joel, who for so many days now had been just a voice on the other end of a satphone line. He was an unusual-looking young man—tall and thin with a shaved head and a bristling set of mutton-chop whiskers. The two men were a real contrast: Marcus dark-haired and muscular, with a bearing that revealed his military past, while Joel had a gangling build and the easygoing air and relaxed drawl of a surfer. I found out later that he lived on a boat in Hawai'i, which seemed entirely appropriate. They were an unlikely pairing but seemed to get on well together, which was all the more remarkable given the trials and tribulations they had been through. For many ocean-rowing pairs, the pressures of a voyage had proved too much for the friendship to survive, so it was a relief to find that the atmosphere on board the *Junk* was amiable.

FIRST THINGS FIRST: WHILE THE *BROCADE* was alongside, Joel went across to pick up the bags of food that I had set aside for them in my sleeping cabin. Much later, he told me that after the less-than-fragrant conditions in their own sleeping quarters ("the *Junk*'s got funk" had become one of their catchphrases), he was quite smitten by the smell in my cabin. "It smelled of *girl*," he later reported to Marcus. It was probably the tea-tree oil that I use to try and prevent saltwater sores on my backside that he could smell, but I was nonetheless pleased to think that I had retained some degree of feminine fragrance during my time at sea.

After Joel had passed the bags of food over to the *Junk*, the men returned the favour by giving me a container full of water and transferring yet more into my empty Dromedary bags. Some of the water had a hint of green in it, probably some kind of algae, but I wasn't in a position to be fussy. They also very generously gave me their spare manual watermaker in case I had to make more. I still have it on my boat now, although fortunately I've never needed to use it.

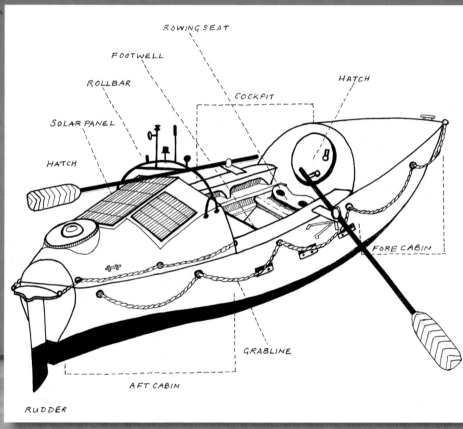

ROWING SEAT

FOOTWELL

ROLLBAR

COCKPIT

HATCH

SOLAR PANEL

HATCH

FORE CABIN

GRABLINE

AFT CABIN

RUDDER

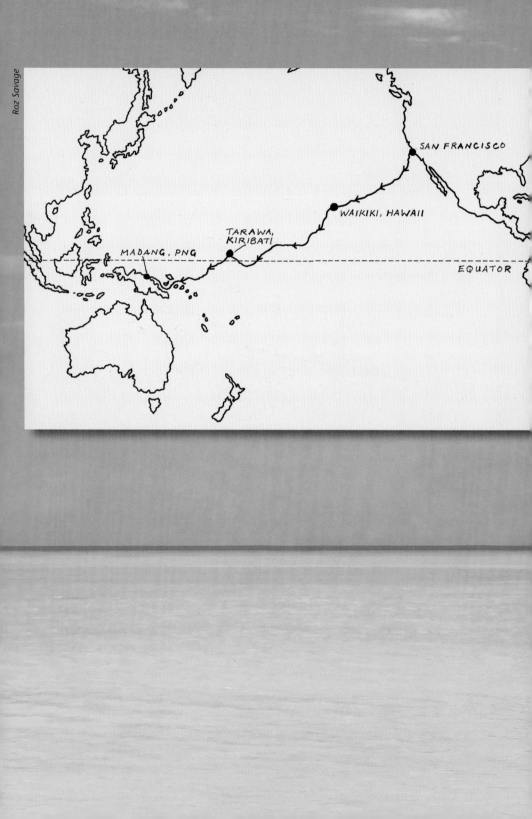

The *Brocade* in San Francisco with four months' worth of supplies

Lieutenant Kevin Winters, Rescue Swimmer Chuck Wolfe, me, and Lieutenant Stephen Baxter

The *White Holly* team. Back row: Eric, me, Melinda,
Vince, Caitlin, Aenor. Front row: Chris, Mike.

Marcus Eriksen

Joel Paschal, me, and Marcus Eriksen gurning at the camera
on board the *Junk* raft

Joel Paschal

With Marcus Eriksen on board the *Junk* raft

Aleksey Bochkovsky

Roz Savage

Roz Savage

Brocade waiting to depart from
San Francisco in 2008

Daily rations

My broken finger

Bedecked with leis in Hawai'i

The Moloka'i Channel

Phil Uhl

Greeting my mother after rowing to Hawai'i in 2008

Phil Uhl

Phil Uhl

RowsTheB

Big smiles on arrival in Hawaiʻi

Rowing past Diamond Head in Honolulu

Beach cleanup in Hawai'i

Barnacles on the *Brocade*'s hull

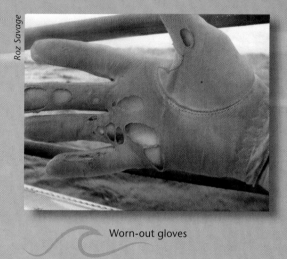

Worn-out gloves

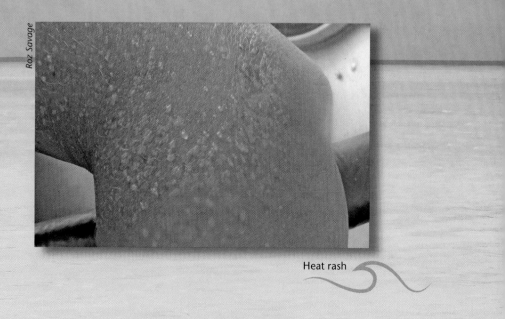

Heat rash

Roz Savage

A booby bird

Hunter Downs

Arriving in Tarawa

Roz Savage

Squishy the Dolphin,
aka Neptune

Roz Savage

One very deceased squid

Rowing into Tarawa—note evidence of the booby birds

Nicole brings me a beer

Carried ashore in Tarawa

Dancers greet me in Tarawa

President Anote Tong of Kiribati

Roz Savage

The usual

Roz Savage

Ship's compass

Turtle with pilot fish

Sunset

A warm welcome in Papua New Guinea

Rowing into Madang

Transfer complete, we allowed my boat to drift a short distance away so that she wouldn't chafe against the *Junk*. The *Brocade* bobbed around about ten yards away at the end of her line. It was strange to see her from the outside—for the last three months she had been my entire world. She was weathering well, and I felt quietly proud of her as she waited there patiently for me.

Joel put on a mask and snorkel and, armed with a harpoon gun, hopped overboard to catch our supper. While his crewmate was fishing, Marcus showed me around the boat. It didn't take long. The small cabin of the Cessna aircraft was messy, with bedding lying in untidy heaps and various instruments and gadgets littering the shelf beneath the cockpit windscreen or fixed to the ceiling above it. Marcus invited me to sign the outside of the cabin, and I added my signature to the many names of well-wishers already written there.

I felt a bit clumsy on board this vessel, so different from my own. The masts that formed the deck were laid in a loose grid with large gaps through which I could see the water beneath. A few garments were tied to the underside of the grid, streaming out in the current. "The laundry," Marcus explained.

Turning to the back of the boat, where a large tiller mechanism took up most of its width, Marcus pulled up an open-mouthed mesh net, a homemade trawl to gather samples from the ocean each day. He showed me the results. Tiny pieces of plastic, still recognizable, dotted the mesh. On a typical day they were finding more plastic than organic matter, by a ratio of around six to one. Plankton, the basis of the entire ocean food chain, was far outweighed by plastic fragments, even many hundreds of miles from land. And, Marcus explained, it was going to get worse. We were a long way from the epicentre of the Great Pacific Garbage Patch, where the ratio of plastic to plankton could exceed 40 to 1.

It was sobering to see with my own eyes the evidence that human-kind has profoundly impacted the oceans. Plastic never truly biodegrades, as far as we know. It just hasn't been around long enough for us to know for sure how many years, decades, or centuries it might take for it to disappear—if indeed it ever does. Plastic has only been in mass production for around 50 years, yet in that time we have deposited many millions of tons of it into landfills and oceans, largely in the form of "disposable" items such as bags, bottles, cigarette lighters, and toothbrushes. It is surely insane to make throwaway items out of an indestructible material—and a toxic one at that. On a finite planet, what goes around comes around, so to continue pumping vast quantities of poisonous substances into our environment is obviously a catastrophically bad idea.

By now Joel had scrambled back on board, proudly bearing a magnificent big mahi mahi as the fruit of his underwater hunting mission. Apparently he had been trying to catch one for the previous few days to ensure that he could keep his promise of a fresh fish supper, but to no avail. So I felt especially grateful that this mission had been successful.

As Marcus expertly gutted and filleted the fish, he told me about another mahi mahi that they had caught a couple of weeks previously. When they opened it up, they found numerous pieces of plastic in its stomach. Being scientists, they knew this was bad news. Most plastic is not an inert substance. It leaches out toxic chemicals and hormone disruptors into its surroundings, especially when mixed with a creature's digestive juices. Given the amount of plastic in its guts, this fish would not be safe to eat; and after photographing the evidence, they threw the dead fish back into the ocean. That fish has now become a poster child for the plastic pollution issue.

Seeing me look rather downcast at all this bad news, Marcus suggested we shoot some lighthearted video and photos to document our encounter. We recorded some jokey footage for their blog and gurned horribly at the camera for some still photos. I think the idea was to look vaguely piratical, but actually we just looked like we're suffering severe facial spasms.

After that it was on to the social part of the evening. It was surely one of the world's more surreal dinner parties, given that we were on a boat made out of empty water bottles floating around in the Pacific several hundred miles east of Hawai'i. We could have done with some cold beers, but they had long since run out, and the dinner guest had turned up shamefully empty-handed. As I sat and enjoyed the luxury of being waited on, Marcus and Joel opened up their cooking range, a large metal box at the side of the Cessna, containing a stove, pots and pans, and a selection of spices.

After cutting some of the fish for us to eat sushi style, Joel fried several batches of the flesh, varying the mix of spices for each course. The meat from near the tail was especially delicious—dark and intensely tasty. The butter was a little rancid, but I wasn't complaining. This was by far the best restaurant in town.

After the first three batches, the boys leaned back and asked if I'd had enough. I hadn't, quite. I had another two generous helpings. I'd like to claim it was my body craving protein, but more likely I was just being greedy. It was the first fresh fish I'd had in months, and I was going to make the most of the opportunity.

(As an aside, I now eat fish infrequently, and many of my friends don't eat it at all, in deference to collapsing fish populations around the world. My plea of mitigation is that this was a very special occasion, and I can guarantee that there was absolutely no by-catch.)

Conversation revolved around the environment—the garbage patch, which Marcus knew well, having made three previous trips there with Algalita—and our respective plans for Hawai'i. We pledged to combine forces once we got there, recognizing that circumstances had offered us the perfect opportunity to collaborate, and hopefully achieve more together than we could do separately.

Just before sunset, I returned to the *Brocade*. After the incessant creaking of 15,000 empty water bottles chafing against each other, my boat seemed blissfully peaceful. She also felt a lot more solid and seaworthy than their crazy craft. I had enjoyed the interlude of sociability, but I felt happy and secure to be back aboard my own boat, especially now that the end of the voyage was in sight and I had a generous supply of water. But I don't mean to seem ungrateful. The Hunks had been wonderful hosts, and I went back to my oars with a full belly and rowed off into the sunset with a smile on my face.

I switched over to green-tinted *Junk* water on 18 August and arrived in Hawai'i on 1 September. It would have been a very miserable last few weeks if I'd had to ration my existing water supplies to stretch to the end of the journey.

Marcus discovered the hard way that it's not a good idea to eat three bags of jerky in an hour when your digestive system has got used to nothing but peanut butter and granola. I will leave you to read his book if you want to know the full details. The state of Marcus's digestive system is beyond the scope of my story.

I FELT INCREDIBLY LUCKY TO HAVE CROSSED PATHS with the *Junk*, but at the same time I acknowledged the role that I had played in creating my own luck. Had I not committed to my blogging duties in order to share my inspiration, adventure, and environmental message, I would never have been made aware of the proximity of the *Junk* raft.

Having read *The Celestine Prophecy* during the formative years of my mid-life transformation, I was fascinated for a while with the idea of there being no such thing as coincidence. Could we really manipulate our experience of the world through operating on the energetic level, attracting into our lives the things that we need? It was a fascinating idea, but in my experience, the best way to get what we want is to be clear about what we're looking for so that we recognize it when we see it, and then to work ceaselessly to create opportunities. Serendipity does play a role, but I've found that the harder I work and the more people I connect with, the more the universe provides. While everything may come to she who waits, I find it comes a lot faster to she who gets off her backside and makes it happen.

I've found the most effective way to go about my life is to maintain a balance between keeping my eye on the goal and paying attention to what's happening in my peripheral vision. I need to know where I'm going so as not to get too diverted, but also to be aware that there are many different paths to the top of the mountain, some of which will provide invaluable opportunities for fun, friendship, and learning.

I ARRIVED IN WAIKIKI A LITTLE MORE THAN A WEEK after the *Junk*. It was the Labour Day weekend, an American national holiday, and the folks at my sponsors' public relations agency had asked if I could please hold off for a couple of days as the local media only had a skeleton staff working over the weekend. I was none too impressed with the suggestion.

"*You* try spending 99 days out here, and see how *you* would feel about hanging around offshore," I retorted. "I want a shower and a shampoo. And champagne. I'm coming in."

I had been a little nervous about making landfall in Hawai'i ever since I set out from San Francisco. There is a good reason why Hawai'i is the surf capital of the world. The waves can be intimidating. My weatherman, Rick, himself a resident of Hawai'i, reassuringly predicted that the conditions in the notorious Moloka'i Channel would be relatively benign for my arrival.

I had already been within sight of land for several days—by which I mean literally that I could see land, but anyone on land would not have been able to see me. I had rowed past the "Big Island" of Hawai'i, then Maui and Moloka'i, but I was no safer than I had been in the middle of the ocean. Even if somebody ashore were looking for me, they would not be able to spy me rowing past in the distance, hidden down amongst the waves. Kayaker Andrew McAuley died in the Tasman Sea between Australia and New Zealand when he was less than 40 miles from his destination. I knew I could not afford to relax until I set foot on dry land.

I now had to try and shoot cleanly down the Moloka'i Channel, heading southwest, to reach Waikiki on the sheltered southern side of O'ahu. The PR people were pressing me for an estimated time of arrival. They wanted to muster the media for a photo opportunity as I rowed past Diamond Head, the distinctive mountain to the east of Waikiki that marks the finish line of the Transpacific Yacht Race. It would make a spectacularly photogenic backdrop as I arrived in Hawai'i.

In an attempt to come up with an accurate guesstimate, I had been calculating my average rate of progress over the last few days. The plan, as agreed upon with the PR staff and communicated to the TV networks, was that I would arrive at the Waikiki Yacht Club sometime between 9 A.M. and noon on 1 September. I was later given a specific target of a 10 A.M. arrival, which even at the time I thought rather unrealistic given the vagaries of the ocean.

We had all reckoned without the "Funnel Factor." The challenge was going to be to make enough progress west, after I rounded the northern tip of Moloka'i, in order to reach the yacht club, while the winds and currents that barrel down the channel between Moloka'i and O'ahu would be trying to push me south.

My last full day at sea, 31 August, started early, when a huge wave crashed into the side of my boat at 4:30 A.M., jolting me awake. If these conditions were benign, as Rick had described them, I thought that I would not like to encounter the channel in a malevolent mood.

The sun rose on a fine day, with scattered cumulus clouds speckling the sky overhead. I could see the green bulk of Moloka'i to the east, hunkered down beneath squally clouds. O'ahu was lost in the haze to the west. The day grew hot. Birds wheeled and swooped around my boat. There was a big swell and a brisk wind; conditions were fast, and pushing me south. I spent most of the day with the boat pointing north-west while I desperately tried to counteract the strong southerly drift. It was a struggle. *Brocade* was sideways to the waves, and I was regularly drenched by huge "boatfillers," the name I gave to the really annoying waves that storm in like juggernauts and fill the cockpit to the gunwales, eliciting a stream of bad language from one very irritated ocean rower. I doubt I will ever reconcile myself to the futility of swearing at an ocean, as it does make me feel so very much better.

As the day went on my concern grew. The wind was blowing 25 knots and my red ensign flag stuck out horizontally as if it had a rod running through it. I was getting pushed too far south, too fast. To have any chance at all of making it into Waikiki, I would have to row all night to keep pushing west. If I stopped to sleep, the *Brocade* would be pushed south and I would miss O'ahu by several miles. I called Rick from the satellite phone to share my concerns with him and let him know the plan. My mother was by now in Hawai'i, and was staying with Rick and his wife, so I spoke to Mum, too. I promised to call her with an update every few hours during the night.

I had also spoken via satphone to Joel from the *Junk*. The Hunks had landed about a week before me, and Joel had promised to sail out in his boat to greet me. He told me that he and a couple of friends, Morgan and Troy, planned to leave from the Ala Wai marina at around midnight to try and intercept me at first light. I was touched that he would do this for me.

As DARKNESS FELL, THE WAVES WERE HIGH, topped with white foaming crests that seemed to glow as if lit from within. There was no moon, and the deck was invisible in the darkness. I took good care to avoid mishap as my boat pitched around restlessly. It would be too bad to have anything go wrong on the home straight. The stars were bright overhead despite the nearness of the orange streetlights of O'ahu, which as I got closer resolved from a general glow into individual dots of light. It didn't look far now. After 2,324 miles, there were just a few more to go. As I rowed I listened to an audiobook of the Jules Verne classic *Twenty Thousand Leagues Under the Sea*. It seemed appropriate. Then the battery on my iPod went dead, so I switched over to the boat's stereo to play a CD of music that Eric had compiled for me. I sang along to drown out the sound of the roaring wind and to give myself courage.

I checked in with Mum at 10 P.M., and again at midnight. The conditions were still rough, and I was zooming along.

Joel would later tell me that he and his friends had had to abort their attempt to come and welcome me. "It was windy and the current was ripping. We were making almost no progress trying to tack around Koko Head. Each time we tried going farther out into the channel and then tack back towards shore, and each time we ended up just a very short distance up the coast. Plus we were getting soaked and beaten up by waves. I figured if we couldn't get to the spot I thought you would be at, that you, being in the same current and wind, would not be there anyway. You'd be far south of that. So we gave up and sailed back to the Ala Wai." Even for a seasoned sailor like Joel, it was a frenetic night in the funnel of the Moloka'i Channel.

On I rowed, the orange lights of O'ahu growing ever closer. By 2 A.M. I was exhausted. I'd been awake and rowing since 4:30 the previous morning. Just a little power nap, I told myself—a quick half hour.

Three hours later I woke up. *Damn!* I checked the GPS. Disaster. I had slept too long and was now south of Waikiki. I had overshot the bottom end of the channel. It was now going to be virtually impossible for me to make the Yacht Club under my own power. Sheepishly, I called my mother.

"Thank heavens you're all right!" she exclaimed. "I was worried when you didn't check in."

"Yes, I'm all right, but I'm too far south. I fell asleep," I confessed. "I'm going to need help getting into Waikiki."

We had thought I might need a tow and had prepared for this contingency. A boat and skipper from the Waikiki Yacht Club were on standby.

"It's a bit early," my mother said. It was 5 A.M. "Can we wait another hour or so before we call Captain Phil?"

"Sure," I said. "I'll row past the line of longitude of the Yacht Club, and do my best to hang around as close to there as I can. But I'll probably get pushed still further south."

We agreed that we would separate the two components of my finish. I would carry on rowing and cross the finish line in my own time. Then I would be towed back to Diamond Head to re-row the last half mile closer to shore, for the cameras.

WHEN I ARRIVED AT THE FINISH LINE, morning was just starting to lighten the eastern horizon, and the stars were winking out one by one. The water was rough, but I was rowing strongly. The track playing on the CD—by accident rather than design, but it couldn't have been more appropriate—was Hawai'ian singer Israel Kamakawiwo'ole's version of "Wonderful World" interlaced with "Somewhere Over the Rainbow."

His soft, wistful voice filled my ears and my mind. I had dared to live my dream, and although it had become a nightmare for a while the previous year, now it had all come good. I thought back to my departure from the Golden Gate Bridge, nearly 2,500 miles ago, and reflected on the highs and lows since then. This had been a hard crossing, but so much less difficult than the Atlantic. I had spent the years since that voyage assiduously dissecting the experience, the process of giving talks and writing a book allowing me to analyse and assess what had happened and to learn from it. I had taken what the universe provided, determined to grow from it. I had internalized the lessons, incorporating them into the way I operated in the world, and those new life skills had paid dividends on this voyage.

I hadn't known in advance of the Pacific launch whether I had fully succeeded in this task. It's easy to believe that you've got it all figured out when you're on dry land, but the ocean has a way of upsetting everything that you thought you knew. After completing the Atlantic voyage, I had been utterly certain that I would continue with my mission to row the world's "Big Three" oceans—the Atlantic, Pacific, and Indian—yet this did not mean that I relished the prospect. Having crossed the Atlantic and hence knowing what I was letting myself in for, the notion of tackling the Pacific had created a tight knot of dread in the centre of my chest every time I thought about it.

So it gave me great gratification to recognise that not only had I succeeded in crossing safely, but also that this voyage had been less miserable than the Atlantic. At times, rowing along and listening to audiobooks, I had even almost enjoyed it. I smiled as I acknowledged to myself that I had matured as a person and as an adventurer. It was indeed a Wonderful World.

AT 5:55 A.M. LOCAL TIME ON 1 SEPTEMBER 2008, I crossed the line of longitude at 157 degrees, 50.550 minutes west. I stopped rowing, whooped in delight, and beamed a huge grin of satisfaction. I had completed the first leg of my solo row across the Pacific in a time of 99 days, 8 hours, and 55 minutes, becoming the first woman to row from California to Hawai'i. I finished it as I had spent most of the previous 99 days—alone.

The last hours had not quite gone according to plan, but in the final analysis it made no difference. I had still done it, and a warm glow of accomplishment filled me as the waters fill the ocean—all the way to the edges.

There was then a bit of a hiatus while the escort boat tried to find me. I had given them my latitude and longitude, but it transpired they didn't have a GPS on board. We were communicating by VHF marine radio, but they simply weren't able to see me. When I heard the roar of engines as a jet took off from Honolulu International Airport, inspiration struck. "I'm underneath the airplane . . . now!" I timed the last word to coincide with the moment when the plane was directly overhead. After two hours of searching, at last they could see my position, and within minutes a little yellow boat with a boxy cabin was zipping across the waves towards me.

They towed me back to Diamond Head, and I did my duties for the TV cameras and press photographers assembled on another, larger motor boat. An underwater cameraman, known locally as Scuba Drew, got some unusual angles by swimming around and beneath my boat. At last the photo call was over, and I was able to head to dry land. By now I was impatient to feel terra firma beneath my feet.

As I paddled into the harbour, a couple of outrigger canoes were there to escort me in. I heard a familiar, Australian-accented voice ring out a greeting across the water, and did a double take when I saw Melinda, not renowned for her athletic prowess, sitting in one of the canoes. I don't know quite how she'd arranged it, but she had somehow coerced the paddlers to come out and greet me and to bring her along. Aenor was waiting on the dock to fulfill her role as expedition doctor.

The photos of my arrival show a skinny, suntanned figure in black capri pants and a turquoise bikini top stepping ashore to hug her mother. Leis are placed around her neck, and there are more hugs. Then a barrage of microphones and cameras being pointed in her direction, engulfing the tiny figure. Bobbie Jennings, the PR chair of the Waikiki Yacht Club, had done a magnificent job of securing a media turnout. The assembled reporters and photographers nearly sank the pontoon.

A glass of champagne, rather warm in the Hawai'ian sunshine, was pressed into my hand, and I sipped as I spoke. It was only later that I realized it had been a plastic glass, as would be sarcastically reported by a sharp-eyed journalist. Just moments after stepping off my boat, I inadvertently made contact with a single-use plastic item, exactly the kind of object I was campaigning against. I was appalled that I hadn't noticed at the time, but can only submit in my defence that after so long alone, I was completely overwhelmed by the sensory onslaught of being back on dry land and being surrounded by so many friendly faces.

By the time we moved over to the buffet lunch, I had recovered my senses somewhat and insisted on a ceramic plate rather than the plastic "disposable" ones that were otherwise in use. The incident brought home to me that plastic has become so ubiquitous that, unless we are made aware of it, we don't even notice how much of it we are using.

After a couple of glasses of champagne, Aenor gently steered me in the direction of the ladies' room. It was time for my medical exam. We had done this before my departure, and now we went through the familiar drill again. As the Coast Guard medic had done, she made me follow her fingertip with my eyes. After so long without alcohol, the champagne had gone straight to my head and I felt a bit woozy, but I more or less passed the test. Then she asked me to push against her resistance with arms, then legs, to check for injury or weakness. She placed bathroom scales on the floor and I stepped on. I had lost 25 pounds. Later testing would reveal that I was down to 11 percent body fat.

"Drink water!" Aenor ordered me, emphatically. "Or you'll dehydrate in this heat."

"'kay," I slurred. "S'long as it'sh not in a plashtic bottle."

Glass of iced water in hand, I joined in with the milling throng in the yacht club bar. Marcus and Joel were there among the well-wishers waiting to greet me. I was relieved to see that Joel had shaved off his muttonchop whiskers. He looked almost normal. I was introduced to Marcus's fiancée, Anna Cummins, who had been acting as their shore manager. Since the voyage of the *Junk* raft, Marcus and Anna have gone on to found the 5 Gyres Institute to investigate Marcus's theory that the Great Pacific Garbage Patch is in fact just one of five such areas around the world, the others being in the South Pacific, North Atlantic, South Atlantic, and Indian Oceans. They alternate their time between scientific research at sea and outreach and education on dry land. Joel has also remained passionately committed to fighting the plastic peril, founding a nonprofit called Sea of Change to develop ways for citizen scientists to collect plastic pollution data at sea.

As Mum and I were given a lift from the Yacht Club to my weatherman's house, I went into a kind of culture shock. The speed of the car seemed unnaturally fast. The skyscrapers of Waikiki seemed dangerously high. And all these people! I felt like a space alien seeing human civilization for the first time. I looked at the shops selling designer clothes, jewelry, and electronics. I was quite perplexed that people would spend so much money on such pointless things. If you couldn't eat it, drink it, or row with it, then what purpose did it serve? A rower's needs are very simple—enough food and water and a few miles in the right direction are enough to make it a good day.

Examining my visceral reaction to the blatantly conspicuous consumption all around me, I realized that although I'd been so materialistic in my early adult life, my values had fundamentally changed. Not only was I not interested in owning much stuff, I was actually repulsed by this flagrant consumerism.

There is still a widespread belief that money can buy happiness, yet this is patently not true. It has been demonstrated scientifically that beyond a certain level of income where our basic needs are taken care of, further wealth delivers very little additional happiness—but it *can* have a major effect on levels of consumption, and hence on our environment. In fact, in some countries, reported happiness even diminishes as average per capita income continues to rise. Some of the most affluent societies in the world are rife with disease, addictions, and unhappiness. It would be easier to understand our obsession with consumerism—or at least forgive it—if it was making us happier, but in most cases it isn't.

I realized that over the course of the past three and a half months, far away from the insidious messaging of advertisers and marketers, my happiness had come from much more authentic sources—from the beauty of sunrises and sunsets, from making progress towards a well-defined goal, from enjoying plenty of fresh air and exercise and a healthy diet, and from my relationships with my mother, friends, and blog readers. By any definition it cannot be said that I had enjoyed a high standard of living while at sea, but I had experienced incredible quality of life.

Looking at the crowds of tourist and shoppers, I saw evidence of overconsumption and overeating. I examined their faces, looking for clues to their thoughts, their emotions. I wondered if they stopped to consider the big questions, like *Why are we here? What is our life purpose? What makes us happy?* The computer revolution was supposed to give us more leisure time, but even the tourists, supposedly relaxing on holiday, seemed busier than ever, caught up in a whirlwind of largely pointless activity. Was all this busy-ness just serving to distract them from uncomfortable questions—and answers?

I felt happy to be free of the burden of stuff—buying stuff, selling stuff, maintaining stuff, fixing stuff, earning the money to buy yet more stuff, all for the greater good of the economy, which in its present incarnation depends on an ever-increasing demand for stuff. We're encouraged to satisfy our desires rather than our needs in a doomed pursuit of infinite economic growth on a finite planet.

THE FOLLOWING THURSDAY, THE *JUNK* GUYS and I held a joint press conference on the lawn in front of the Waikiki Aquarium. I had lost so much weight that none of my clothes fit properly any more, and a friend had to lend me a length of sailing rope as a makeshift belt to hold my jeans up. The *Junk* raft and the *Brocade* were on display, and the press conference included statements from local groups working to reduce plastic waste, including the O'ahu chapter of Surfrider Foundation, Styrophobia, Jack Johnson's Kokua Hawai'i Foundation, and the Beach Environmental Awareness Campaign Hawai'i (BEACH).

From the aquarium, we clambered into a minibus and headed with about 25 volunteers to Kahuku Beach on O'ahu's northeast coast. I was shocked to see the amount of plastic debris on this rarely visited beach. Where I might expect to see lines of seaweed, here instead I saw tidemarks of trash, most of it plastic. Suzanne Frazer from BEACH issued each of us a yellow bucket labeled with the name of a particular kind of commonly found plastic object. I was in charge of oyster spacers. I had never before heard of such a thing, nor had I realized that oysters were in need of spacing, but it turned out that these were plastic rods of various lengths with a hole down the middle, used in oyster farming. It was important that the different types of plastic were kept separate so that the items could be counted, providing useful data on what kind of trash was being found and where it might have come from.

To me it was frustrating to see all this plastic and only be able to pick up a small subset of it. I wanted to clean up the whole lot, to remove it from this once-beautiful beach and restore the site to its pristine state as nature intended. We took away two truckloads of rubbish that day, but there was plenty still left lying on the sand, and an almost endless supply still lurking offshore, in the Great Pacific Garbage Patch, waiting to roll in on the next tide, coming back to haunt us in an endless karmic cycle. Truly, we reap what we sow.

CHAPTER FIVE

WE CREATE OUR FUTURE

"Sow a thought and you reap an action; sow an action and you reap a habit; sow a habit and you reap a character; sow a character and you reap a destiny."

— RALPH WALDO EMERSON

I usually love to see wildlife at sea. Although in one way the ocean seascape is infinitely variable—every sunrise, sunset, squall, and cloud formation is a unique event—it can also seem unbearably monotonous, with nothing but sea, sky, and a little silver boat to occupy the eye, day after day. A visit from a sea creature is usually a welcome relief from the monotony—but I felt I might have to make an exception in this present case.

It was May 2009, and I was en route from Hawai'i to Tuvalu on the second stage of the Pacific crossing. I was rowing along, listening to an audiobook, as was my habit, when something caught my eye. I did a double take. A pointed fin was waving at me from the water's surface.

I'd read reports by sailors of previous centuries of oceans teeming with creatures such as dolphins, whales, sharks, or turtles, but in my experience days could go by with no sighting. This might have been due to my low vantage point, or due to my being in a daze induced by the repetitive motion of rowing, but is also likely to be due to the much-diminished populations of many of these charismatic megafauna of the ocean. So wildlife sightings were rare enough, but to have the wildlife waving to me was rarer still. I moved over to that side of the boat to take a closer look.

It was hideous. Lying on its side while it lazily waved its pectoral fin in the air, the large, disc-shaped creature looked like a truncated version of a fish. Its body went straight from head to tail with nothing in between. The head occupied the front half of its body, and the tail was no more than a frill around the back half. Its appearance deeply disturbed me. Was this mutant a terrible consequence of our pollution of the oceans?

Fortunately not. I mentioned the odd fish in my next blog post, and the social media network provided the answer. It was a sunfish, well known for basking at the surface of the ocean—while waving its fin. I was relieved to find that this was not some unnatural, man-made, genetically modified monster, but actually a rather rare and special fish, made exactly as nature intended it to be: pug ugly.

I hadn't seen many interesting creatures on the first stage of the Pacific crossing, between San Francisco and Hawai'i—a few dolphins, the occasional whale, and birds almost every day. I had to wait until this second stage to hit the real mother lode of marine wildlife.

TURTLES ARE AMONG MY FAVOURITE creatures. They have an air of benevolence and wisdom that convinces me that they're old souls returned to Earth to watch over vulnerable seafarers. While I was scuba diving on a wreck in Hawai'i shortly before my departure, I encountered a huge turtle sitting on the deck of the sunken ship. I sat next to her (for some reason I was sure it was a female) and very slowly, so as not to scare her, reached out my hand and gently touched her flipper. A small cloud of algae, disturbed by my touch, puffed up into the water. The turtle turned and blinked at me lugubriously. She didn't seem to mind, and I felt a momentary bond of kinship with this strange, ancient being.

It makes me sad that they are amongst the creatures most impacted by plastic pollution, especially plastic bags. The turtles mistake them for jellyfish, their favourite food, and eat them. I have seen distressing photographs of dissected turtles, their digestive tracts so bunged full of plastic that they can neither digest nor excrete. It offends me that we expose these peaceful animals to the risk of an unpleasant and lingering death through our carelessness.

I was rather pleased with some underwater video footage I managed to get of a gorgeously patterned turtle as he swam laps of my boat one day, with his little entourage of pilot fish in tow. (For some indefinable reason this one seemed male.) The fish follow turtles around to eat the algae that grow on the animal's shell. It's a mutually beneficial relationship: The fish get dinner, and the turtle gets clean. This fellow spent about ten minutes circling my boat, occasionally popping his head above the water, but mostly swimming purposeful laps, round and round.

SOME OTHER VISITORS WERE LESS welcome. Much as I of course love nature in all its manifestations, booby birds are without a doubt the stupidest, smelliest, most obstinate creatures I have ever encountered . . . although maybe they are not that stupid, because when three of them spotted my small rowboat heading the same way they were going, they decided it would be a great way to hitchhike across the ocean. Why bother flying if you can take it easy while some dumb human does all the hard work for you? Okay, it might be a bit slow, but these birds were in no hurry. And so they moved in and settled on the roof of the forward cabin.

You might think it would be nice for me to have the company—but not this company. It was like having three incontinent strangers move into your living room, take up residence on the sofa, and spend all day squabbling noisily while pooping all over your upholstery. In a short space of time, my solar panels were liberally pasted with bird shit. The boobies would make their deposit and then step in it and shuffle their feet around, as if deliberately spreading it as far and wide as possible.

Each morning I came outside wondering just how much of a mess my unruly visitors had made overnight. It was actually a relief if I found that they had confined their antisocial activities to the forward cabin. It was a less-than-ideal start to the day if they had strayed into the cockpit and pooped on my rowing seat or on the oar handles. The smell was a powerful blend of ammonia and decomposing fish, and my nose would involuntarily wrinkle as I scrubbed away the evidence of their nocturnal misdemeanours. The stench was sometimes bad enough to make me gag.

I couldn't easily see them from my rowing position, as their roost on the fore cabin was behind me, but I couldn't ignore the noise. They jostled with each other for position, pecking and flapping and shrieking as each tried to assert his right to stand on that particular patch of cabin roof. It was like having rowdy teenagers fighting in the back of the car. At times the din drowned out my iPod as I tried to listen to my audiobooks.

I did my best to get rid of my uninvited guests. The Rozlings, as my faithful band of Internet followers had named themselves, offered helpful suggestions: tie some shiny Lärabar wrappers to the boat to scare the birds away, try throwing a bucketful of water over them, and so on. These suggestions were well meant, but were made with no idea of the sheer tenacity of my feathered foes.

Other people posted comments on my blog to the effect that it was the boobies' ocean more than mine, and if I chose to intrude on their environment then I had no right to complain about their presence. This was a valid point. I absolutely acknowledge that all creatures have their role and their place and their rights to freedom of action. But it wasn't really their presence I was complaining about—it was their unhygienic personal habits. They had an entire ocean to poop in, so why did they have to do it on my boat? They could go anywhere they wanted, while I was confined to this small boat of 23 feet by 6 feet, a sitting target.

I started off being terribly British and polite, flapping my hands at them and saying, "Shoo, shoo." This had precisely no effect. They just squawked at me, shuffled their feet a bit more, and stayed put. Their vacant yellow eyes registered no emotion, apart from possibly a slight indignation that I had tried to shoo them off *their* boat.

I decided to set up a booby trap, to use a particularly apposite term. I lassoed the cleat on the far end of the cabin roof and rigged up a network of strings a few inches above the surface. The idea was that they wouldn't be able to find enough space to stand between the strings. But the distance from cleat to cockpit was too great, and the strings sagged. The birds simply stood on top of them. The experiment was mostly a failure, although I did get some malevolent satisfaction from time to time by jerking on the strings beneath their feet. For some reason the boobies never associated this phenomenon with me, but assumed it was one of the other birds jerking their chain and so squawked belligerently at their fellow freeloaders. I found my petty revenge a fine form of entertainment.

As my desperation grew, I would take my red dustpan and shove the birds bodily off the cabin roof. Sometimes I would give them a few brisk bangs on the beak as well, more to vent my boiling frustration than because I thought it would make any difference. They would squawk and flap their wings comically as they slithered off the curved roof into the water, then bob there for a moment, folding their wings while regaining their composure. Then they would take off, fly in a big circle, and come straight back again, as if nothing had happened.

They were absolutely incorrigible. I would have thought that almost any creature could be trained, that they would get the not-so-subtle hint that they were not welcome, that they would get bored of being shoveled off into the sea. But no, they were happy to play this game forever. It would drive me crazy before it had any effect whatsoever on them.

Ultimately, I had no option but to give in. They clearly weren't going to change their attitude, so I would have to change mine. I cranked up the volume on my iPod to drown them out and did my best to ignore the appalling smell. Not long after I had philosophically resigned myself to my fate, about three weeks after their arrival, the birds departed—and pathetic though it is to confess, I rather missed them.

ALMOST AS MESSY, BUT NOT AS PROLONGED, was my encounter with the low-flying squid. I hadn't known that squid could fly, but one day I was rowing along, minding my own business. Suddenly three missiles shot out of the water and thudded to the deck. I nearly jumped out of my rowing shoes in fright. It took me a moment to realize what my marine assailants were: Three squid, no doubt trying to escape from a predator underwater, had taken drastic evasive action by launching themselves into the air. They must have been at least as surprised—and put out—as I was when they found a small ocean rowboat in their way.

The one squid that had landed at my feet was rather pretty. It glowed in shades of pink and mauve, but as I watched, still trying to gather my wits, the iridescence subsided and I realized the poor little thing had died.

The squid that had collided with the bulkhead of the forward cabin was looking less attractive. As it had exited the water, it had evidently been trying to confuse the predator by emitting a cloud of ink, and as it slowly peeled away from the bulkhead and flopped flaccidly to the deck, it left a messy trail of dense, black liquid.

The third squid I didn't find until some days later, slowly decomposing behind the sea anchor.

Being rather squeamish about slimy creatures of the deep, I took out my trusty dustpan and deposited the sad little corpses back into the ocean. Some people have since asked me why I didn't fry them up for my supper. I tend to blame it on my lack of a suitable cooking vessel (I only had a kettle, not a pan), but the truth is that the little pink creatures, about six inches long, made me think not so much of dinner as of John Wayne Bobbitt.

THE MOST BEAUTIFUL CREATURE I have ever seen at sea, although it had a face only its mother could love, was the whale shark.

It was early on a Sunday morning, and the sea anchor had been out overnight to counteract a headwind. It was almost time for me to make my regular weekly call to Mum, but as I was out on deck performing my morning ablutions, I noticed that the wind had changed. I called my mother.

"Mum, it's me. I'll call you back in about half an hour. I just need to bring in the sea anchor."

It was actually closer to an hour before I rang back, during which time my mother probably feared that I'd had a tug of war with the sea anchor and lost. When her phone finally rang, the first words she heard were: "Mum, can you do a quick Google and tell me what a whale shark looks like?" I was fairly certain this was what I'd seen, but I needed to make sure.

Mum quickly found a photo on the internet, and described it to me. "It's got a very big mouth that seems to take up most of its head. It's got a dark grey skin with pretty white markings. And it can grow to up to 30 feet. Why, have you seen one?"

"Yes, yes, I have! That's why I'm so late calling back. When I pulled the sea anchor in, I got it alongside the boat, and when I looked down into the water I saw this big creature. It has just spent the last 20 minutes cruising around my boat, and I was busy shooting video. It was gorgeous!"

Well, *gorgeous* might be a bit of an exaggeration. The whale shark is a strange-looking creature. A vegetarian shark, it feeds on plankton, so it has the large, gaping mouth of a filter feeder. Looking at it head-on, its face is mostly mouth with just a little rim of head around it. Its main redeeming feature is its markings, a regular pattern of white bands and spots checkering a dark grey skin. The one that I saw was a youngster; gauging its size in comparison with the length of my boat, I would say it was only around eight feet long. It must have been attracted by the bright red-and-yellow chute of my sea anchor, following it as I drew it in towards my boat. I felt very privileged to have seen this gentle giant of the seas.

TOWARDS THE END OF THAT MIDDLE STAGE of the row I saw a lot more wildlife, but not so close at hand. One day I noticed about 30 birds, wheeling in a tight flock low above the water about 100 yards away. They seemed to be focused on one particular patch of the ocean. As I watched, I could see that they were diving down into the water, and that the surface of the ocean itself was seething with activity. I could see some large fins slicing backwards and forwards across the area. I assume that some large predators had rounded up a school of fish and then moved in for the kill, and the birds were scavenging the leftovers.

Over the next few days, I saw this scenario repeated on an increasingly frequent basis. Each feeding frenzy would last about ten minutes, after which the party would slowly fizzle out, the water would return to normal, and the flock of birds would disperse. A little later it would start up again somewhere else. I was never really able to see clearly what was going on, as it was mostly under the water and too far away, but since it might involve large predators in a hungry mood, I didn't feel the urge to dive in for a closer look.

This is the frustration of ocean crossings. I knew that there was an incredible world of wildlife down there, just feet below the hull, but mostly it was invisible to me. Only occasionally did the aquatic world break through to the surface. I dream of designing a glass-bottomed rowboat so that I can row along while watching the marine world going about its business beneath me.

Sadly, there is a lot less wildlife in the oceans now than there was even a few decades ago. It's hard to know exact figures, precisely because it is too difficult to see what is going on beneath the waves, but there is enough evidence from the distances that fishing fleets have to travel, and the reductions in both the size and number of the fish that they catch, to prove that many fish populations are on—or over—the brink of collapse. The size of our human population, devouring more fish than ever and using wasteful industrial fishing practices, has taken its toll. No longer are there plenty more fish in the sea.

I am a firm believer in the power of accumulation, how billions of daily, individual acts add up to enormous consequences. Rowing across oceans, one small oar stroke at a time, has strongly reinforced this for me. There is strength—and horror—in the power of accumulation. If we do the right things, day after day, we can accomplish great feats. But if we allow the days to slip by without checking our internal compass to make sure we're heading the right way, we are in danger of one day discovering that we have wandered far off course and it is too late or too difficult to achieve our goals.

Over the years, I've had people pour scorn on my endeavours: "What difference does it make if I use a plastic bag? Or fly? Or drive an SUV? Or eat fish? Everybody else is doing it. What I do doesn't make any difference." Of course, it is up to each individual to square with their conscience how they feel they can and should act in relation to our environment. But it makes me wince to hear people say that their actions don't matter. We are all making a difference, and it is up to us to choose what kind of a difference that is.

With everything that we do, we are contributing to the collective consciousness and to social norms. Knowingly or not, we are spreading ripples of change. If I remember to bring my own bag to the shops so I don't have to use a plastic bag, the customer behind me in the queue might notice and resolve to remember to bring their reusable bag the next time. By not eating fish and explaining to my companions why I don't, I spread information and awareness. One person at a time, we change the definition of generally accepted behaviour. One day we will reach a tipping point, when environmentally unhygienic behaviour is regarded as a selfish act to be stigmatized. Through the steady accumulation of our positive actions, we create real change in the world. The collective significance of our choices becomes clear.

THIS IS TRUE NOT JUST IN AN ENVIRONMENTAL context. At the time when I wrote the two versions of my own obituary, I was leading a perfectly normal, comfortable life. Day to day, there seemed to be nothing wrong with it. But when I took a different perspective, looking into the future to see where that progression of ordinary days would take me, I discovered that it was leading me towards a life of mediocrity, and that was not where I wanted to go.

To use the analogy of my voyages, it took me about a million strokes to get to Hawai'i from San Francisco, and if I'd stood under the Golden Gate Bridge thinking that one oar stroke wasn't going to make any difference, then I would still be standing there. But I've demonstrated by putting one oar stroke after another that in sufficient numbers, even tiny actions can add up to something significant. From the fate of whale sharks in the Pacific to the survival and happiness of people we interact with every day, we're creating our future.

CHAPTER SIX

I AM NOT MY THOUGHTS

*"The gem cannot be polished without friction,
nor man perfected without trials."*

— CHINESE PROVERB

My poor bottom never has a happy time on the ocean, despite my having tried every possible cream, oil, salve, and ointment under the sun. On the Atlantic, I suffered terrible saltwater sores and boils, Pacific Stage 1 likewise. This time around it was different—and even worse. The skin was raw and sore, and sometimes when I sat down it felt like a million evil elves were sticking red-hot pins into my backside. Unable to see the problem for myself—I'm bendy but not *that* bendy—I took my camera and, stretching my arm to its full length, gathered photographic evidence. It was a horrifying sight—a huge red rash, entirely covering both buttocks, a bottom worthy of a baboon. Knowing how bad it looked somehow made it feel even worse.

I took a couple of days off from rowing, hoping the condition would clear up. I spent most of that time lying on my front, allowing the air to circulate over the painfully inflamed skin. It helped a little, but I couldn't stay off my backside forever. Doctor Aenor urged me to take antibiotics, but I refused. Maybe it's old-fashioned of me, but I don't like ingesting substances that I don't understand (with the notable exception of alcohol, and that only while I am on dry land). The red moon of my bottom would continue to wax and wane throughout most of the voyage, not fully clearing up until after landfall.

I was also having problems with my teeth. I had been diligent in brushing regularly, despite the general inconvenience of not having running water, but had become rather lax about flossing. I paid the price when my gums became inflamed. It was on Day 86 of my row, when I was probably the farthest from a dentist it is humanly possible to be, that the pain reached a sufficient state of seriousness that I resorted to a "no-chew" regimen, as I noted in my logbook.

For a week I mulched all my food. For breakfast I would have porridge enriched with coconut-milk powder. Most of the Lärabars had nice big chunks of almond in them, but I had to avoid those and choose the softer bars instead. Peanut Butter Cookie flavour was in; Ginger Snap was out. The easiest ones to eat were the JamFrakas bars, Lärabar's child-oriented snacks, which consisted mostly of puffed rice and were a lot easier to squish between my tongue and the roof of my mouth. For lunch and dinner, I had to take my raw-food crackers and soak them in water for an hour or so until they turned to the consistency of baby food. The resulting mixture didn't look very appetizing, somewhat resembling cat vomit, but it tasted better than it looked and didn't hurt my teeth, which was all that mattered.

MY OTHER MAIN PROBLEM WAS that it was hot, phenomenally hot, and I do not function well in the heat. I am English. I grew up in a temperate climate. My father had ginger hair, and I have inherited his fair complexion. In the tropics, I feel as if my brain is being boiled in my skull. My skin breaks out in itchy red rashes. In short, I wilt.

In desperation, I began taking cooling dips in the ocean. Previously I had been very nervous about getting out of my boat; I felt exposed and scared when not safely aboard. Scrubbing barnacles off the hull was my least favourite job. But now my fear was outweighed by my desperate need to cool down. I got quite blasé about hopping overboard at the end of every rowing shift. Compared with the prospect of being baked alive, it was by far the lesser of the evils and allowed at least a brief respite from the relentless heat.

I would stand on the gunwale and gaze down into the blue depths, looking before I leaped to make sure that I wasn't about to dive-bomb a shark. That would have been bad news for both of us. It was quite mesmerizing looking down from the side of the boat, the sunbeams slanting through the water to form a corona around my shadow.

I would then launch myself into the water in a bomb position to prevent myself going too deep. As the ocean closed over my head, I relished the sudden wet coolness against the prickly heat of my skin, soothing my mind as well as my body. Mindful that it was absolutely vital not to get separated from my boat, even before I surfaced I would already be reaching out with one arm to grab the black safety rope that looped around the sides of the *Brocade,* attached firmly to eyebolts screwed right through the hull. I could have used an ankle leash to attach myself to the boat, but that would have been too constraining, and I made sure that I swam only on calm days when I could be quite sure that the boat and I would not drift apart while I was resurfacing. On rougher days, the welcome breezes were enough to help me maintain a reasonable temperature without the need for a swim.

If I was feeling energetic, I would swim a couple of laps of the boat, straying no more than an arm's length from the reassuring presence of her silver sides. Otherwise I just hung on to the safety line and bobbed gently in the water for a couple of minutes, enjoying seeing the world from a different angle—a turtle's-eye view, say.

I would look down through the clear blue water at my toes and marvel at the fact that about two miles of ocean dropped away beneath me. I would imagine my way down into the depths, as if I were a superhuman free diver, plunging through the upper layers where the light still penetrated and fishes played, down farther into the oceanic twilight where larger creatures lurked, and eventually all the way into the inky depths, where mysterious monsters ruled.

It didn't scare me to think about these creatures. On balance, it seemed to me that they have much more to fear from us than we do from them. In the last 60 years, we have wiped out about 90 percent of big fish such as tuna and swordfish. We kill about 100 million sharks per year, while they kill about eight of us, on average. I hoped that if I left them alone, then they would return the favour.

It was easy enough to get back onto the boat. If I swam to either of the aft corners of the cockpit, I could clamber up using the grab rope and stowed oars as footholds and handholds. I became quite addicted to my quick plunges, looking forward to the next swim almost as soon as I had finished the previous one.

However, one day my overboard forays came to an abrupt end. I had enjoyed my cooling skinny-dip and was just about to climb out of the water when I felt something small and slimy attach itself to my right buttock. I re-acted—some might say overreacted—strongly, disgustedly, and swiftly. I doubt anybody has ever exited the water quite so fast. As I grasped the oar and shot out of the waves, I looked down over my shoulder to see a small, grey fish gaping gormlessly at me as it clung to my backside. I squealed and slapped it away.

The revulsion I felt was out of all proportion to the size of the of-fender. I can only account for it by hypothesizing that there must be something in the primeval brain that reacts vehemently to having a small creature glom onto a very personal part of one's anatomy. Having been evicted from my person, the remora, as I later discovered it to be, took up residence on the hull of my boat, attaching itself permanently to a point right next to the corner of the deck where I normally made my entry and exit. Any time I thought of taking a swim, I looked over the side and saw its ugly little face looking up at me, its gills pumping repulsively, and gave up on the idea for fear of further assaults on my dignity.

I realize there is no rational explanation for being quite comfortable about the notion of sharks, but completely intimidated by a six-inch rem-ora. I cannot even attempt to explain. I like to think of myself as being generally a calm and rational being, but in this drab little fish I had met my nemesis.

With or without the swim, the heat rash bothered me most when I was in my cabin at the end of a hot day's rowing and it came time to write my blog post. There is barely enough room to sit upright in the cabin, and certainly no space for a comfortable chart table such as you might find on a more spacious boat. I have to balance my laptop on my knees while I type. Computers generate their own heat, and having a hot laptop on my sweaty, rash-ridden legs was a very uncomfortable and itchy experience. I tried all kinds of alternative positions, but it was too difficult to keep stable in a rocking boat while lying on my belly and resting on my elbows. Lying sideways, Roman style, didn't work any better. Eventually I just resigned myself to my fate. (It would be almost another year before the first iPad came on the market and I'd think that my prayers had been answered. But to my great disappointment, I found it didn't yet interface with the Iridium satellite phone that serves as my data modem.)

These were minor inconveniences, but nothing too serious—or nothing I wanted to blog about. I was a little embarrassed about my toothache, and, being British, felt that the state of my bottom was not a suitable subject for online discussion. The main drama of this stage, and the most public one, would turn out to be a matter of navigation.

It was Tuvalu versus Tarawa. This does not refer to a war between two small atoll nations in the mid-Pacific, but to my difficult decision about where to make landfall between Hawai'i and the far side of the Pacific Ocean. Tuvalu would set me up better for an eventual arrival in Australia, and so I had set that as my goal—but now I was out in the sweltering doldrums of the equatorial Pacific, and Mother Nature seemed to have other ideas.

Both were tiny targets. With a land area of just ten square miles, Tuvalu is the fourth smallest country in the world, and can be found a few degrees south of the equator. It may be best known for having sold its .tv domain name extension for a large sum of money. Tarawa is just north of the equator and is the main island of the Republic of Kiribati (pronounced *kee-ree-bas*), which is the only country in the world to straddle all four hemispheres. It has a land area of 313 square miles, split into 33 pieces and strewn across 1.3 million square miles of ocean, an area considerably larger than the United States.

It would have been possible to complete the crossing nonstop, but I was keen to explore a new part of the world. It was also fitting that 2009 was to be the year that the 15th Conference of the Parties (COP15) to the United Nations Framework Convention on Climate Change would take place in Copenhagen. The fate of these small island nations would be determined by the outcome of the conference. If a fair and binding deal could be achieved, there was some hope that rising seas caused by climate change could be kept to a level that would allow these islands to survive. If no such deal was reached, they faced submersion beneath the ocean. The governments of Tuvalu and Kiribati were already in the market to find a new homeland for their citizens. I was keen to visit one or the other. It is not often you get the chance to visit a country that may not physically exist 50 years hence.

THE COPENHAGEN CONFERENCE HAD BEEN DUBBED "Hopenhagen," and indeed there did seem to be reasons for optimism. In November 2008, America had elected its first African American President, Barack Obama, and anything seemed possible. "Yes, we can" had been his campaign slogan, and my liberal American friends wanted to believe it.

The environmental world was abuzz with preparations for the conference. Newsletters and e-mails were flying around the globe as various campaigns rallied the troops to save the world. Huge momentum was building. After decades of slow-burning activism, Copenhagen had come to represent a pivotal moment in the environmental movement. There was a real sense that if we didn't win this battle, the war was as good as over.

I had been invited to be an "Athlete Ambassador" for 350.org, a nonprofit organization whose name refers to the maximum number of parts per million of carbon dioxide in the atmosphere that can sustain human life as we know it, in the long term. At the time I'm writing, the atmosphere has just been measured at over 400 parts per million, and it's rising. The United Nations had designated me a "Climate Hero," a title I found slightly embarrassing for its faint whiff of the comic strip, but which was of course a great honour. There were several Climate Heroes around the world, selected for having gone above and beyond the norm in pursuit of their environmental missions.

Having spent that winter mostly in Hawai'i, but with side trips to the mainland and the UK, I had travelled to Nashville, Tennessee, shortly before launching the second stage of my Pacific row, to speak at the annual conference of The Climate Reality Project. The organization was founded by former U.S. Vice President Al Gore to spread awareness and information about climate change and consisted of several hundred presenters, all trained to give the PowerPoint presentation made famous by the film *An Inconvenient Truth*. I spoke alongside such luminaries as Rajendra Pachauri, the co-recipient with Al Gore of the Nobel Peace Prize, and the renowned Canadian geneticist and environmental campaigner

David Suzuki. Speeches and offline discussions revolved around the most effective ways to communicate climate change, prospects for Copenhagen, and what might happen if it failed—something that nobody really wanted to contemplate.

It was a cruel irony that the countries where I was considering making landfall at the end of Stage 2 of my Pacific row had among the smallest carbon footprints in the world, yet would be the first and worst affected, while the affluent nations that had created the problem had more resilient infrastructure and were better equipped to adapt to a new climate. This was not just an environmental issue; it was about human rights.

DURING MY PREPARATIONS FOR THE VOYAGE, I had discussed my route with Mick Bird, the only other person to have rowed a similar course across the Pacific, making landfall along the way. About ten years previously, he had set out from Fort Bragg in California. Like the Turkish ocean rower Erden Eruç, it had taken him three attempts before he finally succeeded in departing the California coast. He had stopped in Hawai'i, the Marshall Islands, and the Solomon Islands before making landfall in Cairns, Australia. Given that winds and currents can vary enormously from year to year, he recommended that I aim straight for Cairns, and see where I was when I got about halfway there. It might be the Marshalls, or it might be Tuvalu, or it might be Tarawa, which was where the British adventurer and circumnavigator Jason Lewis had stopped off with his pedal boat. This approach seemed a bit vague to me. I wanted to have a more definite idea of where I was going—that's just the kind of person that I am. So I had settled on Tuvalu as my stated destination.

I knew that getting there would be difficult. The main problem would be crossing the equator; Tuvalu lies at eight degrees south, and just a couple of degrees west of the international date line (IDL). The previous year, Erden Eruç had launched from Bodega Bay in California, aiming for Australia, and it had been agonizing to watch his difficulties as he tried to cross into the southern hemisphere. He would get within a few degrees of the equator, only to be caught in an adverse current and whisked north again. His course was a wiggly worm westwards, bobbling along within a few degrees of the equatorial line.

It took five months of frustration before Erden finally found his way through, and by then he had lost his chance at Australia, which now was too far to the south for him to cut across the west-flowing currents. He simply couldn't make a sufficiently southerly course to get to his intended destination and eventually made landfall in Papua New Guinea. This did not set an encouraging precedent.

As it turned out, I had an easier time than Erden crossing the equator, but a harder time than Mick. By Day 45, as I crossed eight degrees north, I was already starting to debate the merits of Tuvalu versus Tarawa. Even from this far out, Tarawa seemed like a safer bet, given the way the wind was blowing and the potential challenges at the equator. There was no point making life excessively difficult for myself. But there was still a long way to go. I reassured myself that there was no need to decide yet.

However, I found the state of indecision very demotivating. More than once I abandoned a rowing shift early, unsure of whether I should go speeding downwind to the west towards Tarawa or continue to slog south towards Tuvalu. "A sailor without a destination cannot hope for a favourable wind," as the saying goes. I was inclined to agree.

By Day 50 I had reached six degrees north and had entered the Intertropical Convergence Zone (ITCZ). Better known as the doldrums, this is the twilight zone of the Pacific, notorious amongst mariners as a region of deathly calms and sudden squalls, thunderclouds, and lightning storms. It overlaps with, but is not the same as, the Equatorial Counter Current (ECC).

A brief geography lesson may be useful here. The Pacific contains two enormous rotating *gyres,* or circular currents. The North Pacific system turns clockwise, heading north up the coast of Japan and Russia, across the Arctic Circle, and down the California coast, before turning west at the equator to head back to Japan again. The South Pacific gyre turns in the opposite direction, anticlockwise, flowing up the coasts of Chile and Peru, across the equator, down past Australia, and through the islands of the South Pacific back to South America. It is in the centre of these gyres that plastic and other debris accumulates.

Because the flow in the northern hemisphere goes clockwise, and the flow in the southern hemisphere goes anticlockwise, this means that both currents are heading west at the equator. This is good news for ocean rowers heading from California to Australia, as I was attempting to do. The not-so-good news is that between those two helpful currents, a fraction north of the equator, there lies a contrary band of east-flowing water—the ECC. It varies in width according to longitude and time of year, but generally it occupies a horizontal stripe about 240 nautical miles wide, between two and six degrees north. So although it is narrow in the overall scale of the vast Pacific, it's plenty wide enough when you attempt to row across it. It moves at up to one knot, and I move at about two knots while rowing, so its effect would be quite significant.

ALMOST BANG ON CUE, AT SIX DEGREES AND five minutes north, I found it—or rather, it found me. Having been heading quite happily south for 50 days, I woke up one morning to find that I'd been pushed three miles north overnight.

This was when I started to realise that the ECC would be an even trickier adversary than I had anticipated. As well as trying to push me back towards the Americas, this contrary little bugger of a current also generates a variety of eddies along its edges, where the east-flowing water meets the west-flowing water. These are invisible and unpredictable sub-currents that can unexpectedly whisk a rowboat way off course. It is like an oceanic game of snakes and ladders, played on an invisible board. Some days I would find myself in a helpful current, a ladder helping me towards my destination. Just as often, I found myself slithering down a snake, helplessly watching my hard-won progress slipping away in the numbers on my GPS.

To endure the vagaries of the ECC and the ITCZ at the same time was to dice with madness. Sailors have traditionally dreaded this region. Usually sailboats have an easier time than rowboats, as they gain enough momentum from the wind to fly across the top of tricky currents. But at these latitudes, where the air is often stagnant, a sailboat could drift aimlessly for days, the crew desperately hoping for a breeze to aid their escape. In a rowboat, at least I could row my way out, although progress was slow and hot and sweaty, and the air weighed heavy on the soul. With no high waves to limit the view, the ocean stretched out to infinity, and land seemed no more than a distant memory.

My logbook records days of sultry, calm, overcast conditions, with the ocean so still and silent I could hear the fish jumping, or, as I put it in one of my tweets, "It's quiet enough to hear a fish flatulate." At other times winds were frustratingly variable, in both strength and direction. I had to adjust the rudder frequently to try and stay even vaguely on course. Sometimes I had no sooner put the sea anchor out to stop myself being blown backwards, than the wind would wheel around and I would have to go through the 20-minute process of hauling it in again. Squalls drenched me, to be followed moments later by blinding sunshine. Black thunderheads rolled across the sky, and after dark I was often treated to spectacular displays of lightning flashes as they lit up high-piled cumulus clouds from within. Rainbows and double rainbows abounded—and one night I saw a moonbow. The full moon was exceptionally bright, and in the opposite direction I saw a monochrome arc rising above the sea. I hadn't even known that such a thing existed, but after I mentioned it in my blog, my online followers corroborated that this was a known phenomenon. These were strange days indeed.

The combination of odd winds and unpredictable currents drove me as close to insanity as I have ever been—which, to be honest, is not very close, my mind seeming to have a particularly strong grip on reality. But I did become obsessed with the line on the GPS that represented my course. I zoomed the chart's scale way up so that I could detect an adverse current as soon as I ran into it, and I watched the numbers as keenly as a day trader might watch the stock market when he has bet his last dollar on pork bellies. My obsession reached unhealthy levels, my mood a hostage to those little numbers on the GPS screen as wind and currents pushed me this way and that. One day I recorded in my logbook, "After 6 hours and 4 squalls, have nearly completed a jagged circle." And a little later: "Hard to stay upbeat. So much effort, so little reward."

Eventually a trusty follower intervened, concerned that I was losing perspective. "Zoom down the scale!" he implored. "Overall, you're still making progress!"

I complied, and things immediately looked much better. It was an important lesson in focusing on the bigger picture rather than getting bogged down in the little setbacks that are an inevitable part of any major project. In *Zen and the Art of Motorcycle Maintenance,* by Robert

Pirsig, these setbacks are called "gumption traps." There are catastrophic consequences for the unwary, the traps sucking them into a dark hole of negativity and despondency. Get-up-and-go drains away, leaving the victim confronted by a seemingly intractable problem. It takes perspective—or the help of a good friend—to escape the trap, set aside the spiraling thoughts, and get back to the task at hand.

OVERALL, I WAS SLOWLY EDGING MY WAY towards the equator. Some days I went south, other days I went north, but gradually the degrees ticked by. Five degrees north, four, three . . . I got almost down to two degrees when I found myself in a strong adverse current and heading north. Over the course of the next three days, I was pushed nearly all the way back up to three degrees, my worst setback yet.

It was heartbreaking to lose so much ground. I resorted to scream therapy, a technique I had learned on the Atlantic for venting my frustration. Then it had been followed by an almost immediate improvement in the conditions. Superstitiously, I hoped it might yield the same result this time, so I stood at the bows of my boat and hollered my frustration at the ocean. But no luck. The trick didn't work, but it did make me feel a little better, apart from the sore throat.

A small boost to morale came that night with the discovery that powdered coconut milk is a magical addition to freeze-dried Thai curry. The restorative effect of a tasty dinner is quite remarkable. When the going gets tough, the tough get cooking. As was my habit, I ate my dinner while watching the sunset. I sat on top of the life raft, my feet in the footwell, my back resting against the hatch to my sleeping cabin—not desperately comfortable, but by far the most comfortable seat on the boat. And most important, it positioned me facing the bow, towards the sunset.

Sunrise, sunset, moonrise, moonset—these were the highlights of my day, the ocean rower's equivalent of prime-time TV. I loved watching the dying moments of the day, with the best of the colours usually appearing after the red disc of the sun had dropped into the ocean. I sometimes exclaimed out loud in appreciation of the afterglow in the west as the sun lit the clouds from below, and the subtler hues of rosy pink reflected on cumulus banked around the other points of the compass.

Nothing can compare with the end of a day on the ocean, when you can reflect virtuously on a full day of fresh air and exercise, while eating a well-earned hot meal and admiring a full 360-degree Technicolor sunset. I have hundreds of photos of the sky taken during those precious moments at either end of the day. The novelty never fades.

HEADING SOUTH WAS STILL my primary focus. I had decided that I wouldn't consider the Tuvalu/Tarawa question again until and unless I crossed the equator. It was so difficult to predict how long that might take, or what longitude I might reach before it happened, that it seemed pointless to debate the issue at this stage. But despite my determination to release my unproductive thoughts, the debate was always there, hovering in the back of my mind, unsettling me.

The decision suddenly became more critical. On Day 86, the watermaker broke. I had replaced its electric motor in Hawai'i, the critical component that had rusted to death on the first stage of the row, and the rest of the machine had been thoroughly overhauled. When it lost all pressure and refused to work, I was at a loss as to what the problem could be. It was certainly not the motor, which I could hear running with its reassuring hum. I cleaned the mesh of the pre-filter, which removes the larger particles from the seawater, to no avail. Even though I was sure it wasn't the cause of the problem, I replaced the feed pump—I carried two spares with me after the problems of the previous year—but again to no effect. I checked to make sure all the connections were tight, and they were. I was baffled.

Luckily I had enough water in ballast bags to last the remainder of the voyage, and I didn't have to resort to using the manual watermaker that the *Junk* guys had kindly donated. But this did give a greater urgency to the matter of my destination.

The question was complicated by the fact that I was in transition between my existing weatherman in Hawai'i and a new one, Ricardo in Lisbon, Portugal. I had met Ricardo on a couple of occasions and knew him to be a charming young man with Mediterranean good looks and a laid-back attitude. Not that good looks are an important attribute in a weatherman, of course, but they don't hurt, either.

On Day 87, the day after the watermaker broke, Ricardo told me that he had a good "gut feel" that I could still make it to Tuvalu, despite my difficulties in making convincing progress south. This feeling was based on his analysis of the weather and currents on my patch of ocean, and in retrospect, I can see that I wanted to believe him for several reasons. Tuvalu had been my original stated goal, and I was keen to stick with my initial plan if at all possible. Also, Ric and I were establishing a new professional relationship, and to doubt his word would not be a good start. Added to that, Nicole had expressed a preference for Tuvalu from the environmental public relations angle. Virtually all the islands in the South Pacific will experience a significant impact from the rising oceans, if the climate scientists are correct, but the Tuvalu government had already been highly vocal on the issue of global climate change. Several Tuvaluans had already posted comments on my blog to express their welcome in advance. So in a rash moment, I recorded a video post, declaring my intention to hold out for Tuvalu—absolutely, decidedly, definitely Tuvalu.

WHEN WILL I EVER LEARN? NOTHING ON OCEANS is ever absolute, or decided, or definite. It ain't over till the now-not-so-fat lady makes landfall. Even as I uploaded the video, I was already starting to doubt the feasibility of my plan.

On Day 89, I crossed the international date line. For a while I had wondered if I might manage to cross the IDL and the equator simultaneously. That would have been quite an achievement and would have qualified me to be an Emerald Shellback, the term bestowed on the few human beings who have managed to cross the intersection of those imaginary lines at 180 degrees west and 0 degrees north. But it was not to be. I was still 46 miles north of the equator when I lost 31 August to the peculiarities of time zones and took a shortcut into September. My celebrations were muted. It didn't feel like such a big deal, compared with the much more pressing question of my destination.

Over the next few days, my concerns grew due to a number of factors. I discovered by zooming around on my new chartplotter that the coordinates I had been given for Tuvalu weren't for the main island, but for an outlying island that had little infrastructure and would not be a good place to land. The outlying island would be easier navigationally but a poor choice logistically, while the main island would be better logistically but an awful lot harder navigationally.

Around the same time, Ricardo sent me a text saying I had 142 nautical miles of longitude left—that is, another 142 nautical miles west, during which I would have to push hard south to get down to the latitude of Tuvalu. This disagreed with my figures. I believed I had only around 100 miles of longitude, which would make my task much more challenging.

I grew still more concerned when he set me a target of making three miles east every day while I headed south, in order to maximize my chances of reaching Tuvalu. If I failed to make this goal one day, he said, I had to add the shortfall onto the next day's total. There could be no ongoing slippage if I was going to reach Tuvalu. But this was nearly impossible. Now that I had emerged from the east-flowing equatorial countercurrent, the water would be pushing me to the west. Every time I stopped rowing I would lose ground against the schedule.

Once again I temporarily put my worries to one side, this time as I made the final countdown to the equator. As zero degrees approached, I planned my celebrations. The IDL had not meant much to me. It was just an arbitrary, manmade line, directly opposite the equally arbitrary, manmade line of the prime meridian that ran through Greenwich in London.

But the equator was a proper, natural delineation, the line of equidistance between the North and South Poles, those far-flung points at the top and bottom of the world that marked the axis of the Earth's rotation. The equator felt much more significant. On a more mundane level, it also meant I could open the package that a friend in Hawai'i had given to me just before I departed. A small yellow drybag, it bore the instructions in capital letters: "Not to be opened before 0 degrees." I had a sneaking suspicion that it contained at least a small quantity of alcohol. Not that I'd been squeezing the bag like a naughty child checking out the parcels under the tree before Christmas Day. No, of course not—not me. That would have been downright childish.

Equator Day dawned fine and calm. I had to make 11 miles to the south in order to reach my goal. Conditions were flat, windless, and unhelpful, and it took me most of the day. I started rowing at 6:30 in the morning, and at 5:05 in the evening I crossed the legendary line. I had been sharing the countdown of the last few miles on Twitter, posting an update each time I checked off another mile. I fondly imagined my online followers celebrating along with me as I turned on the video camera to record my own festivities for posterity.

First things first: Homage had to be paid to King Neptune. On cruise ships, they usually have a crew member dress up as the god of the ocean. I didn't have a crewmate handy, so I turned to my small menagerie of cuddly toys—two ducks, a robin, and a dolphin. It may not seem appropriate for a 41-year-old woman to have taken a collection of stuffed toys to sea, but over the years various schools had entrusted me with their beloved mascots. The students eagerly awaited news of the toys' maritime adventures via the blog, so it did not behoove me to eschew their cuddly companionship.

The choice was easy. This was clearly Squishy the Dolphin's big day. I propped him up on his tail and gave him a fork to use as a trident. I didn't have a crown handy, but he looked regal enough without. I genuflected to Neptune/Squishy a couple of times before turning my attention to the yellow goody bag. It contained various random symbolic objects—a wooden spatula, a string of plastic fish beads, a couple of snack bars. *Aha, this is what I was looking for!* I pulled out a mini-bottle of champagne, containing the equivalent of about two glasses. I already had a plan for this.

I unclipped the string bag that usually held my bean sprout pot to stop it from being washed overboard, and popped the champagne bottle inside. I attached it to a longish piece of rope and dropped it over the side. I waited a while. At least two minutes. Then I decided that the water was so warm that it probably wouldn't have much cooling effect anyway. And what if a shark came along and stole it? That would be a disaster. Best to drink it now. I pulled the line in again.

The bottle was, predictably, warm. But champagne had never tasted so good. I sipped it respectfully. I hadn't had a drink in three months, and very soon my mind was buzzing pleasantly. As the sun dipped in the sky, I enjoyed the sweet nectar and prattled away to my video camera about how wonderful life was and how all my dreams were coming true. For the first time since I had left dry land, I forgot all my problems, past, present, and future, Tuvalu and Tarawa, and relaxed into the moment.

As I sipped, I spotted a cruise ship a mile or two distant. It didn't seem to be moving. I halfheartedly tried to hail them on the VHF radio—mostly to ask if they could please pop over with another bottle of champagne, as it was going down quite well—but got no reply. They were probably too busy with their own celebrations, inflicting the ritual humiliations on those crossing the equator for the first time and making the transition from Pollywogs to Shellbacks. This cruise ship would turn out to be the only other vessel that I saw on this stage of the row. If you ever feel the need for some peace and quiet and don't mind a bit of warmth, I can recommend the doldrums of the Pacific. With the possible exception of the polar regions, nowhere else will guarantee you such solitude.

I drained the last drop from my little champagne bottle and treated myself to an extra-special dinner: my new favourite dish of curry with coconut milk powder, followed by some whole-food treats given to me by another friend in Hawai'i—some carob nuggets and raw-food cookies. They were much more delicious than they sound, take it from me. At last I had reached the southern hemisphere. After all the frustration and struggle I felt an enormous sense of achievement and satisfaction. It was a good day.

THE NEXT MORNING, CELEBRATIONS OVER, the worries returned. I had promised myself I would put my navigational decision on hold until I crossed the equator. Now I couldn't postpone the decision any more. If I was aiming for Tuvalu, I now had less than 500 nautical miles to go. All that day I did my best to obey Ricardo's instructions to row east, but I found myself almost paralysed by the impossibility of the task. Every time I stopped rowing I was pushed west by the current. It was utterly demoralizing. It seemed that Ric's target would be unachievable unless I rowed 24 hours a day for the remainder of my voyage, and maybe not even then.

In my heart of hearts, I knew that Tuvalu was impossible. But part of me still resisted changing my mind. It was my stated destination. My imminent arrival had been announced on the radio, I was due to meet with members of the government, we had arranged storage for my boat—and of course I wanted to find out more about how they intended to become the world's first carbon-neutral nation.

That night I slept badly. The cabin was hot and airless, and I lay there, itching and sweating and churning the question in my mind. *Tuvalu or Tarawa? Tuvalu or Tarawa?* It became unbearable inside, so I went out on deck to cool down. I looked up at the stars and the setting moon. The night sky helped calm my thoughts and give me a sense of perspective. I sighed. I realized I knew the answer; I was just having difficulty admitting it to myself because I was embarrassed to have to change my mind so publicly.

If I persisted in aiming for Tuvalu, the worst-case scenario was pretty bad. There was a substantial risk of running out of water and possibly missing the island altogether and spinning off into the great blue yonder. The food situation wasn't looking too good either. I definitely had enough to get me to Tarawa, but the delays and backslidings in the countercurrents at the equator had cost me valuable time, so I would have to ration if I was to push for Tuvalu. Going hungry while rowing 24 hours a day was not an appealing prospect. I could have a fallback plan of calling for a boat to tow me in if it looked like I would miss it by a few miles.

Ultimately, although the message was important, I reasoned, it definitely helps if the messenger (a) is alive, and (b) has not had to rely on some fossil-fuel guzzling means of transport to come and rescue her if/when she seemed in danger of disappearing over the horizon with no water and no food. So it seemed the choice was clear. The sensible, responsible, if rather embarrassing thing to do would be to change course for Tarawa. I could reach it relatively easily—or as easily as ocean rowing ever lets it be—well before I ran out of sustenance and without having to rely on outside intervention.

Ultimately, I had to put survival first. The decision was made. Now I just needed to persuade my team that it was the right thing to do.

I CALLED RICARDO FIRST. ALTHOUGH IT WAS the middle of the night where I was, it was a reasonable time of day in Lisbon—not that this mattered to Ric, who seemed to be awake at all hours of the day and night, judging from the time stamps on his e-mails. He told me that he was completely supportive of whatever I decided to do, and we talked it out until we had agreed that I would aim for Tarawa.

Then I called Nicole. I was worried about how she would react. She had been in touch with people in Tuvalu and had already found somewhere I could store my boat for the nine months until the next stage of my row. She'd made provisional plans for flights and accommodation and logistics. This would mean starting over. When I gave her the news, the briefest of pauses betrayed her disappointment, but she took it like the professional that she is. She agreed to put plans in place for Tarawa instead.

Next, the really humiliating part. Having declared so adamantly that I was going to head for Tuvalu, I would have to confess to my online audience that I had changed my mind. I just had to hope that they would understand my reasons. Ultimately, the watermaker's breaking had been the deciding factor, and I doubted anybody could argue with that. Nobody ever died of embarrassment, as far as I know, but many people have died of dehydration.

Uncomfortable though it had been, I was hugely relieved now that the decision had been made and communicated to all interested parties. The cloud of doubt that had hung over me for so long had dispersed, and the sunshine of certainty was shining. Having fought so hard to get south across the equator, I needed to cross it again to get to Tarawa, which lies at one degree north. I turned my bows to point downwind, and was soon flying along, relishing the joy of working with the elements rather than against them.

Within hours, Nicole e-mailed to let me know she had rebooked the flights and found accommodation. She would be in Tarawa within four days to prepare for my arrival. Conrad (a cameraman) and another friend from Hawai'i would be coming with her. It looked like everything was falling beautifully into place. I relaxed for the first time in weeks and wondered why I had been so apprehensive about breaking the news. It's funny how our thoughts can take over, and how often our fears prove to be unfounded.

With perfect timing, the audiobook I was listening to at that point of the voyage was *The Astonishing Power of Emotions,* by Esther and Jerry Hicks, in which they advised, "Nothing you want lies upstream." I very much doubt that this was intended to be applied to ocean navigation, but it did seem more than coincidental that choosing to go with the flow had unleashed a remarkable run of good fortune.

THERE WAS A FINAL MAGICAL MOMENT in store for me on that stage of the row. It was still unbearably hot in my cabin, so one night I decided to try sleeping out on deck. It might not be long before the next squall came along to drench me, but it was worth a try. I took my sleeping bag and dragged it out to the cockpit, making it into a cozy nest between the runners of my rowing seat. I snuggled in and lay there, gazing up at the stars.

As my boat rocked gently on the waves, I found myself suddenly marvelling at the strangeness and splendour of my life. It was as if I rose up outside myself for a moment and looked down at this little naked woman lying on the deck of her small silver boat, completely alone in the vast darkness of the ocean.

Who would have thought, ten years previously when I was still working in an office in London, doing a job I didn't like to buy stuff I didn't need, that one day I would find myself here, in the middle of the Pacific, well on my way to becoming the first woman to row across the world's largest ocean? There had been some scary moments over the years that had tested me almost beyond my limits, but they had also helped me become stronger, to form a character that could withstand the vicissitudes of life—not just on the ocean, but on dry land too. I thought back to that unhappy, underachieving management consultant who had dragged herself into the office every day because she thought she had no choice. I was immensely happy that I had reached that fork in the road, and that I had chosen the road—or ocean—less traveled.

I snuggled in deeper, and marveled at the beauty above me. So far from the nearest light pollution, the stars sparkled across the night sky like a jewel-encrusted cape. The Milky Way swooped diagonally across the heavens, reminding me of my utter insignificance, and at the same time my complete interconnection with everything. I was just a tiny speck of consciousness, and yet I was consciousness itself, omnipresent and omnipotent. I was suddenly overcome with a profound sense of joy—which lasted until the clouds blotted out the stars, a squall blew in, and I beat a hasty retreat to the shelter of the cabin.

~~~~

CHAPTER SEVEN

ONE WORLD

*"When the power of love overcomes the love of power
the world will know peace."*

— ATTRIBUTED TO JIMI HENDRIX

As I began the final 20 miles to Tarawa, I'd had less than 6 hours of sleep in the previous 48, and the heat was brutal. The sun beat down from an almost cloudless equatorial sky. As usual, I was rowing naked, and I could feel the impact of the sun's rays on my skin, striking me with their powerful heat as if to penetrate me to my core. Only a few tiny, fluffy cumulus clouds broke the endless blue, giving no relief. The ocean was like a mirror, the first time I had seen it so flat in the 100-plus days I'd been at sea. There wasn't a breath of breeze, and the sweat ran down my back in rivulets. I stopped rowing for a moment to glug down some water, but it was warm, tasted of plastic, and failed to refresh. I yearned for an ice-cold drink—preferably one with bubbles and alcohol in it.

Since giving up on Tuvalu as a destination, I had looped back up to re-cross the equator into the northern hemisphere. I had already made it safely past the island of Abemama (where Robert Louis Stevenson, author of *Treasure Island, Kidnapped,* and *The Strange Case of Dr Jekyll and Mr. Hyde,* lived for a while), but it was no straightforward matter trying to hit the tiny target of Tarawa in such a huge ocean. I could see from my GPS where I was and where I wanted to end up, but connecting the two was proving to be difficult when winds were pushing me this way and that, and there were islands and reefs in the way.

But at last Neptune decided to give me a break. Having had great fun at my expense ever since our tussle at the equator, it was as if the god of the sea now decided I'd been out on the ocean for long enough and could finally be permitted to land. Late in the day a useful southeasterly wind arrived, which lasted only three hours, but that was long enough for me to ride it all the way up the east side of the island of Maiana and line myself up nicely for Tarawa.

I rowed late into the night until I could be sure I was well clear of Maiana. I tried to grab a quick nap in the cabin, but couldn't relax enough to sleep. I kept opening one eye to squint at the GPS to make sure I wasn't going to shipwreck on a coral reef. Eventually I realized that this was ridiculous—I wasn't sleeping anyway, so I might as well get up and row to make sure I made it safely through this maritime obstacle course. It would be a real shame to get this far only to destroy my boat on a reef within sight of the finish line. So I resigned myself to a sleepless night, kitted up, and headed out onto the darkened deck.

UNLIKE MY APPROACH INTO HAWAI'I, NO ORANGE streetlights revealed the presence of humanity. The land was indistinguishable from the ocean. I had to navigate by instruments only, unable to see Maiana in the darkness. As day broke the next morning, the dawn revealed the thin green line of the island only about a mile distant. In terms of the vast Pacific, that had been a close shave.

When I got within nine miles of Tarawa, I started to wonder if I was going to make it. Without having slept the previous night, and after rowing 3,000 miles, I was sleep-deprived and bone-weary. The last few miles seemed to loom very large. I put some good rocking music on my iPod to help me through.

Slowly, stroke by stroke, I covered the closing miles of my voyage. After each mile, I posted another tweet to report my progress to my online audience, as I'd done at the equator, and I had a bite of food. I kept looking over my shoulder to scan for the escort boat that would take me through the narrow gap in the reef. Nicole had been in Tarawa for nearly a week now and had been sorting out local logistics. She and I had been communicating daily by satellite phone since she arrived, finalizing the plans for my arrival. I had alerted the team when I reached the last ten miles to land, and I expected them any moment now.

At last I spotted them, the escort boat skimming across the mirror of the ocean like a mirage. Like the boat that had come out to greet me in Hawai'i, this one, too, was yellow. It had a blue deck and red sun canopy. After so many days of seeing nothing but blue sea and blue sky, its bright primary colours made for a cheerful change.

The boat pulled up alongside me. On board were Nicole and two other familiar faces: Hunter from Archinoetics, a Hawai'ian research and technology company that had provided technical and Web support since I first met them in Honolulu the year before, and Conrad, our cameraman. The boat owner, who stood at the helm, was introduced to me as Emile. Another unfamiliar figure was introduced as Rob, the New Zealand High Commissioner. I had imagined high commissioners would wear suits and ties, but this one had on a baseball cap and white rash guard that complemented his muscular physique. Although no longer a young man, he was evidently very fit, and I found out later that in his heyday he'd been a successful adventure racer, a particularly challenging form of athletic endeavour usually involving two or more endurance disciplines with some orienteering thrown in for good measure. Now he nonchalantly launched a sea kayak over the side of the boat and steered over to paddle alongside me.

"G'day," he said, as if greeting a bikini-clad transpacific rower was the kind of thing he did every day of the week.

"Pleased to meet you," I said, which sounded oddly formal, but was entirely true.

IT WAS VERY HELPFUL HAVING ROB alongside during that last mile. As always, I was facing backwards, so it was useful to have a forward-facing kayaker to tell me what adjustments were needed to keep my boat on course.

The drawback to having him there was that, rather unnecessarily, I felt the need to keep pace with him. I keep thinking I've overcome my competitiveness, but I keep proving myself wrong. My boat weighed 2,000 pounds, whereas his probably weighed no more than 20, but I still felt I needed to maintain some professional pride and look good for the last mile.

It was seriously hard work. The heat was unrelenting, and I was, not to put too fine a point on it, knackered. I could feel my skin burning and my body getting depleted. That last mile seemed it would never end. Rob told me I was rowing against the tide, and that mile most definitely took a lot longer than any of the previous nine had done. I knew this for a fact, by looking at the time intervals between my final few tweets. I was reduced to counting oar strokes. Just ten more strokes. Then another ten. Then another ten. My eyes were fixed on the display screen of the GPS, willing the "Dist Next" number to reach zero.

At last I crossed the finish line of latitude, level with the southern tip of Tarawa and about 400 yards from shore, and collapsed backwards off my rowing seat, shattered. I had not an ounce of energy left in me. I felt I would never be able to row another stroke as long as I lived. I lay there with my eyes closed, utterly spent.

NICOLE KNEW WHAT THIS SITUATION demanded. Through the haze of exhaustion, my senses dimly registered some sounds of splashing and laughter. A few moments later a voice piped up just inches from my right ear.

"Beer?"

I opened my eyes to see Nicole's head peeking over the side of the boat. It was joined by an arm, rising up like the torch-bearing arm of the Statue of Liberty. The arm was holding a can of Australian beer.

"You absolute star," I gasped.

The beer was rather warm after its dip in the ocean, but I wasn't in a mood to be picky. I cracked it open and necked several large gulps before remembering my manners and inviting Nicole on board. I directed her to the safety rope and oar arrangement that I had used so many times to clamber back into the cockpit after my brief ocean plunges, and she scrambled onto the deck. It was great to see her again, but at the same time a little strange and oddly crowded to have another person on the *Brocade*.

By the end of the beer, I had recovered sufficiently to make it to shore. As I approached the town jetty, I was amazed to see about 500 people gathered along the harbour wall. This was an impressive turnout for a country of only 100,000 people, many of whom lived up to 2,000 miles away on distant islands and atolls.

Following Rob's directions, I paddled up to the boat ramp where islanders were waiting to greet me and take care of the *Brocade*. I stepped ashore, setting foot on dry land for the first time in 105 days. Or was it 104? The international date line had confused me. Either way, it had been a very long time since my feet had touched solid ground.

This was now my third landfall after prolonged periods at sea, so I wasn't surprised when the ground seemed to lurch beneath my feet. My brain had adapted to being on a constantly pitching boat, so now it was overcompensating when I stood on terra firma. I looked up at the crowd that had come to greet me and wondered if my first act upon arriving in Tarawa would be to topple over like a drunkard.

Fortunately help was at hand. Two muscular, tattooed men approached, wearing traditional grass-mat skirts, with sashes, armbands, and coronet-shaped headdresses made out of the same material. They knelt in front of me, forming a cradle with their arms.

Got to love local tradition, I thought, as I sank gratefully onto the proffered seat. From my position aloft, I had to bend to accept garlands of plumeria flowers that a woman placed around my neck and on my head.

The tattooed men carried me to a plastic chair a few yards away on the boat ramp and then rejoined a group of a dozen or so men and women to perform a local dance of welcome. It resembled the haka that the All Blacks rugby team perform to intimidate the opposition before a match, although with less eye rolling and sticking out of tongues. I felt a bit like the Queen must do when being entertained on royal tour. A girl in traditional garb presented me with a young coconut, refrigerated and cool, its top lopped off so I could drink the refreshing, sweet coconut water inside. It was exactly what I needed. I could almost feel the electrolytes flowing back into me, restoring mind and body.

A woman standing alongside me whispered, "You don't have to drink it if you don't like it."

But it was delicious and I couldn't get enough. I gulped it down in very un-Queen-like manner, trying not to dribble too much down my chin.

There followed a generous speech of welcome from a venerable gentleman, whom I understood to be a local dignitary, which was translated into English by a woman who introduced herself as Linda. Nicole had told me on the way in that Linda and her husband, John, comprised the main media presence on Kiribati and had also organized the troupe of dancers. Nicole had evidently explained my environmental mission, and their speech made me feel as if I were their last great hope for promoting awareness of their environmental plight. I felt uncomfortable and a little daunted by the faith they appeared to have in my ability to help. I would of course do my best, but I was not a major celebrity, able to elevate an issue to centre stage the way, say, Leonardo DiCaprio or Julia Roberts can. It made my heart ache to think of these people, in the back end of beyond as far as most of the world was concerned, living in fear for their homes and their future but lacking the economic and political clout to make their voices heard.

After the various formalities, including a completely unrehearsed speech in which I pledged to do all I could to help their cause, the crowds dispersed. I saw my boat safely into the custody of Emile, Hunter, and Conrad, who were going to take her to the Marine Training Centre (of which more later), and we departed. Nicole drove us in a rented car to the Hotel Otintaai where she and the rest of the team had already set up base camp.

AS WE DROVE, I PEERED EAGERLY out of the window to see what kind of a place I had landed in. From some basic information that my mother had e-mailed to me, I knew that prior to 1979, the country now known as Kiribati was comprised of the Gilbert and Ellice Islands, Phoenix Islands, and Line Islands. When the country was unified, it found itself straddling the international date line, an eventuality that the fine gentlemen of Greenwich could not have foreseen from the vantage point of 1851. In those far-off days when the sun was said never to set on the British Empire, my beloved little upstart of a country had fought off the claims of places as diverse as Philadelphia, Lisbon, Paris, Pisa, Mecca, Kyoto, and the Great Pyramid of Giza to claim Greenwich's Royal Observatory as the global prime meridian, and that its opposite, which was on the backside of the Earth as far as the British were concerned, would be the temporal fault line where today leaps into tomorrow. It was as if this messy zipper in the fabric of human timekeeping was faintly repugnant to them, so they had positioned it as far away as they could, out of sight and out of mind.

Even if they had foreseen the possibility, it probably wouldn't have bothered them overmuch that a few unfortunate Melanesians would one day face the considerable inconvenience of having the Gilbert and Ellice Islands already in tomorrow, while the Phoenix and Line Islands were still in today. I can barely imagine how New York City, say, would function if it found itself thus divided. Would cab drivers charge double for having to drive all the way into tomorrow and back again? The effective working week would be only four days long, because one half of the city would still be enjoying Sunday brunch while the others were suffering the Monday blues; half would be relaxing into their Saturday, while the others were still saying "Thank God it's Friday." It's unimaginable.

Fortunately, in Oceania, the pace of life is less hectic. The only natural resource of Kiribati is phosphate, a polite word for guano, or bird shit, and even this solitary natural resource ran out in 1979, coincidentally (or not) the year that the United Kingdom granted them independence. Thanks to the boobies, I had just re-imported quite a quantity of bird shit, but not enough to revive the ailing industry. Now much of the population appears to spend the day lying in hammocks, so today, tomorrow, later, or never is about as specific as schedules need to be.

The new nation of Kiribati tolerated the situation for fully 16 years before declaring in 1995 that it had had enough of being a nation divided, and that henceforth the Phoenix and Line Islands would join Gilbert Island time, being 12 hours ahead of Greenwich Mean Time instead of 12 hours behind, and a substantial kink was created in the international date line to accommodate the unification.

As we drove, Nicole told me that in the early 1990s, South Tarawa had one of the highest population densities in the world, similar to Hong Kong's, but unlike the towering skyscrapers of that island, I didn't see a single building more than two storeys high, and very few of those. Most of the houses were small huts, thatched with palm leaves or roofed with corrugated tin, crowding in on either side of the road. Some had cinder-block walls, while some had no walls at all, just a roof supported by wooden uprights above a platform on stilts. Once in a while a small store, little more than a kiosk, punctuated the line of densely packed huts, a homemade sign proclaiming its name. These were usually composed of the names of two family members put together, such as Taotin,

Tokaraetina, or Mili. Village gathering halls, known as *maneabas,* were spacious constructions with high, pitched roofs dipping down so low that you would have to duck to enter, but once within, the thick thatch of the roof would provide welcome shade and respite from the sun. Inside, they were hives of both activity and inactivity. People sat in huddles, chatting or weaving mats, or lay on the floor sheltering from the heat of the day.

This was a country where life was lived out of doors, with the citizens returning to their homes only to sleep. People (predominantly men) lounged in hammocks, while children, pigs, and dogs ran around or ferreted in piles of rubbish. Women carried groceries or used brooms to sweep piles of rubbish off their land onto that of their neighbours. There was rubbish everywhere, much of it plastic. We drove past the city dump, discernible as a higher concentration of plastic more or less restrained from blowing into the sea by a chain-link fence. With no point of land more than a few feet above sea level, there was nowhere on Tarawa for a landfill site, so there was no choice but to leave everything sitting on top of the ground.

We drove past a small inlet, dotted with the tall trunks of dead palm trees. "That's apparently evidence of the rising ocean," Nicole said. "Those trees used to be on land; now they're in the lagoon."

She had quickly become accustomed to the local way of driving. In some countries they drive on the left, in others on the right. In some Mediterranean countries they drive in the shade. In Kiribati, they drive around the potholes. I would soon become used to the erratic behaviour of the battered, rusty vehicles that plied the town's few roads, but initially it was rather alarming.

EVENTUALLY, SAFELY, WE ARRIVED AT the Hotel Otintaai. To fully convey the impact of this arrival, I should explain that when I set out on an ocean voyage, I hold a clear vision in my mind of my destination. I picture the joy of landfall, the first hot shower, the first glass of wine, the first proper meal. I think of the rediscovery of simple pleasures—turning on a tap, taking a walk, appreciating the shape and colour of a tree or flower. Each day, I focus on what I need to do to get myself a bit closer to there. I just take it one day, or one rowing shift, or one oar stroke at a time. And eventually I get there.

Now, at last, I was on the verge of realizing my vision. For months I had been picturing the comfortable, clean hotel with its crisp linen sheets, white fluffy towels, and delicious food.

The Otintaai would comprehensively fail to deliver any of these things.

It was a desperately plain two-storey building. The main hotel in Tarawa, it was wholly owned by the government, a rather surprising arrangement to my mind. To say that in my first, startled assessment I thought it resembled a low-security prison, with its high chain link fence and concrete façade, would be slightly harsh, but only very slightly.

Nicole parked the car in the dusty, unpaved car park. The room with twin beds that she and I were to share had no hot water, so I used Hunter's bathroom. The shower was hot, and the water pressure was respectable, both significantly redeeming features. After nothing but a bucket and sponge for the last three and a half months, and now that I had given up on the white-fluffy-towels scenario, I was not a fussy customer.

That evening around sunset, we assembled on the beach in front of the hotel restaurant. We pulled up some plastic chairs around a plastic table and examined the menu while we drank sundowners. The alcoholic repertoire of the hotel was limited to expensive imported beer and wine, but the team had taken the precaution of buying maximum allowances of liquor in the duty-free shops on their way out. One way and another, we managed to make a party of it.

The menu was not too exciting, but considering the limited range of food products available to the chef, the number of options was actually quite impressive. His powers of creativity would have been hard pushed to do much better. Fish ten different ways, and any vegetable you wanted so long as it was cabbage or frozen mixed veg. Chicken, beef, and pork were also available, but fish seemed likely to be the best bet. I would have given anything for a huge fresh salad, but on an island with no soil, only sand, this was unlikely. A trip to the main supermarket the next day yielded little to excite the palate—row upon row of cans, jars, packets, tubes, and boxes. Think 7-Eleven convenience store and you more or less have it. A gourmet's paradise this was not. I later found out that diabetes is rampant on the island, a result of eating large quantities of white rice and other over-refined foods.

THE FOLLOWING NIGHT WE HAD THE BEST meal of our entire stay, at the home of David and Tessie Lambourne, the power couple of Kiribati. David, an amiable Australian, was the Solicitor General. His elegant I-Kiribati wife, Tessie, was the Foreign Secretary. I had met David for the first time that morning. He had taken Team Roz under his wing during the week before I arrived, offering them the use of his office, which had the fastest Internet in town. This was not saying much. It was the speed of a very slow dial-up connection, and many Web pages (such as Facebook) simply refused to load. Conrad had been up all night editing the video of my arrival, from six hours down to six minutes, in order to get it over to the Associated Press. It would take him all day to complete the upload.

Nicole had marginally better luck filing the press release, but the slow Internet, lack of mobile phone coverage, and our obscure time zone all contributed to making Kiribati a PR professional's worst nightmare—even worse than Crescent City. Many potential interviews fell by the wayside due to our communication problems. Exasperated with the local infrastructure, I continued to use my satphone to upload blog posts and tweets, just as I had done from the boat.

David was incredibly kind to us. Nothing was too much trouble. A couple of days after my arrival, I had carelessly mentioned that I would love a massage to ease my aching shoulders, and he immediately replied that one of Tessie's relatives could do a great traditional Tarawan massage. A quick call, and it was arranged. He drove me to his home, which turned out to be more of a small estate, comprising various peripheral buildings as well as the main house, and introduced me to a large gaggle of his wife's relatives, sitting in a row of small, shady, thatched cabañas on the lagoon side of the island, whiling away the hot hours. Two of them tended to me, while a small audience of aunts, sisters, and children watched nearby. I sat on palm matting under the thatch while I was rubbed down with oil and water, and my aching back muscles soothed with long, gentle strokes. Then I was sponged down with a wad of coconut wrapped in muslin and dunked in hot water. Coconut milk ran down my skin. A gentle breeze wafted in from the lagoon. It was all very pleasant indeed. I smelled like a piña colada.

My masseuse and I chatted as best we could across our differences of language and culture. She was the same age as I was—41—but had eight children and three grandchildren, while I had none. Her eldest child was 26 and the youngest was 7. Her husband had died of cancer four years previously. I looked up the stats later and found that life expectancy here was low—60 years for men and 66 for women, putting Kiribati 170th out of 221 countries in the world ranking.

I spent the rest of the afternoon writing in my journal in the cabaña, covering several pages with my reflections while the relatives chatted amongst themselves in the melodious language of Kiribati, played dice, crocheted, ate, and snoozed in the shade. A litter of new puppies slept in a furry heap underneath the cabaña. A pig lay in its pen, also dozing. I couldn't remember the last time I had ever had such a lazy day.

Towards dusk, David's wife, Tessie, came home, and David himself arrived with Nicole, Hunter, and Conrad. We sat in the cabaña drinking toddy, the diluted sap of the palm tree. It was unlike anything else I'd ever had, and it was delicious. It smelled strangely of hot dogs, but tasted much better—sweet and fresh. Conrad begged to differ, though, and barely touched his. David told us they gather it by climbing to the top of a palm tree and shaving the bark at the site of a new palm frond to get to the rising sap beneath. As we had driven around the island, we'd seen the jars attached to palm trees to gather the juice.

After sunset, we sat on the beach under the palm trees, watching the moon rise over the lagoon. Conversation was varied and interesting, including talk of climate change, which was very much on the minds of the Kiribati government. David explained how the country is especially vulnerable. It has one diminutive hill of 81 metres (265 feet) on the island of Banaba, but most of the country lies at less than six feet above sea level.

The first problem they would encounter would be the contamination of their freshwater supply, he told us. They have no streams, springs, or rivers. Drinking water comes from a freshwater lens that forms between the coral bed of the island and the sand that lies above it as a result of local rainfall. The inhabitants dig wells just a few feet deep to reach this fresh water. But when there is a storm large enough to send waves crashing in over the fringing reef, the water becomes brackish, and it takes a while before the salt settles out and it once again becomes fresh enough to drink. Long before the islands disappear beneath the oceans, the water supply will become permanently compromised. With tragic irony, there would be water, water, everywhere, but not a drop to drink.

Neither Tessie nor David were making any moves towards the kitchen and my stomach was starting to rumble when Tessie said, "Come on, let's eat." I turned around and saw to my surprise that a long table had silently appeared on the sand behind us, and it was laden with an array of platters. We walked over and helped ourselves to the buffet—coleslaw with local tuna, chicken, and white rice, washed down with coke, cold beer, or a very nice New Zealand Pinot Noir, according to choice.

This, I learned, was how their household functioned, in a perfect state of symbiosis. David and Tessie worked to support the relatives financially, in return for which the 20 or so members of the extended family provided them with cooking, cleaning, and massage services.

THE NEXT MORNING, IAN TULLER ARRIVED on the island to help out with the boat. Ian was one of the angels of my Pacific row. I truly do not know what I would have done without him. It is one of the many perks of my unusual work that over the years amazing people have gravitated towards my adventurous projects, wanting to help in some way. My boat and I may be the most visible part of the picture, but I never could have achieved as much as I have without an ocean of support from Ian and my other volunteers.

A retiree from San Francisco, Ian has a boat of his own, a small sailboat called the *Phoebe*. She is usually docked in Sausalito, California, and I have stayed on her at various times when in need of a bed. Ian worked hard during his career and was now enjoying a full and active retirement, regularly traveling overseas, hiking in Yosemite, or flying halfway around the world to lend a hand to a certain British ocean rower. Twice he had come out to Hawai'i to help me, at his own expense, and now he came to Tarawa. The best word to sum up Ian would probably be *solid*. Physically, emotionally, practically, he is solid. He's stocky yet fit, with a balding head and glasses. He rolls up his sleeves and gets on with things. He tells it as he sees it, and he makes me laugh. There's no hidden agenda; he just wants to help. I would trust Ian to the ends of the Earth, and indeed that was where we now found ourselves. We picked him up from the airport, and headed over to visit the *Brocade*.

One of my big concerns before making landfall had been whether I would be able to find somewhere to store the *Brocade*. In Hawai'i, I'd had tremendous problems finding a suitable place. For the last couple of months there, she had resided happily at Pacific Shipyards, but apart from that one final staging post, the rest of my search for appropriate storage in Hawai'i had been a frustrating saga of dead ends and dashed hopes. If it had been such a challenge to find boat accommodation on a relatively spacious, well-developed island such as O'ahu, I feared that the chances of finding somewhere suitable on a tiny sandbar in the middle of the Pacific would be slim indeed.

But we were in luck. Tarawa was the location of the renowned Kiribati Marine Training Centre (MTC), where cadets trained to become some of the best-respected merchant marines in the world, going to work on foreign ships and sending money home to their families. Established in the same year that I was born—1967—the Marine Training Centre was an oasis of efficiency, organization, and military discipline amidst the general atmosphere of gentle chaos that characterized South Tarawa. This would be the *Brocade*'s temporary home.

When we arrived at the MTC, the guards swung open the big chain-link gates to allow our car to drive in, and after parking, we were issued day passes at the sentry box. We were escorted through the grounds, past neat borders of red flowers, and up an outside staircase to the Captain Superintendent's office. The door opened in response to the sentry's knock, and Boro Lucic, a tall, burly Montenegrin, greeted us cordially and welcomed us into his office. It was air-conditioned and cool, a welcome respite from the heat outside. Maps, photographs, and nautical memorabilia adorned the walls. This was evidently an establishment with a strong sense of pride in its history and its reputation, and justifiably so.

Boro was keen to help. In his strong Eastern European accent, he promised a round-the-clock guard, a room in which to store the *Brocade*'s contents, and boat-cleaning services. After all the problems I'd had in Hawai'i, when I was always being made to feel my boat was an unwelcome oddball that nobody wanted to shelter, this was a dream come true.

Nicole, Ian, Boro, and I went over to take a look at the *Brocade*'s new residence. It was a sturdy structure, with a corrugated tin roof resting on four stocky columns. A lattice of metal struts crisscrossed the underside of the roof. Judging from the array of towels and garments dangling from the struts, it was mostly used by the cadets for drying their laundry.

If her shelter looked perfect, *Brocade* did not. She was a mess. The boobies had done their worst, and white bird poop was liberally spattered and streaked across her forward cabin. Despite my best efforts to keep them at bay, gooseneck barnacles studded her sides, and her port side was thick with dark green algae. The deck paint had peeled in the sun. I was embarrassed by her shabby appearance.

"We need to clean her, I think," Boro opined. "I will get the men to help."

In fact, the men did more than help. They did it all. About 20 cadets were assigned to the project and set to work with buckets, sponges, and a lot of enthusiasm. Many hands made light work, and within an hour, *Brocade* was almost as good as new, her silver paint gleaming, her solar panels booby-poop-free.

We attempted to rally the cadets for a team photo, but they were unwilling to be distracted from their task. "In a minute, in a minute," they said, as a couple of them still scrubbed away at the last stubborn spots of green algae in a corner of the deck. To my embarrassment, a couple of them had even found my bedpan and were scrubbing that too.

At last they were satisfied that the *Brocade* was as clean as she would ever be and consented to line up for a photo with Nicole and me. The picture shows them striking jokey poses in front of my boat, their smiles gleaming nearly as brightly as the *Brocade* did.

Besides the cleaning, there was much else to do, and Ian and I spent most of the rest of the week at the centre, cleaning, sorting, and storing equipment in the section of the MTC kit store that had been set aside for our use. Ian then turned his attention to the mystery of the broken watermaker. As I described, a few weeks before I arrived in Tarawa the system had lost all pressure and refused to produce water, so I had been surviving on the reserves of water in the ballast bags ever since.

For a couple of days it defied all Ian's attempts at diagnosis. He called Spectra, the manufacturers, but they were unable to offer much in the way of helpful suggestions. I grew concerned. The watermaker is a highly specialized piece of equipment. The MTC was able to offer me a lot, but I doubted they could offer me a trained watermaker engineer. If Ian was unable to fix this problem, my entire Pacific bid might be in jeopardy. It was unimaginable to set out to sea without this piece of equipment, relying purely on the reserves in the Dromedary bags, but the alternative—quitting—was equally unimaginable. Flying out an engineer from California, plus a week of his time, plus accommodation, would be prohibitively expensive.

One day, after I had been at David Lambourne's office trying and mostly failing to access e-mail, Nicole and I drove to the MTC to collect Ian, who had once again been labouring over the watermaker. By this point I had all but given up hope, so it was a wonderful surprise to see him grinning broadly as our car pulled up in front of the entrance gate.

"I've found the problem!" he exclaimed. It was a punishingly hot day and his T-shirt was soaked in sweat, but I had never seen him look happier. "It was the pre-filter cup!"

I had suspected that it was something to do with the pre-filter, but I hadn't realized that the problem lay not in a mucky mesh, but in the outer casing. The pre-filter consists of a wire mesh tube inside a clear Perspex cup, and it resides in the footwell. Other than the intake hose, it's the only part of the watermaker that is fully exposed to the elements, the rest being housed in a locker under the rowing seat. Its job is to filter out the larger particles—of phytoplankton, zooplankton, and, of course, plastic—before the water progresses to a finer filter, and then finally to the membrane where the salt is removed by a process of reverse osmosis.

Adding together the combined days of the Atlantic crossing, the aborted attempt of 2007, and the first stage of the Pacific in 2008, this filter had now spent 212 days at sea in all weather. Its cup had become crazed by prolonged ultraviolet exposure, causing the loss of pressure. Ian had figured this out by isolating each part of the watermaker in turn, until all components had been found innocent apart from the culprit.

Even if I had been able to figure this out while at sea, I didn't have a spare pre-filter cup on board. To guard against future problems I ordered not one, but two, new cups from the manufacturers—thus almost guaranteeing that it would never go wrong again.

ONE DAY TOWARDS THE END of my time on Tarawa, I found myself sitting on a leatherette sofa in the office of Anote Tong, the President of Kiribati. Unlike the Oval Office, this looked like a proper work space, the President's desk piled high with neat stacks of folders and documents. Orange curtains sagged slightly at the windows.

The President sat on a matching sofa on the other side of a low coffee table, a slim man with a dapper moustache, wearing an elegant lavalava, the traditional sarong-like garment. His fingers steepled together, he was telling me about his concerns for the future of his people. Conrad was recording the interview on camera, so the words that follow are selected from the transcript.

He told me what he had seen on his family's home island. "There is no longer what was there," he said. "Where they used to have their homes, the sea is there. We don't know how to explain it to people. As a young child I was living there, and the village was there, but now I go back and it is no longer there. On a daily basis we are getting complaints from people who are losing their homes. I thought we had a long time, but the projections are getting much worse. The time frame is getting shorter. I have grandchildren, and I wonder where they will be in 50 years' time."

"Where will you go to?" I asked, "when you can no longer stay here?"

"We would much prefer to stay here, but in the face of all these uncertainties, it is important to keep exploring all the options available. I don't think we will focus on a single option. I think we will use a combination of options. They are not mutually exclusive. Personally, I would like us to build up some of our islands, so we still have somewhere to call home."

He told me that he was soon to meet President Obama, to ask him for aid money to finance defence measures against rising oceans. He hoped to secure enough money to pay for vocational training for his 100,000 people, so that when they were forced to relocate to other countries, they could find gainful employment.

"It's the least painful for all concerned, because it falls in line very much with the integration policies of the different countries that do accept migrants, so all we need is assistance with the training of our people, so they can become qualified, and so we would be able to fill in the skills gaps where they exist in the countries that would be able to accept our people. If we do migrate, if we do relocate, I'd much prefer to see it to be on merit, with dignity for our people, and to be as worthwhile citizens that will make a contribution to their new communities."

I wondered out loud how his people generally felt about climate change, whether their thoughts, as they lay in their hammocks, were often troubled by concerns about the future.

President Tong said, "You've been here some time, and I think you have seen our lifestyle, very simple. We tend to live on a day-to-day basis, and so we don't plan for 50 years. Hardly anybody plans for 50 years, but as leaders, we must be able to do that. I would like to be able to reply to the question 'What did he do?' and say yes, at least I provided the option, whether they take it up or not. There are options which take time to do. Building up the islands, all it requires is a lot of resources. But to train our people, to up-skill them, it's going to take a lifetime, a generation."

He told me that he had faced dissension from within his own ranks. "I am being criticized. In the last parliament I was being called a defeatist because I am advocating this migration policy."

I heard later that even the President's older brother, Harry, who had fought him for the presidency in 2003, had argued publicly that God had sent the rainbow as a token of his pledge to Noah that he would never again flood the Earth.

"So we will be fine," Harry had said, "because God has made his promise."

The President also planned to ask Obama for funding for sea walls, to buy themselves extra time from the encroaching waves. "I don't know if the international community will be willing to help us with it, but I think they should. I think they owe us that."

Third, he would make a plea for mitigation, beseeching the United States and other developed countries to limit their emissions of greenhouse gases in the hope that other low-lying countries might be spared a similar fate. He explained, "We might be on the front line. Others will follow. This is what carbon trading is about—so that the next line does not fall. But we have fallen. Something must be done about the victims."

I looked at this dignified, university-educated man sitting across the table from me, and asked him what his hopes were for that December's COP15 climate change conference.

"What I would like to see in Copenhagen is quite a lot more common sense than we have seen so far. We need a sense of commitment, of sacrifice. Without that spirit of commitment and sacrifice nothing can be achieved. We have to give up some things. I hope that there will be some compassion. After all, we are human beings, and human beings are blessed with compassion. If we can start off with that, then we have a chance of achieving something."

In response to my question about what he planned to say to the global leaders in Copenhagen, President Tong replied: "I think a lot of people know climate change is happening but they don't want to accept it. For their own different reasons, I think a lot of countries don't want to do that. I've had to argue with leaders from countries like India at different meetings to say, no, no, no, come on, it's not about economic growth, it's about survival—we're talking about the survival of our people here. Yes, I think really what the message should be is: Let's have some common sense about all of this. We've not used that over the last few decades, maybe centuries, in our quest for growth, progress, technological development, and I think it's time we become a bit more realistic about it, that we realize that everything we get comes at a price. And unfortunately the people who get the benefits don't always pay the price. It's those others that pay the price, and I think there's got to be more responsibility."

The words that struck me most came towards the end of our interview. The President looked sad and said, "It's not just about the polar bears. But also about the people. People will die, in masses."

A COUPLE OF NIGHTS LATER, I WAS WATCHING a group of local teenagers playing in the ocean. They were running and jumping off a stone pier, their leaps becoming progressively more elaborate and daring. They were grinning and laughing. I thought of their future as unwilling climate migrants, forced to leave the country of their forebears, and I wondered how I would feel if it were my country. The places where I had been born, grown up, gone to school, got married, and raised children—all gone forever.

The President's words came back to me: "When a nation no longer has a land, what becomes of its people?" he had asked, rhetorically. "Its economy? Its sovereign rights?"

The I-Kiribati themselves had a subsistence lifestyle. Their carbon footprint was inflated by their need to import almost everything, but even taking this into account, their emissions would amount to a fraction of a comparable community of 100,000 Americans or Europeans. Their close neighbour Tuvalu had pledged to be carbon neutral by 2020, which though commendable, was largely symbolic given their negligible contribution to the problem.

I felt I had seen the human face of climate change. Now it was a brown, broad-featured, Micronesian face. But within the century it would be other kinds of faces too—European, Asian, and African faces—and American faces. Climate change recognized no national boundaries, and we had to work together as humans—as one world, not divided as nations—to tackle this, the biggest human challenge of all time.

CHAPTER EIGHT

DO NOT LOOK OUTSIDE YOURSELF FOR THE LEADER

"It is time to speak your truth. Create your community. Be good to each other. And do not look outside yourself for the leader."

— HOPI ELDER

From Tarawa I was whisked into a hectic whirl as I promoted my first book, *Rowing the Atlantic*, in seven major U.S. cities. The tour kicked off in New York, where I stayed with friends, so my first hotel after the rudimentary Hotel Otintaai was the famous Beverly Wilshire in Beverly Hills, where *Pretty Woman* was filmed. The receptionist upgraded me to a junior suite with two bathrooms. The level of luxury felt almost obscene after the austerity of life on board my little boat. Just one month previously, my facilities had consisted of a bucket, a bedpan, and a sponge. Now I had two spotless bathrooms all to myself, stuffed full of more white fluffy towels than I knew what to do with. I firmly closed the door to one of them and tried to make it as clear as possible that it would not require cleaning.

The book tour was enormously enjoyable, a nonstop blur of presentations, signings, media interviews, airports, and hotel rooms. I marveled at the contrasting extremes of my life, from solitude to sociability, from speaking once every few days to speaking all day, from spartan simplicity to the lap of luxury. The old me, the materialistic, consumerist me, might have had her head turned by the celebrity treatment, but ocean rowing has a way of deflating even the biggest ego, and the effects linger long after the return to land. It would be hard to get too impressed with myself when, within very recent memory, I had been rubbing tea tree oil on my baboon bottom and scrubbing mould out of my sleeping cabin. It seemed I was making progress in staying grounded, finding perspective and some greater meaning that could keep me anchored throughout the dramatic shifts I was experiencing.

From the speaking tour, I returned to the UK to prepare for the climate change conference in Copenhagen. I had resolved to get there in as eco-friendly a way as possible, so with a group of trusty female friends, I hiked 250 miles from Big Ben in London to Brussels, Belgium, taking a ferry across the North Sea. After our two-week trek across wintry northern Europe, I was happy to let the train take the strain for the final leg and joined the United Nations Environment Program's "Climate Express" for the journey from Brussels to Copenhagen.

The conference started out well enough. During the first week, I spent several days at the Bella Centre, where the main action was happening. A huge hangar of a conference venue, it was teeming with activists, bloggers, delegates, and politicians. An air of intense activity and a strong aroma of coffee hung over the proceedings. The activists petitioned for support, the bloggers camped out at the huge banks of PCs or trailed cables across the floor to their laptops, the delegates bustled around with bundles of papers, looking important, and the politicians were mostly invisible. Plenaries, the meetings being attended by all official parties, were going on in vast conference rooms behind closed doors, while elsewhere side events, workshops, media interviews, and informal meetings took place in any available space. Already it was a conference of two halves—the decision makers insulated from the hubbub outside by barriers of protocol and security.

By the end of the first week, the representatives from non-governmental organizations (NGOs) were gradually being excluded from the Bella Centre as the top-level negotiations gathered pace. Each day, fewer and fewer entry passes were being granted. This did not go down well with the NGOs, who felt they had a right to be represented, but their protestations fell on deaf ears.

As we entered the last few days of the conference, all eyes were on the Bella Centre. The global heavyweights had arrived—Obama, Indian leaders, the Chinese delegation—and were in there slugging it out. Or so we assumed, but the building was now an impenetrable fortress. We were not allowed beyond the high chain-link fences that surrounded it. Outside, we held our collective breath and waited to see what would happen next.

As we now know, what happened next was—not much.

I KNEW THE WRITING WAS on the wall. I had tried to keep an upbeat attitude, but my relentless optimism was about to run slap bang into reality. As it turned out, Copenhagen comprehensively failed to deliver the hoped-for deal, the draft agreements eviscerated by a powerful cabal of up-and-coming nations who understandably aspire to the same affluence that the developed world has been enjoying for the last 50 years or so. All the numbers that mattered were removed, substituted by meaningless expressions of unenforceable intentions.

While the climate talks were in their final throes, I was having dinner with President Anote Tong and the rest of the Kiribati delegation in a curry restaurant in downtown Copenhagen. The President was open about his feelings: "We are trying to maintain our composure, but I am very sad . . . We were naïve and vulnerable . . . I wish I was so much more ruthless." That evening the negotiations ended in failure.

The next morning, as I walked through the cold winter sunshine of central Copenhagen, my mood was decidedly "morning after the night before." The city squares, which for two weeks had been full of exhibits, trailers, tents, and people, were almost deserted. Everything had been broken down and removed with almost indecent haste.

I observed with a little bitterness that it is often the most long-awaited and eagerly anticipated events that signally fail to deliver satisfaction, while the really good and memorable things happen serendipitously and unexpectedly. I had spent much of the last year planning for this event, trying to figure out how I could be of most service. I had been obsessed by COP15. And, predictably, I had woken up the morning after feeling rather disappointed and wondering what went wrong.

I wrote in my blog that day:

> I will leave Copenhagen more jaded than I arrived, but more realistic too, and hence hopefully more effective. I'm not going to believe that every international negotiation is hopeless. The truth lies somewhere in between my former idealism and my present cynicism. To see the world as it is, rather than as I wish it was, is no bad thing, but having one's illusions shattered is never a pleasant experience.
>
> I leave Copenhagen tomorrow, with my heart a little heavier, my head a little wiser. I'll be pondering on what has happened here, and starting to evolve my environmental mission for 2010. As 2009 draws to a close, I'm looking forward to a period of reflection and rejuvenation, and preparation for challenges of the year ahead.
>
> And a final note—a definition of Post-COPulation Syndrome: a feeling of anticlimax, disillusionment, cynicism. Leading to increased fire in the belly.

I had begun to realize that we couldn't sit back and wait for our leaders to step in and save the day. For too much of my life I had held to the myth of the white knight. Beguiled by fairy tales and Hollywood legends, I expected somebody else to protect me and make sure my world was safe and happy, abdicating responsibility to parents, teachers, boyfriends, husband—or governments. But in Copenhagen I had grown up and realized nobody had a magic wand. This challenge was too big, and too important, for us to leave it to a handful of humans cloistered in a conference room. We would all have to step up and take part.

AFTER RETURNING TO THE UK to regroup and spend Christmas with my family, I spent the early part of 2010 staying in a borrowed apartment in Devon, writing and working.

That spring, I spoke at a TED conference that took place on a small cruise ship in the Galapagos Islands off the coast of Ecuador. TED stands for Technology, Entertainment, Design, and their tagline is "Ideas Worth

Spreading." For the last few years, all TED Talks have been available on-line on YouTube, as I had discovered a couple of years previously when a friend sent me a link to a presentation that he thought would be of particular interest to me. As I browsed the site, I found a treasure trove of presentations from inspiring, enlightening, thought-provoking, mind-expanding speakers, a veritable who's who of 21st-century culture, all giving 18 minutes of their best.

This particular TED conference was to be the first of its kind, specifi-cally focused on one particular issue—the oceans—and the conference was accordingly dubbed TED Mission Blue. It had been inspired by dis-tinguished American marine biologist Dr. Sylvia Earle and the prizewin-ning TED speech in which she described her wish for the oceans: "To ignite public support for a global network of marine protected areas, hope spots large enough to save and restore the ocean, the blue heart of the planet." The hundred or so attendees on board included the ac-tors Leonardo DiCaprio, Edward Norton, Glenn Close, and Chevy Chase; musicians Jackson Browne and Damien Rice; various top-tier business-men, wealthy philanthropists, and heads of some of the most respected nonprofit organizations in the world; and a brace of Cousteaux—Jean-Michel, son of Jacques, and his daughter, Céline.

OVER THE COURSE OF THE PREVIOUS few years, I had unavoidably become aware of the problems facing the world's oceans. Although I saw myself more as an Earth advocate than an oceans advocate, not believing that we can isolate any one component of our biosphere from the others, I'd inevitably been involved in various conferences, film festivals, websites, and other projects concerned with the 70 percent of our planet that is blue. Acquaintances often sent me links to articles about the plight of the oceans, assuming that I would be particularly interested in news relating to my chosen field (so to speak) of operation. As time went on, by dint of repeated exposure to relevant information, I did indeed become inter-ested for reasons beyond this merely being my place of work. It became increasingly clear to me just how crucial the oceans are to our future well-being. If we want to live on a healthy planet, we can't afford to ignore the large portions of it that are covered in water.

As I had thought more deeply about our environmental challenges, I had perceived that a holistic approach was required. There was a bewildering multitude of information and difficulties, but ultimately they were all manifestations of a single fundamental problem: humanity's estrangement from nature. We used to know on a visceral level that we're part of nature, unable to survive in isolation from every other component of our biosphere. It made sense to treat our fellow residents of planet Earth with respect, because we knew that we needed them—possibly very indirectly, but in this intricate web of life everything was ultimately interconnected, so to harm or even remove any part of it would be to risk destroying the whole.

And what was happening in the oceans, I knew, was a cause for serious concern. Over recent years I had received a steady drip, drip of bad news—but it would take TED Mission Blue to make me fully realize just how bad the situation was. It turned out to be a crash course that would bring home to me like never before the scale of the destruction that had been unfolding beneath the hull of my boat while I rowed along largely oblivious on the surface. By the time I left the conference I would no longer have just a shallow, intellectual appreciation of the challenges. Quite literally, my concerns deepened.

Species extinction, ocean acidification, collapsing fish stocks, coral-reef destruction, fossil-fuel extraction, sewage, runoff, sea dumping, mining, agricultural waste, plastic pollution, and the acronym barrage of PCBs, DDT, POPs—the roster of reasons to be fearful, rather than cheerful, seemed endless. I tried to maintain some degree of optimism, standing by my "every little helps" credo. But it seemed woefully inadequate in the face of such an onslaught of depressing news. I felt like a latter-day King Canute, trying to hold back an incoming tide but being submerged by a tsunami instead.

The only glimmer of hope I could find was in Brian Skerry's assertion, backed up by his photographs of marine reserves in New Zealand, that when the ocean is left alone for a while it has amazing powers of recovery. In as little as 20 years, life returns and equilibrium is restored. Nature is incredibly resilient, but it needs to be given a chance. The creation of more marine reserves—and the larger, the better, to allow the fabric of the underwater ecosystem to mend—is absolutely key to the future survival of the seas. If we want oceans once again teeming with life, as they did not so very long ago, we can start by leaving them alone for a while and giving them a chance to heal.

As I reflected on my time at TED Mission Blue and my realization from Copenhagen, that we each have the responsibility to act as a leader, I made some new resolutions and shared them on my blog in the hope of spreading a few ripples of change—for the sake of the oceans.

1. Reduce even further my use of plastic. Recycling isn't good enough, and comes with its own environmental impacts. We need to stop it at source.
2. Eat less protein, and/or get more of it from organic vegetable sources. Avoid farmed salmon (salmon are carnivorous, so it takes many pounds of wild fish to produce one pound of farmed salmon), shrimp (horrendous by-catch), and don't even think about eating bluefin tuna.
3. Support organizations campaigning for more marine protected areas.

I rounded off the blog with one of my mantras: "If we all pull together, we can make a world of difference." And I just hoped that we could make enough of a difference, and soon enough, to save the oceans.

I WENT STRAIGHT FROM TED MISSION BLUE to Kiribati—or at least, straight there via a two-hour boat ride, then flights from Galapagos to Quito, to Houston, to Los Angeles, to Fiji, and finally Kiribati. The journey took about two days, but it was still a lot faster than rowing there.

As we flew across the Pacific, the man sitting next to me on the plane leaned across to look out of the window.

"That's a whole lot of ocean down there," he commented.

I smiled wryly and replied, "Yes, it is."

I looked at the glittering expanse beneath us and thought of the times when I had been on my boat, looking up at an aeroplane's contrail and wondering if anybody on the plane noticed the tiny vessel below them, a microscopic dot in the vastness of the ocean. To put it in perspective, if the Pacific Ocean were three statute miles across, my boat would be less than one-tenth of an inch, about the size of a pinhead.

My trusty Director of Boats, Ian Tuller, had refused to come back to Kiribati. When he left the island the year before, he had brought home an unwanted souvenir—a parasitic infection. He had not been the only member of my team to suffer: Conrad and Nicole had contracted stomach bugs, and Hunter a nasty bout of conjunctivitis, but Ian's problem was much more persistent. Seven months later it still hadn't cleared up.

"That just doesn't work for me," Ian had said.

I was disappointed, but I completely understood. To ask one's friends to travel halfway around the world to help launch a rowboat is a tall enough order, but asking them to risk serious long-term health consequences is just too much.

Luckily, my friend Liz Fischer had volunteered of her own free will. A Virginian living in Hawai'i, she had traveled extensively in the Pacific and knew more or less what she was getting herself into. Forsaking the Hotel Otintaai, we stayed at the Betio Apartments. Our twin-bed room, one of a row of similar rooms opening onto an outdoor walkway, was basic, but clean enough.

The only problem was that, as we looked out of our room window, it appeared that the Betio Apartments had been built in a lake. The weather had been quite pleasant the last time I was in Kiribati, but now it was raining. Or, to do it full justice, I would have to say that it was a deluge. To describe this weather as rain would be like saying that the Pacific is quite large, an understatement of heinous proportions. The unpaved yard in front of our apartment was flooded to ankle depth, and the potholes in the road were filled with water. The entire island was awash already, and still the rain fell in torrents from the sky. It was like a glimpse into the future of Kiribati, as if the oceans were already triumphing over the land.

On Saturday morning, Liz and I headed along the short walkway to a roofed area that served as a congregating spot for the guests to have coffee and our self-catered breakfast. We sat there on the upholstered sofa, watching the raindrops cascading off the thatched roof, topping up the mini-lagoon of the courtyard, and wondered when it would ever stop, or if one day I would be able to row my boat right up to our front door.

Normally a bit of water wouldn't have bothered me. I was about to row across a couple of thousand miles of the stuff. But this was a lot of water, in a place where I hadn't been expecting it, and it was very inconvenient. We hadn't planned to spend much time in Tarawa. I wanted to get ready and get out as quickly as possible. I'd already pushed back my start date so that I could speak at TED Mission Blue, and I also reasoned that the less time I spent on the island, the less risk there was of contracting an infection. That would be the last thing I needed at the start of a long voyage on a boat with minimal bathroom facilities.

We had a lot to do, and not much time to do it. Almost as soon as we arrived in Tarawa on Friday, the cadets moved the boat out from under the laundry shelter for us. We needed to seize the offer of manpower before they went home for the weekend, as most of the things that remained to be done required the boat to be out in the open. For example, I couldn't set up the bimini (a nautical term for a sun canopy) until the short antenna masts were up, and I couldn't raise the masts under the limited headroom of the shelter's roof. But we would have preferred to work in the dry than in a monsoon.

We had had plenty to keep us busy indoors—sorting and packing food and kit, testing technology, completing a few final e-mails and interviews. But if this weather continued for the rest of Saturday and into Sunday, we were going to be struggling to be ready in time for me to leave early Monday morning. The rain had begun at five o'clock Saturday morning and seven hours later showed no signs of relenting.

Somehow we managed. One of our most important tasks, not for survival but for PR purposes, was to put my sponsors' logos onto the boat—but we needed dry weather. Due to the rain, we didn't have time to put the stickers on the boat before she went in the water. On Sunday afternoon, during a brief easing of the downpour, Liz did a commendable job of applying some of the decals by leaning out of the aft hatch of the sleeping cabin. Unfortunately the dampness was just too much for the glue, and when we arrived at the boat on Monday morning for the launch, the letters of "Green Heart by Sony Ericsson" (an environmentally conscious mobile phone) had slithered across the slick surface of the cabin to form a higgledy-piggledy alphabet soup. There was nothing to be done about it, so that was how they stayed. The photos of my arrival in Papua New Guinea would show my boat proudly endorsing the "en Hat by Sony Ercsson."

ON MONDAY MORNING, THE RAIN gave us a break. I would be starting from the Marine Training Centre at 6:45 A.M., partly to get away before the worst heat of the day, but mostly so that the President could come and see me off before attending Parliament. Liz and I got up early and drove over to the MTC. I was still sitting in the rental car, signing a few copies of my Atlantic book as gifts for our friends in Tarawa, when Liz rapped on the window to let me know the guest of honour had arrived. I hastily penned the last few words and leaped out of the car to walk over to where the President, Captain Superintendent Boro Lucic, and John and Linda Anderson were standing on the grass by the lifeboat launch pool, where my boat had been lifted out of the water nine months previously. The cadets of the MTC stood in a well-ordered group, their ceremonial uniforms as brilliantly white as a laundry-detergent commercial in the soft grey of the early morning light.

President Anote Tong, whom I had last seen in a curry house in Copenhagen, said a few words and wished me a safe voyage, thanking me for my work in bringing attention to the plight of his country. I recall him using some phrase like "ultimate sacrifice" to describe my commitment to the cause. I sincerely hoped it wouldn't come to that. I was willing to make many sacrifices, but not the ultimate one. Many movements have had their martyrs, but I continue to feel strongly that I am more useful alive than dead.

Linda Anderson also said a few words of thanks on behalf of Kiribati, and placed a headdress on my hair as a token of good luck. It was not made out of plumeria this time, but from silk flowers and plastic drinking straws "to demonstrate our commitment to sustainability."

I said a few words, too, thanking the people of Kiribati for their hospitality, and Boro and the men of the MTC for taking such good care of my boat, and pledging to do all I could to promote sustainable living through my adventures.

As I spoke, I glanced over at Liz. She was watching me with a strange expression. It was a look that mingled a sense of pride in being associated with my adventures with a sense of mystification that this ordinary-looking woman could be capable of achieving such extraordinary feats. I had a sudden rush of emotions that probably generated a similar complexity of expression on my own face. Almost simultaneously, several realizations dawned on me.

The first was the power of my adventures to draw people in and engage them (which with the benefit of hindsight, I have identified at earlier points in the voyage and already mentioned several times in this book). I had seen it in everybody from schoolchildren with an infinity of possibilities still open to them, to people in their 80s who saw in me either their own young and idealistic selves, or maybe the life they wished they'd lived.

The second was that people felt a vicarious sense of pride in getting involved. Over the past five years, literally hundreds of people had done so much to help me financially, logistically, and emotionally. From venture capitalists to journalists to psychologists to paddlers—whatever their skills, they had found a way to help me towards my goals and had been willing to put their time, money, and energy at my disposal.

The third—and here Liz represented everybody who had ever supported me—was that I had not been a very gracious co-worker that week. I get a bit uptight just before a launch and don't always show enough appreciation to those who are helping. Liz had done so much for me. Not only had she worked incredibly hard on my boat, but she had also given me many of her own possessions to remedy the shortcomings of the shops in Kiribati. My flip-flops had expired in Tarawa, the uppers ripping out from the soles one day as I waded through the ankle-deep water in the yard at Betio Apartments. Liz had given me hers. Being an accomplished world traveler, her pack was full of many other useful things that she had unhesitatingly donated to me in case they might come in handy: sunhat, clothes pegs, cord, and many other things besides. Totally focused on the launch and under the pressure of time, I suddenly felt I had not shown enough gratitude, and now it was too late.

All this rushed through my mind in a moment. I had to make an effort of will to pull myself back to the present, and focus on the here and now. Everyone was looking at me expectantly. It was time to go.

As he walked me over to my boat, the President asked me how I felt at this stage, setting out on a new adventure. I replied, truthfully, that I try not to think about it too much until I am past the point of no return, for fear that I might talk myself out of it. He smiled, and I wondered how many people who take on major challenges, be it an ocean crossing or a presidency, truly know what they are getting themselves into. There is a lot to be said for stepping up to take on something that needs doing, without hesitating to consider all the potential problems and pitfalls that may lie ahead. It is so easy to think too much about all the things that could go wrong. It is much better to commit, prepare as best you can, and just figure out the rest as you go. As the saying goes, plan roughly, and execute superbly.

I boarded my boat, still wearing the headdress. The fine young men of the MTC broke into song. Liz and I had overheard them rehearsing the day before. Their voices resonated around the rusty metal sides of the lifeboat pool as I paddled carefully out of its narrow entrance to the ocean beyond. This was it. If all went according to plan, by the end of this leg I would have become the first woman to row solo across the Pacific Ocean.

As soon as I got away from land the weather improved, to my considerable relief. Wet skin chafes much more than dry, and I had not relished the prospect of rowing in the rain for the next few months. But soon I had the opposite problem. Once I escaped from the cover of the clouds, the day was swelteringly hot, with nary a breeze to ease my sweaty discomfort. By 3:20 p.m. the thermometer was registering 42.7 degrees centigrade on deck. That's about 109 degrees Fahrenheit, and in plain English it was bloody hot.

But I was prepared. After the itchy, unsightly heat rashes of the previous year's row, I had resolved to do whatever I could to make this year's effort more comfortable. I had purchased two 12-volt electric fans, designed for use in cars. They weren't marine grade, just cheap Chinese fans, so I wasn't sure how long they would last in the salty humidity of the ocean, but it had to be worth a try. One had already been doing sterling service in my cabin. It was time to press it into action out on deck. Luckily it had a good long lead that could reach all the way from the bank of six cigarette-lighter sockets inside the sleeping cabin out to the cockpit. Its brand name was Roam, which seemed appropriate—surely few fans would have roamed so far.

I clipped it to the bar that arched across the deck above my rowing shoes, a bar which had served so many purposes over the years: bracket for my gimbaled cooking stove, grab handle as I emerged from the sleeping cabin, cleat for the sea anchor trip line—and now electric fan support. Much to my surprise and delight, the fan whirred away faithfully and reliably, hour after hour, day after day. It wasn't particularly powerful, but it made life more tolerable when nature failed to provide any breeze.

During my midday siesta, I would unclip the fan from the bar and relocate it to one of the guardrail oars so that it could keep me cool as I lounged in the shadow of my makeshift sunshade, fashioned from a sarong slung between the bimini and the guardrail, with the sea anchor bag as my pillow. On the rare days when it was calm enough to lie on deck without being constantly soaked by waves coming in over the side, it felt decadent indeed to seek refuge from the baking sun, my naked skin cooled by the soothing breeze of the fan as I lay between the runners of my rowing seat. The deck was hard and unyielding, but if I arranged myself carefully, I could find a relatively comfortable position. If I'd had a rough night in the stultifying stuffiness of the cabin, my heat rashes itching, this midday snooze was absolute heaven as I felt the gentle waft of air moving over my skin.

As I LOOKED AT THE FAN, I sometimes thought about the Chinese workers slaving away in their huge factories, making cheap electronic goods like this. There's a film called *Manufactured Landscapes* that opens with an eight-minute continuous sequence of workers in a Chinese factory, frighteningly reminiscent of chickens in a factory farm as the camera slowly tracks at constant speed past row upon row upon row of human beings in matching yellow uniforms, silently working on a production line. It was hard to believe that any manufacturing facility could be so vast. The scene went on, and on, and on.

I had thought ocean rowing was boring, but it was nothing compared with the monotony of this work. Even one day of it would have had me running for my life. Occasionally a worker would look up and stare into the lens of the camera as it slowly passed by the end of their line of workbenches. I wondered what was going on behind those eyes. How could they possibly stand this? What job satisfaction was there? What motivation? What legacy? Did they really go home at the end of the day proud of what they had achieved? To me, it seemed inhuman—and inhumane. What in their psyche enabled them to tolerate this mind-numbing work? Did they in fact tolerate it, or was it slowly driving them insane?

An interview later in the film revealed a little of what their feelings might be. Some men working on the Three Gorges Dam said, "It's work. We get paid." They had been working on the dam for ten years. Maybe this was all it meant to them: spending 8, or 10, or 12 hours a day, for years on end, mere ants on an anthill, just to get paid. I almost couldn't stand to watch the film. It made me want to scream. It made me want to cry.

Whoa—easy girl. It's amazing what tangents of thought can be inspired by one electric fan. But that electric fan had become my new best friend, the object that was right in front of my eyes for 12 hours a day as I rowed, and it ultimately became a focus for my thoughts.

I have to be very careful what I place within my field of view on the boat. I'd berated Liz for a crooked sticker on the bulkhead of the aft cabin, saying, "I'm going to be looking at that for 12 hours a day, for maybe three months. It's got to be straight!" I knew that I wasn't an easy taskmaster, but it was of almost vital importance to me.

No matter who made it under whatever political and industrial regime, the fan was a very welcome addition to the boat. Each time I went out on the ocean, I tried to refine the setup. What I was doing was tough enough already; there was no need to be unnecessarily masochistic about it. If I could find a way to make it a little less uncomfortable, then life was good.

BUT NOT ALL TECHNOLOGY IS AS QUIETLY HELPFUL as the fan. I have a very ambivalent relationship with the satellite phone, and on the final stage of the row, this was to be truer than ever before. On the sixth night, I rowed for a couple of hours after sunset, enjoying the slightly cooler air. I grew sleepy after the long, hot day's rowing. It was time for bed. I bathed and brushed and flossed and had no sooner got into my cabin than the phone rang.

To understand the full impact of this, you need to know that my phone *never* rang. Only a handful of people had the number, it's about ten dollars a minute to call, and I was hardly ever in the cabin to answer it—in fact, it was usually switched off and packed away in a waterproof case—so this was not good. Apprehensively, I picked up the phone and pressed the green button.

It was my poor, long-suffering mother, wanting to know if I was still alive. I was able to reassure her on this point. Yes, I had picked up the phone. Therefore I was incontrovertibly alive. But apparently my positioning unit had not been reporting my whereabouts, and I had been too busy trying to stay cool to tweet as much as usual today. So one way and another, there had been no news from *Brocade* for more than 18 hours. According to our impeccably documented emergency procedures, this was about the time to start panicking. My mother was duly following the protocol.

I had to sigh. Time was when sailors would set off around the world and nobody would hear a peep out of them until they arrived—or sometimes didn't—at their intended destination. Months could go by with no word. But not anymore. Regular check-ins were now expected, and indeed required. From then on, to save my mother from more worry, I promised to be more regular with my tweeting. Twitter has been appropriated for many things, but this voyage may have been the first recorded use of the platform as a marine-safety technology.

By Day 15, the satphone had become a much greater bane. When at sea, I use it as a data modem to post text and photographs to my blog. It's slow, but it usually works, more or less. I write my blog post, then I plug a cable into the USB port of the laptop and connect it to the satellite phone. I launch a software application called SkyFile, a very basic e-mail client, and through that I send my blog post via satellite to a server on dry land, from whence it is posted to my blog on WordPress.

Or at least, that is how it's supposed to work. This time I had been persuaded that the new Iridium 9555 satphone was a significant improvement over its predecessor, the 9505A. So at enormous expense, I had bought one. It was, from beginning to end, a complete disaster. I would have switched back to the 9505A, which I still had on board as a backup, but it refused to recognize its own SIM card. To cut a very long and boring story short, it was buggered.

Here's how I reported it in my blog:

> BIG techno hassles today, as you may have gathered from the very belated appearance of my blog. After trying for an hour last night to upload my blog, and another half hour this morning, I then spent an hour on the phone to Rob at Remote Satellite Systems trying to resolve the problem. We tried various things, none of which worked. Then it just started working randomly, without any further changes being made. Gaaargh! Intermittent problems are just the worst—almost impossible to find out the root cause. I've also found out that my Tweets are not being posted to Twitter. I don't know why this is. Half the time my phone rejects my Tweet anyway, neither telling me why, nor allowing me to resend it.

When things start breaking down on the ocean, there are generally three possible outcomes:

Fix it. Straightforward enough with low-tech objects such as oars, but with exponentially diminishing chances of success as the complexity and technological sophistication of the object increase.

Decide you didn't need it anyway. On the Atlantic, the demise of the camping stove had fallen into this category. Faced with little choice, I decided there are worse things in life than cold freeze-dried food. Not many, but some.

Find a workaround. This is my usual approach. I try to have a backup plan of some sort, and even if I didn't have one before I set out, it's amazing what complete isolation in the middle of an ocean does for one's powers of resourcefulness and creativity.

With the satphone, I eventually resorted to option 3, when the problem escalated from difficult to impossible.

I had spent a whole morning on the phone to Rob at Remote Satellite Systems, who was incredibly generous with his time, especially as it was a Sunday, and we tried to solve the problem. My whole cabin was strewn with bits of computer, satellite phones, and cables, as we tried every possible permutation to find a combination that worked. We failed, and as the morning wore on, I got crankier and crankier at being cramped in my hot, stuffy cabin while rowing conditions outside were relatively cool and pleasant. Rowing 12 hours a day isn't necessarily at the top of my list of favourite things to do, but it's all relative, and for once I was impatient to get back to the oars and away from delinquent technology.

EVENTUALLY I HAD HAD ENOUGH. MORE THAN enough. Keeping meticulous notes in my Rite in the Rain waterproof notebook, I had tried every possible option. Sometimes I had come tantalizingly close to succeeding, only to fail at the last gasp. It was with an enormous sense of relief that I finally declared the system to be beyond hope. I simply could not stand to waste another moment on a project that I was convinced had no chance of success. I hope that, given the scale of the projects I pursue, you know I am not a quitter. But now it was time to abandon the technology and move on.

I felt the need to purge my living quarters of evidence of the techno fiasco, so I gathered up every last bit of defunct kit from my sleeping cabin, shoved it disgustedly into whatever waterproof receptacles I could find, and relegated it to the forward storage cabin. It left my control panel looking strangely denuded, but I couldn't stand having all that stuff lying around being useless. Now it was out of the way and I could forget about it. There was nothing to be done about it until I got back to dry land.

It could be worse, I reflected. On the Atlantic I'd had no communications at all for the last 24 days, when my one and only satphone had broken. My transponder had still been working, so my progress was visible on the online map, but I was totally incommunicado apart from one occasion when I had managed to make radio contact with a passing ship to let my mother know I was okay. I had actually been more than content in my glorious isolation for those precious few weeks. I'd felt it to be a rare privilege to be truly alone in this day and age, when on one level we have so much communication, but on another level so little connection, so much information but so little understanding.

Now, on the Pacific, Mum and I devised a workaround. I would type blog posts on the laptop, then use the satphone to call a special voicemail account that my mother had set up. I would dictate the blog post, inserting notes on spelling and punctuation where necessary, and hang up. My mother would receive the message as an mp3 file in her e-mail. The big advantage of this over normal voicemail was that she could pause, fast forward, or rewind the message. She would transcribe it and post it to my website via the WordPress interface. Not for the first time, I was grateful to have such a technologically competent mother, especially impressive as she was already over 70 years old, and many of her con-temporaries barely knew what a blog was. Yet again she helped keep the show on the road—or the row on the show.

In many ways I preferred this streamlined version of blogging. It was a shame, but not the end of the world, that I was no longer able to post photographs from the ocean. And there was much during this crossing to keep me cheerful. I was making unexpectedly fast progress westwards. Despite having wasted so much time on the phone, conditions that Sun-day conspired to give me my best day's mileage ever—around 60 nauti-cal miles closer to my target, including some good progress south.

"Praise be to the weather gods, and long may it continue," I dictated for my blog.

In addition to my speedy progress, I had a new friend. There was a little spider that had been with me since I left Tarawa. I couldn't figure out what he was finding to eat, but he seemed pretty full of energy. He moved so fast that it was hard to catch him on camera, but I managed to grab a blurry photo or two of Alf the Spider. I hoped my little stow-away would manage to survive the voyage. I enjoyed the company. The conversations weren't great, but on a solo rowboat, you make the most of what you have.

SADLY, ONE OF THE MOST NOTABLE THINGS about this stage of the row was the amount of plastic trash I saw littering the ocean. Between San Francisco and Hawai'i I'd seen many small fragments, distributed throughout the water column, but here, closer to land, I saw many pieces of litter that were still all too recognisable.

On one particular day, I saw about 30 individual recognisable pieces—drinks bottles, yogurt pots, bits of packaging. There was something upsetting about seeing a beautiful blue ocean, glinting in the sunshine, marred by a plastic bottle bobbing along on its surface.

Appalled by the ugliness of the sight, I shared in my blog:

> I would love to see a ban on all plastic drinks bottles. It's easy enough to avoid using plastic water bottles—just buy a Brita water filter and keep refilling your own reusable water bottle. But what about the other drinks, even health drinks like smoothies, that come in plastic bottles? I hate the hypocrisy of selling a drink that is supposedly good for your body, packaged in a substance that is so bad for the planet.
>
> For decades—centuries, even—we used glass bottles. They can be returned for a deposit, or recycled, and even if they end up in landfill or the ocean they are at least inert and don't leach out nasty chemicals into the environment. I don't know the cost/benefit analysis of glass versus plastic, but if you factor in the REAL cost of plastic—environmental as well as financial—I'm fairly certain this would swing the argument.
>
> After all, beer still comes in glass bottles. So why can't everything else? Maybe we should boycott all other drinks, and just drink beer and wine. Think this could catch on as a campaign? SAVE THE WORLD. DRINK BEER.

A waggish commentator on my blog suggested an even better slogan: "Save the whale. Drink more ale." When my mother told me about it, I had to laugh. Sometimes you have to laugh, or else you'd cry.

GIVEN MY DEEP-ROOTED AVERSION to marine debris, it was ironic that this final stage of the row would also become notable for objects going overboard. The first harbinger of the trend was the electric kettle. Although electric kettles are not an efficient use of solar energy—anything involving light or heat gobbles up electricity at a phenomenal rate—by this point I had simplified my technological setup so much, and had such a plentiful supply of sunshine, that I had more than enough solar energy to spare. It took the kettle about 20 minutes to reach a boil, but I was in no hurry. I wasn't going anywhere.

On the evening of Day 13, I was bringing the kettle out on deck, ready to rehydrate my dinner. A sudden wave lurched the boat, and I grabbed hold of the starboard guardrail with the same hand that was holding the kettle. The kettle toppled out of its stand and dropped into the water.

I didn't even stop to think. Even if I had, I'd have done the same thing. It wasn't the kettle that mattered (I had a spare); it was the fact that I couldn't possibly drop plastic in the ocean and just leave it there. So with barely time for a quick expletive, I followed my kettle into the water, sun hat and all.

This was not the time I would have chosen to go for a swim. It had been stormy and chilly most of the day, and the ocean waters had been sullied by a long windrow of plastic shreds in the ocean, accompanied by small, slimy green blobs and occasional jellyfish. It was a nasty, dirty, polluted bit of ocean and the last place I wanted to go for a dip. But it had to be done.

I retrieved the kettle and, trying not to think about jellyfish, to which I have a lifelong aversion, I splashed my way cack-handedly back to the boat. I don't suppose that many people have tried to swim with an electric kettle in one hand, so take it from me—it isn't easy.

Unsurprisingly, the kettle no longer worked too well. The light came on to show it was receiving power, but it wouldn't heat up—which rather defeats the point of the thing. So I had to resort to the spare, but hoped that Kettle 1 might recover when it had had a chance to dry out. Meanwhile, Kettle 2 did a grand job, and after my unscheduled swim, I was soon looking forward to some nice hot rehydrated fish pie, extra welcome on such a dank, gloomy day.

THE NEXT TIME I WENT OVERBOARD after a stray object, the outcome was nearly a lot more disastrous than a ruined kettle. 15 May 2010 was nearly the last day of my life. I was so embarrassed by my own stupidity that it took me a couple of days before I decided to share the story on my blog, and even then I felt the need to defend myself first.

It is confession time, and please, before you are tempted to wag your finger at me, bear in mind that I didn't have to tell you this. I could have kept it quiet, and you would have been none the wiser. So please resist the urge to tell me what I already know, that I shouldn't have done it.

You'd think that a near-death experience would be many things, but *embarrassing* would probably not be near the top of relevant adjectives. Yet that was my overriding emotion, because my premature demise would have been entirely my own stupid fault.

When I embarked on the Atlantic crossing, my first time alone at sea, my foremost fear had been that I would do something terminally stupid. Back then I had been constantly conscious of the need to be very, very careful, because solo seafarers get no second chances. But as time had gone on, I had relaxed my guard, even become a little complacent, and it was nearly my undoing. The motives for my act of consummate stupidity were good, but that would have been scant consolation to either me or my mother as my head disappeared beneath the waves for the last time.

On this final stage of my row across the Pacific, I nearly got separated from my boat.

To PROTECT MYSELF FROM THE INTENSE afternoon sun once its arc had moved beyond the slender protection of my triangular sun canopy (which had been dubbed the "G-string" due to its resemblance to a certain item of underwear), I had improvised an extension to the shelter involving a sarong and the telescopic boat hook. Normally I kept everything on deck attached to the boat with lanyards, but not on this occasion—the first link in the chain towards potential disaster.

As I was rowing along, listening to my iPod, the boathook slipped from its mounting and dropped overboard. The sudden movement, rather than the faint splash, caught my attention. My first instinct was to go after it, just as I had gone after the electric kettle. I briefly considered that I could manage without it, especially as I had a spare boathook in the fore cabin, but it just wouldn't do to leave a manmade, non-biodegradable object floating around in the ocean.

By the time I had removed sun hat, rowing gloves, iPod earbuds, and sunglasses, the boathook was starting to look rather distant. That crucial delay was the second link in the chain of disaster. I mentally measured the growing distance from the boat to the boathook. Not good, but I couldn't just leave it there. So I jumped in and started swimming.

As I swam out, I was already starting to have misgivings. I felt very vulnerable being so far from my boat.

I got to the boathook, picked it up, and started to head back towards the boat, but swimming with the rod in one hand was no easier than swimming with the kettle. I didn't seem to be making any headway at all. It rapidly became apparent that I couldn't possibly make it if I held on to the boathook.

So, reluctantly, I abandoned the hook to its fate, hoping that a fisherman from a nearby island might pick it up and put it to good use before it drifted out to the deep ocean beyond. But even without the hook in hand, I struggled to narrow the distance between me and my fast-drifting boat. I am not a speedy swimmer. I can plod slowly along for a long time, but sprinting is not my style. Yet right now a sprint was what I needed. My life depended on it.

I could feel my body starting to tire. My fingers were already stiff from grasping the oars, and now they weren't strong enough to pull through the water effectively. I was trying to cup my hands, to more effectively grab and draw the water past me, but my fingers trembled and I could feel the water slipping between them. Every few strokes I glanced frantically towards the boat, but it didn't seem to be getting any closer.

I struggled on, feeling my heart pounding a desperate drumbeat of exertion and rising panic. The boat was my everything, my life-support capsule, my only refuge in this massive ocean wilderness. The nearest land, Bougainville Island, although relatively close in Pacific terms, was still dozens of miles away—much farther than I could swim. Unless I could get back to my boat, I would eventually become exhausted and slip beneath the waves to my death.

My strength was starting to fail when a memory rose up in my panic-numbed brain. A few months before, my mother had told me she'd had a nightmare in which they had found my boat empty and abandoned, with nobody on board. She had been distraught when they told her the news, for she knew it meant I had been lost at sea. Even as she told me about the nightmare some time later, she had almost been crying at the traumatic memory. I had hugged her and promised her that I would never let it come true.

Was I now going to keep that promise? Or would I leave my mother to mourn for her elder daughter, lost at sea in an accident that she had foreseen? I couldn't do that to her. I owed it to her, if not to myself, to come back safely.

I dug deep, found an extra ounce of strength, and at last the boat began to get perceptibly closer. With an overwhelming sense of relief, I felt my outstretched fingers finally touch the black rope grab line. I had probably been in the water no more than 15 minutes, but it had been the longest 15 minutes of my life, and almost the last.

I COLLAPSED ONTO THE DECK, MY CHEST HEAVING, and felt the fear ebb away to be replaced by a powerful realisation of my own foolishness. Of all the things I had said I would never do, this was the most obvious. *Don't leave the boat!* And to be sure, I never would again. If I had been in danger of being complacent or blasé, this was the wake-up call that I needed.

As I felt the reassuring solidity of the warm deck against my back, I reflected that in the context of expeditions, nature rarely kills. It is much more likely to be human error—a poor choice of equipment, underestimating the conditions, or a bad judgment call. Robert Falcon Scott, Sir John Franklin, and George Mallory were all in very hostile environments, but ones in which others had survived. It only takes a single mistake at a key moment, or a series of minor mistakes that combine to create a catastrophe, to make the difference between life and death. Dropping a boat-hook is not in itself a disaster, but crucial moments had been lost while I shed garments and earbuds, and even the decision to try and salvage the hook was arguably a poor one, although my motives had been worthy.

The American novelist and newspaper editor Edgar Watson Howe once said: "A good scare is worth more to a man than good advice." I was inclined to agree. I had scared myself silly but the lesson had been well learned. As I vowed at the end of my confessional blog post, "From now on, no matter what goes overboard, I don't."

THAT NIGHT I HAD A DREAM. I WAS in the waves and could see my boat in the distance. I was trying to get back to it, but it was too far away. I was swimming and swimming, but to no avail.

Then there were millions of people in the water with me. We were all swimming as hard as we could, trying to get to my boat, except that now she was no longer my boat. She was a blue and green Earth, spinning gently on the waves like an enormous inflatable beach ball. The waves darkened, and sparkling stars of phosphorescence appeared.

Then we were swimming through space, our arms thrashing vainly in the vacuum. We had drifted away from our Earth, and now we were trying to return, but it was too late. We had become separated from our only life-support capsule, our solitary life raft in the big black vastness of the universe. Now we realised that we needed it, that without it we were lost and would die. But we had drifted too far, become too distant, and there was no way back. We were doomed.

I woke up with a jolt as the sound of a dying wave reverberated around the cabin. I felt sick and clammy and stuck my head out of the cabin hatch to get some fresh air. I looked up at the Milky Way and prayed that we would rediscover our connection to the Earth while there was still time.

CHAPTER NINE

ACHIEVEMENT

"Optimism is the faith that leads to achievement.
Nothing can be done without hope."

— HELEN KELLER

Having been fully prepared to spend the usual 100 or so days at sea, I was rather taken aback to find that I was clearly on track for a much faster crossing. By the time I was halfway through the third week, it looked like it might be just another two or three weeks before I made landfall. I would soon be entering the Solomon Sea, so in one sense the crossing of the Pacific Ocean proper would already be over, and from there it would not be far to Papua New Guinea.

I recorded in my blog:

> Given the unpredictability of where I would end up, let alone when, we have all been taken rather by surprise. For the last few days my mother and I have started to discuss arrival logistics, but there is a lot to do and a rapidly diminishing window of time in which to do it.

I had long since given up on my original goal of Cairns in Australia. I had known from the moment that I finally decided to head for Tarawa rather than Tuvalu that it would be all but impossible to make it to Queensland. Even supposing I was fortunate enough to make it into the Coral Sea, which lay between the Pacific and the eastern coast of Australia, the winds and currents in that stretch would all be coming out of the southeast and pushing me north while I was trying to get south. Even though, on a map of the world, Cairns may appear to be just around the corner from Papua New Guinea, not all ocean miles are created equal. Winds and currents can conspire against a slow-moving craft in such a way that, as my new weatherman, Lee Bruce, put it, "you can't get there from here."

So I had decided to follow in the footsteps, or wake, of Erden Eruç, and to aim instead for Papua New Guinea. This turned out to be a good plan. The currents in the western Pacific were astonishingly powerful. This was later explained to me by an oceanographer as follows: As the world spins, the currents bunch up on the western side of any major body of water. Waves work the same way; the greater the "fetch," or distance over which a wave gathers momentum, the larger it grows. It is like a rolling snowball, gaining more mass as it goes. The result of this was that the currents on this third and final stage of the Pacific were propelling me rapidly westwards.

There was a second reason that I was very open to the possibility of landing in Papua New Guinea. During one of my many conversations with Jean-Michel Cousteau at TED Mission Blue, we had discussed my final Pacific destination. "Oh, don't go to Australia. Eez boring!" he had declared in his charming French accent, which was so beguiling that no-body—not even an Australian—could possibly take offence at his words. "Madang eez very interesting. I spent a lot of time zere wiz my father"— meaning, of course, the legendary Jacques Cousteau. Jean-Michel had a way of saying things with such an air of authority that it allowed little scope for doubt or debate. If he said Madang was interesting, then interesting it must be, and there I would go.

AND, ULTIMATELY, I HAD LITTLE CHOICE. THE CURRENTS were so strong that I eventually covered the 2,248 miles in just 46 days, at an average rate of 49 miles a day. To put this in perspective, my previous personal best mileage for a single day had been a mere 42 miles.

On the one hand, this was very good news. I would be back on dry land much sooner than expected and would have time to enjoy the reward I had promised myself on completion of the Pacific project—a few weeks traveling in southeast Asia. The not-so-good news was I had been fully confident of losing the usual 20 to 30 pounds during my voyage, so I had cheerfully chowed down plenty of food to build up my bodily reserves before I set out. As I approached land, I still had plenty of bodily reserves remaining. I doubted I could fit back into my jeans. That's oceans for you—just when you think you've got them all figured out, they find a way to surprise you.

As I contemplated this unexpectedly early end to my row, I confided in my blog:

> It's quite exciting to think that I could be sipping sundowners in Madang around the end of the month, but it has its downsides too. Tonight, as I sat eating my dinner and watching one of the more spectacular sunsets to grace the skies during this crossing, I couldn't help but feel a little melancholy at the thought of arriving in Madang. I doubt that there will be any familiar faces there to greet me. Nicole has important commitments in Hawai'i. Mum isn't up to taking the long flight from the UK.
>
> So instead of a grand welcoming party, it could just be me pootling up to a dock, getting my passport stamped, and having a solitary beer in a yacht club bar. And then trying to rope in some local manpower to help me clean and prep the Brocade for her next voyage (the Indian Ocean).
>
> After a four-year, eight-thousand-mile adventure, this would be, well, a bit on the anticlimactic side. But I suppose that's the price I pay for landing up half a world away from most of my friends. I'll look at it this way—it will be a great opportunity for me to get to know new friends I haven't met yet.

WITH THESE THOUGHTS OF ARRIVAL, I WAS in danger of getting ahead of myself. The ocean had a few challenges in store for me yet. Day 26 did not get off to a good start. When I checked my GPS at about 4:30 A.M., I was in for a nasty surprise. I had gone to bed happy with my good west-by-southwest course. This would have got me safely past Cape Henpan at the northern tip of Bougainville Island, which marked the boundary between the Pacific Ocean and the Solomon Sea. But during the few hours between my bedtime and 4:30 A.M., the current had changed, and now the cape and I were on a collision course. Clearly the cape wasn't going to get out of my way, so I would have to get out of the cape's. Out I went into the deep darkness of the new-moon night to row my way out of potential disaster. It was not a very relaxed start to the day.

It didn't get much better. By lunchtime I had managed to break the arm off my one and only pair of sunglasses—one of the few things for which I had no spare—and my watermaker had droned to a halt for no apparent reason and refused to restart. I had no idea what the problem might be. Battery? Motor? But I didn't have time to investigate—I was still rowing strenuously west to try and avoid land.

As the current dragged me closer, I could see cliffs, dense trees, and white sandy beaches. It all looked lovely in a picture-postcard kind of way, but it held no appeal for me. There was nothing to be gained by attempting to land on the beach, and potentially much to be lost, including my rudder.

My mind flickered back to a conversation I'd had with Captain Vince of the *White Holly*. He, Nicole, and I had been standing on the bridge of his ship in Sausalito some time after our emergency mission to salvage the *Brocade*, chatting about the Pacific crossing. He had been rifling through the drawers of his chart cabinet to see if he had any maps of the Pacific that he could give me. He had found a chart that spanned the entire ocean from California to Australia. It had been printed in the 1950s, according to the legend in the bottom right-hand corner, so it was rather out of date but better than nothing. The future Republic of Kiribati was still labeled as the Gilbert and Ellice Islands, Phoenix Islands, and Line Islands.

As we discussed my options for landfalls en route, Captain Vince pointed to an island on the left side of the chart. "You don't want to land there," he'd said. "They still eat people." He jabbed his finger at a couple of other island groups. "Or there, or there."

Nicole had looked up from the chart to stare at me, her eyes as big as saucers. "Really?" she had asked. "Oh Lordy."

I HADN'T BEEN SURE IF CAPTAIN VINCE was telling the truth or if he was just teasing. At the time it hadn't seemed to matter much either way, as I was planning to aim for Australia, well to the south and, to the best of my knowledge, mostly cannibal-free. But now the conversation came back to haunt me. Where had those islands been? Weren't they around here somewhere? Could it really be true that cannibals still existed?

It was just then that I saw three small boats heading across the water towards me. I started to move the oars just a little faster. I was sure I was being ridiculous. Surely cannibalism had died out centuries ago. But I didn't want to find out the hard way that I was wrong.

I was about a half mile offshore when the men reached me. They were in dugout canoes with outriggers, using large carved wooden paddles. The first man to approach wore a faded red T-shirt with "Digicel" emblazoned across his chest and a baseball cap bearing the legend "USA." The next to arrive had dreadlocks and a pair of sunglasses propped on his forehead. He was stripped to the waist to reveal a well-muscled torso. The third kept his distance.

Mr. Digicel bared his teeth at me. They were stained dark red. *Cannibal!*

Or, to put it another way, when I came to my senses and banished Captain Vince's disturbing words from my mind:

Mr. Digicel smiled at me. He had been chewing betel nut. *Friend!*

The betel nut is the round green nut, or to be more botanically correct, the drupe, of the areca tree. When chewed, usually with lime, it has a mildly stimulant effect. Like tobacco chewers, betel chewers tend to spit frequently, and I would later see gobbets of red liquid staining the roads of Madang. To the uninitiated, the visible effects of betel-nut chewing are rather alarming, as the nut permanently stains the teeth a dark crimson.

During a trip to India a few years previously, I had seen streaks of betel-nut juice, usually misdirected in the general vicinity of litter bins, so I knew enough to realize that Mr. Digicel had probably been chewing on the fruit of the areca rather than on human bones. The sight of a spool of fishing line and a collection of lumps of coral to use as weights in the bottom of his dugout canoe reassured me that he was much more interested in eating fish than small female ocean rowers.

Digicel and Dreadlocks grasped hold of the gunwales of my boat and said something to me. They didn't seem hostile, so I assumed that it was some form of greeting, and greeted them in return.

This initial exchange of pleasantries over, our conversation stalled.

I cast around for a way to show my friendly intentions. I pulled out the chart from my sleeping cabin, and tried showing them where I had come from, relative to where we were now. Digicel took hold of the chart and peered closely at it as I pointed at the relevant outlines of islands, but I didn't see any flash of recognition. It may well have been the first chart that he had ever seen. I didn't suppose they had much need for them. Their world probably consisted of their village, the coastline, and a few choice fishing spots. I wondered if he even understood the concept of a chart.

I do not in any way intend to cast aspersions on his intelligence. I have no doubt at all that if it came to a fishing competition, he would beat me hands down. I simply mean that charts are, when you think about it, not completely intuitive. If you had lived completely in a three-dimensional world of forest, beach, and ocean, then what would these random two-dimensional squiggles on a yellowing sheet of paper mean to you?

As conversation flagged once again, challenged beyond survival by the lack of a common language or even a common frame of reference, I resorted to the international language of food. I offered them each a Lärabar, which seemed to please them. I wasn't sure what they would make of the chewy, fruity, nutty bars, but I felt that at least I had shown an appropriate degree of hospitality.

Having completely exhausted my repertoire of non-language-based gestures of friendship, I unshipped my oars and departed, giving them a cheery wave. I watched, slightly nervously, as I rowed away, wondering if they would follow, but they obviously had more important matters to attend to and headed in the opposite direction. I have no idea what they made of me and my strange craft and my odd piece of paper with strange shapes on it.

I pondered the contrast between our lives. I had lived in places such as Cambridge, Oxford, London, New York, and San Francisco, while they lived in thatched huts on Bougainville Island in the Solomon archipelago.

I ate in restaurants and bought my food from supermarkets. They picked coconuts and caught fish. Until recently I had never heard of Bougainville Island. And maybe they had never heard of London, somewhere on the opposite side of the globe. We were literally worlds apart. Neither was better or worse, but they were undeniably different. I was as anomalous in their world as they would have been in mine. I knew that there were places in Papua New Guinea where first contact between white men and indigenous people had taken place within living memory. Globalisation is in every sense a foreign concept here. In some ways this planet feels like a small and ever-shrinking world, while in other ways still mind-bogglingly diverse.

As the next few days passed and I continued into the Solomon Sea, I became increasingly concerned by the number of vessels I was seeing. No dugout canoes, these, but enormous container ships. Compared with the second stage of the row, when I had seen only one ship in 104 days, there were times on the Solomon Sea when I could see 5 at one time. It felt very crowded, and it made me nervous.

Although I have always told myself—and my mother—that the bow wave of a container ship would probably push my little boat to one side like a cork on the water, I am not completely convinced of this and sincerely hope never to put it to the test. I kept my Sea-me radar target enhancer turned on at all times. The Sea-me (which, as Boro Lucic of the MTC had proudly told me, was made in Montenegro, just like him) is a white pole, about two feet high, fixed to the top of my sleeping cabin. It is designed to make my boat look much larger than its actual size on the radar of any nearby vessels. It connects to a unit inside my sleeping cabin that flashes a red light and sounds an alarm when it detects a ship's radar scanner. This is not conducive to a good night's sleep, but is preferable to being run over in the dark.

Most nights I would be awakened from my shallow sleep by the alarm, and responding groggily to its urgent beeping, I would stick my head out of the cabin to take a look. Sometimes I could see nothing at first and would have to clamber right out of the cabin to get a 360-degree view. Even then, sometimes there would be only a distant dot that would soon disappear over the horizon. The Sea-me is an invaluable piece of safety equipment, but I often wished that those industrious Montenegrins had devised a way to make the alarm indicate the proximity of the radar-emitting vessel, either in the loudness or the frequency of the beep. It might have resulted in fewer false alarms and more sleep.

Feeling extremely vulnerable, I would have liked a lot more lights on my boat. Usually I prefer to be stealthy, not seeking out contact with other vessels nor wishing to attract their attention. But at this point I would have preferred to be lit up like a Christmas tree. I improvised an all-round white light from the refractive plastic casing of one of my solar-powered rail lights, fitted over an LED light that was a relic from an old video-camera system. A few cable ties held the casing in place. When I plugged the LED light into the 12-volt socket to give it power, it looked like a very miniature, and very homemade, version of a lighthouse. It wasn't especially elegant, but it worked and at least gave me the happy delusion that I was marginally more visible to any passing ships.

ONE DAY I WAS, IF ANYTHING, TOO visible. I turned around at the end of a rowing shift to see a small container vessel a few hundred yards away. As usual, I was rowing naked, so I quickly dived into the cabin to put on shorts and a sports top. There was no point in trying to hide, because there was absolutely no doubt that they had seen me and were coming over to take a closer look. So once I was decent, I picked up the VHF radio to make contact.

The voice on the radio was friendly and asked if I needed food or water, or if I wanted them to pass on a message. I thanked them and said I had more than enough provisions and adequate communications. I was tempted to ask if they had any ice cold drinks—I wouldn't really mind what it was, so long as it was cold and didn't come in a plastic bottle— but I resisted the impulse.

They called back a minute later to confirm the spelling of *Brocade*. They said they wanted to report my position. I was none too happy about this, but couldn't think of any valid reason for asking them not to. So I reluctantly spelled out my boat's name for them.

As I rowed on, I could just imagine what they might be saying. "Hey guys, you'll never guess what we just saw. There's this crazy naked Englishwoman rowing across the ocean. Check it out!"

The next thing that happened was that my post-lunch siesta was interrupted by a loud droning noise. I lifted the sunhat off my face and scanned the sky. A helicopter was rapidly approaching. I hardly had time to dive back into the cabin and scramble into my clothes again before they were about 50 yards away, hovering just feet above the water. We had a vague kind of exchange over the VHF radio, but it was mostly drowned out in the din of their engine. After about five minutes they roared off into the blue sky, leaving behind one distinctly discombobulated ocean rower. Even though I was now drawing close to land, I had got very used to having the ocean all to myself and my pelagic friends, and I did not at all welcome these human intrusions.

In fact, I was starting to feel like an exhibit at a zoo. I hadn't realized I was within helicopter range of land. But surely that had to be the end of unwanted attentions for the day. So I went back to my usual ocean outfit of sun hat, rowing gloves, and iPod, and carried on rowing. I had my earbuds in, listening to the excellent audiobook of *Hotel on the Corner of Bitter and Sweet,* so I didn't hear the next helicopter until it was too late. When I finally noticed, it was hovering about 30 yards away, the crew waving to me from the open door of the cockpit. With a girly shriek I let go of the oars and tried to cover as much of my nakedness as a wide-brimmed sun hat could be made to conceal—which was nowhere near enough.

I kept my clothes on for the rest of the day, so of course nobody else turned up. I grumpily supposed that I would have to keep myself clad for the remainder of my voyage. It would be terribly inconvenient. Clothes get sweaty and smelly and are less easily washed than skin. And in the future I had also best check the horizon and skies before I used my open-air bathroom.

All in all, I simply felt that I had not had my full quota of me-time for the year. Although on dry land I am gregarious enough and can happily go out every night for months on end, I appreciate my social life all the more for its contrast with the decidedly unsocial part of my year spent at sea. I can enjoy each extreme because I know it is only a matter of time before I find myself back at the other end of the spectrum. If I get too much of one or not enough of the other over a 12-month period, I feel decidedly out of balance.

It wasn't as if I were lonely. I was getting really rather fond of the little entourage of yellow fish that had gathered beneath my boat and kept me company for many hundreds of miles as I rowed across the ocean. When I paused and they didn't have to swim to keep up, it was fun to watch them taking time out to squiggle around, flipping and flopping at the water's surface. They were loyal little fellows, and I wondered what they would do when I was finished.

BUT LAND WAS COMING UP FAST, READY or not. Now that I had entered the Solomon Sea, I had to loop to the south. The currents in the Solomon swirl in a clockwise direction. I had entered this rotary system at its two o'clock position, and wanted to exit it at ten o'clock. To try and take the shortcut there by going anticlockwise, via twelve o'clock, was impossible. I would be going head to head with the current, and it would win. So I would have to go the long way around the system clockwise, via the bottom of the dial, instead.

After narrowly avoiding bumping into Woodlark Island lying at seven o'clock, I continued clockwise towards the Vitiaz Strait at ten o'clock. The strait is an 18-mile-wide corridor between the main island of New Guinea, the second largest island in the world, and the smaller island of New Britain, which together with a few more islands comprise the nation of Papua New Guinea. Overall, the land area of the country is slightly larger than California, or twice the size of Britain. The Vitiaz Strait represented the final stage of my journey to Madang.

As I neared the strait, the shipping traffic intensified. It looked as if everyone was heading to and from the same waters where I was bound. I'd planned to try and shoot straight down the middle, keeping a safe distance from land on either side, but decided that wouldn't be such a good idea if it put me right in the middle of a major shipping lane. Instead I decided to try and get through the strait in daylight and to keep to the northeasterly, or upwind, side so that I would be unlikely to get swept ashore. Once through the strait, I guessed that the ships would take the shortest route, so if I stayed a bit farther offshore I should be safe.

On Day 43 I was up and rowing before sunrise, and as it got light I could see the outline of Papua New Guinea to the southwest, looming high on the horizon, green and mountainous. Its craggy silhouette reminded me of the Hawai'ian island of O'ahu. As I got closer to the Vitiaz Strait, there was considerable maritime traffic, including a container ship that got rather too close for comfort, passing less than 100 yards from my bow. As it rumbled past I could easily see its name emblazoned down its enormous side: *Golden Shui*. It was about 300 yards long.

It is hard to describe the sheer scale of these monsters of the sea, which are so much bigger than anything that could travel on a road. I can only describe it as being like seeing a huge office block sweep past at 15 knots. I hardly ever saw a person on board these enormous vessels, nor was I able to raise them on the marine radio. These were huge, impersonal, scary juggernauts.

A little later there was a mild commotion amongst the fishy followers under my boat. A large shape lurked beneath. I got some fleeting footage on my video camera, which defied later identification, but I suspected it was a shark. As I was leaning over the side to try and capture it on film, the big critter made a sudden movement towards the bow of my boat, punching through the surface of the water and making me jump. Memories of *Jaws* came to the fore, and I emitted a frightened squeal. Just because I could appreciate the desperate plight of the world's sharks didn't necessarily mean I wanted to get up close and personal with one, unless perhaps it were a vegetarian, like the whale shark I'd seen on the middle stage of the row.

That afternoon the wind picked up considerably, resulting in the windiest day I'd had thus far. It was coming out of the south and made for choppy rowing conditions. The good news was that it helped put me exactly where I wanted to be—to the northeast side of the strait, out of the main shipping route.

After the roaring winds of the day, the following night was eerily quiet and dark. In daylight I had been able to see land all around—Papua New Guinea, New Britain, Umboi Island, and various low-lying rocks— but as the sun set it all disappeared into the darkness. No lights. No ships. No moon. Just the occasional flash of distant lightning illuminating the clouds, and my little boat an oasis of brightness in the darkness.

DURING THOSE LAST FEW WEEKS, ONCE we realized how soon I was going to arrive, my mother had been hard at work establishing local contacts.

Thanks to David Lambourne, our guardian angel in Tarawa, we had been put in touch with the former governor of Madang, Sir Peter Barter. As I closed in on the town, the timing of my arrival became critical. Sir Peter was keen to organize a proper welcome for me, involving some of the local people, so he needed to know when to expect me. Yet it was almost impossible to predict my arrival time with any degree of accuracy due to wild fluctuations in my speed.

On 1 June, just to the south of Long Island, I ran into some of the most extraordinary conditions I had ever encountered. Standing waves like white-water rapids slowed my progress to barely one knot. That afternoon I escaped the rapids, and in a fast-flowing current my boat speed rose to nearly five knots, the fastest speed I had ever sustained for more than the time it takes to coast down a wave.

The one date that had been ruled out was 3 June, as this was when Sir Peter had a prior commitment and could not be available. But whichever way I ran the numbers, it looked almost certain that I would arrive on 3 June. I couldn't go fast enough to arrive there earlier, nor slow enough to arrive there later. A phone call to Sir Peter established that his meeting was in the morning, so he could make himself available in the afternoon, and that became the target.

In fact, I would meet Sir Peter for the first time a day earlier, on 2 June. But by "meet," I don't mean in the sense of shaking hands. That would have been rather difficult, as he was busy flying a helicopter and I was busy rowing a boat, so our hands were otherwise occupied as well as being some considerable distance apart. I had been warned that Sir Peter might be dropping in, so I had the opportunity to ensure that I was appropriately clad.

I saw the sleek blue helicopter as it approached, swooping low over the waves. As it came closer, the wind from the rotors beat the water into concentric rings and blew my sun hat off on one side of the boat at the same time that a bucket, dropped from the helicopter, plopped into the water on the other side. After making a split-second decision, I lunged for my trusty and cherished hat and retrieved it first, before stepping smartly across the boat and over the guardrail, executing a neat dive into the blue waters to retrieve the bucket. After my near-fatal misadventure with the boathook, when I'd almost been separated from the boat, I could have been forgiven for being a little nervous about jumping overboard. But with the helicopter hovering overhead I felt sure that I wouldn't be left to drown. I reached the bucket and sidestroked back to the boat, pulling it alongside me.

Having seen that I was safely back on board, Sir Peter dipped the helicopter and peeled away, leaving me to pull off the masking tape that bound the lid to the bucket and discover the goodies within: a ham-and-cheese sandwich in a Styrofoam (oh dear) takeout box; three cans of beer packed with ice (hurrah); a thermos bowl containing a tropical fruit salad; a mobile phone still in its packaging; and an information pack comprising a newspaper announcing my imminent arrival, a covering letter from Sir Peter welcoming me to Madang, and a brochure from the Madang Resort. This was Sir Peter's resort, and he had already offered me a room for a month as his guest. It looked very luxurious, holding rich promise of the yearned-for white fluffy towels and crisp, clean sheets. I was impressed. This was the kind of welcome I could get used to.

THE FOLLOWING DAY I MET ANOTHER RESIDENT of Madang. In marked contrast to Sir Peter and his shiny, dark blue helicopter, Jan Messersmith came out in a scruffy little yellow-and-blue dive boat (what was with it me and yellow boats?), aptly named the *Faded Glory*, to find me. As the boat approached, I could see a compact, trim man at the wheel. He had a long white ponytail, a close-cropped white beard, and an extensive collection of tattoos. He was wearing shorts, a vest, and a big pair of aviator sunglasses.

He had heard that I was on my way towards Madang and on a whim had set out to try and find me—a task that, without knowing my current position, would be like trying to find the proverbial needle in the haystack. I would later find out that he had spent a couple of hours searching for me before flagging down a passing banana boat to ask them if they had seen "a woman in a big rowboat." They reported that they had seen "something over there," and Jan had followed their vague wave in my general direction. A few minutes later, he had spotted me through his binoculars and approached.

I generally do not appreciate visitors at sea, so I very much appreciated Jan's diffident, almost shy, approach. After greeting me and introducing himself, we discussed whether I was going to make landfall before dark or if I would have to wait until the next morning. Jan was a photographer and was keen to capture some images of me rowing past the iconic Coastwatchers' Memorial, a lighthouse flashing a tribute to those who stayed behind enemy lines during World War II to report on Japanese troop and ship movements, located at the entrance to the Dall-man Passage. After rowing an entire ocean, it would indeed be a shame to squander this photo opportunity by arriving after nightfall. But I knew I was running out of daylight hours. Jan offered to give me some space while I pushed ahead, and we could convene again in an hour or so to assess the situation. He revved his engine and guided the *Faded Glory* to a respectful distance. I returned to my oars.

A while later, as promised, I saw the little yellow boat approach once more. I had been running the numbers and reckoned I would probably arrive at the Coastwatchers' between 7 and 9 P.M.—too late. Jan had also been running the numbers and agreed. My arrival would have to wait until the next day.

Jan offered to keep me company, but in such a tactful way that I felt able to say I would just as soon be by myself. As I neared the end of my voyage, I wanted to cherish these final moments of solitude. So he handed over a plastic bag containing a few cans of beer (more beer!) and some potato chips, opened up the *Faded Glory*'s throttle, and headed back to port.

Jan's visit had been in the morning, and I continued rowing throughout the heat of the day. Sir Peter had suggested that I check in at regular intervals using the mobile phone to keep him updated on my estimated time of arrival, which I duly did.

During one of the phone calls he had asked me what foods I had been missing, and did I like seafood. Already feeling thoroughly spoiled, with the care packages from both him and Jan (but also a little put out that I had accumulated as great a volume of trash in the last 24 hours as in the previous 45 days), this was like having my fairy godmother grant me three wishes—not that Sir Peter bore any physical resemblance to a fairy godmother, as I would later find out, being a burly, middle-aged

Australian with sun-freckled skin. He said he would come out again to-wards sunset to see how I was getting on.

He was as good as his word. Late in the afternoon, I saw a large yacht heading towards me at a brisk clip. Sir Peter's boat, like his helicopter, was new and shiny, a large white motor cruiser with the words *Kalibobo Spirit* inscribed in bold blue letters down its side.

There was quite a party on board. People crowded the rails as the yacht motored over to me and stopped. Sir Peter stepped onto the swim deck to personally hand over two enormous platters of seafood and fresh fruit, and a bottle of champagne. I tried to find suitable places to put them, no mean feat on a boat more accustomed to meals in mugs than large silver salvers. There was enough food to feed a men's heavyweight rowing eight.

Sir Peter introduced various smiling faces. I have to confess that the only ones I can remember are Richard Coleman, the English principal of the Papua New Guinea Maritime College, and his wife, Tekla. I am not very good at grasping names at the best of times, and after more than six weeks of isolation, suddenly there was an awful lot of sensory input.

As the sun was setting, the yacht left to return the partygoers to shore, Sir Peter promising to come back later to escort me in. I looked forward to my last opportunity for several hours of peace before the *Kalibobo Spirit* returned. I gulped down a load of the fresh fruit and got back to the oars. A stitch in my side soon made me regret my gluttony.

THE FINAL FEW HOURS OF MY PACIFIC CROSSING, after the return of the *Kalibobo Spirit*, felt psychologically hectic. It was dark by now, and the main challenge was navigation. I was sure I had the right coordinates for the entry to the Dallman Passage, as provided by my trusty weatherman, and I could see clearly on the screen of my GPS where I needed to go. But I kept receiving phone calls and booming announcements over the tannoy of the *Kalibobo Spirit*, telling me to correct my course. I had been rowing since 3 A.M. and became increasingly grumpy about this interference. I fondly reminisced about my arrival in Hawai'i, when the crossing of the line of longitude of the Waikiki Yacht Club had been a peaceful, serene, and solitary moment.

At last, at 11 P.M., I finally passed the Coastwatchers' Memorial. As I entered the Dallman Passage, the tannoy voice stopped booming, and I sighed with relief. I had arrived.

Well, almost. I wasn't allowed to set foot on land until I had cleared customs, and the customs officials had long since gone home for the night. We tethered my boat to the back of the *Kalibobo Spirit*, and I spent the night on board the larger vessel. I considered making the most of the opportunity to spend a final night on my boat, but ultimately the deciding factor was access to a proper bathroom. Having seen far too much human waste fouling the Solomon Sea on my way in, I did not want to add to the problem, especially this close to land.

Staggering into my cabin around midnight, wobbly-legged and exhausted, I took a wonderful hot shower and collapsed into the most comfortable bed I had ever had the pleasure of sleeping in. It was blissfully soft and downy. I felt like I was sleeping in a warm, dry cloud.

FIVE SHORT HOURS LATER THERE WAS A BRISK RAP at the door of my cabin, rousing me from a deep sleep. It was time to get up for the ceremonial arrival. We towed *Brocade* back out to sea, and after a quick phone call to Mum, I took up my oars again and re-rowed the last segment of my journey. The first local people to congratulate me were a few early fishermen, paddling their outrigger canoes, who formed an orderly line to pass close to my boat and shake my hand.

They were just the first of many. As I neared the harbour, a flotilla of about 20 canoes, bedecked in traditional garlands of leaves, came out to join me and escort me to the dock. A helicopter buzzed overhead, shooting video and photos. Everybody was smiling, especially me. I kept stopping to wave to the crowds, who waved back enthusiastically. I wished there were a way to row and wave at the same time.

As I got closer to the dock, the crowds on the shoreline thickened. Schoolchildren in uniform created blocks of colour, red and blue. As I rounded the corner towards the Madang Resort, the harbour wall was absolutely packed. The estimated number was 5,000 people, and I don't think that was an exaggeration.

The customs officials had set up a makeshift office on the dock, and as I stepped off my boat I was escorted to a table where I sat down opposite a row of uniformed men and one woman. It was a faintly surreal scene, an office out of doors, on a quayside. I handed over my passport, answered questions, and signed forms. Once we had completed the formalities on the dock, I was free to step ashore. I was met by the governor of Madang, Sir Arnold Amet, who explained the meaning of the traditional offerings I was being given. Not just garlands but also string bags, known as *bilims,* were placed around my neck, like outsize necklaces. I later noticed that most people wore their bilims in similar fashion, rather than slinging them over their shoulders as a Westerner might.

As Sir Peter escorted me through the crowd everyone was reaching out to shake my hand or touch me. Brown faces crowded in on every side. Mobile phones pushed into my face as people took photographs. It was quite overwhelming to be surrounded by such a crush of humanity after 46 days at sea, even though it was less than half the time of my previous rows.

I was startled when a woman pushed back my baseball cap and slapped white powder onto my forehead. I was later told that this was a traditional welcoming gesture, but at the time it was quite a surprise. The baseball cap fell off, and such was the crush that a young man caught it before it even hit the ground. He asked me if he could keep it. I hesitated. I had become rather attached to that hat. But what the heck, it would probably mean more to him than to me.

"Sure," I nodded. "Have it."

Sir Peter guided me to a microphone set up at the waterside and I said a few words. A group from the Madang Technical College, standing beneath a homemade banner depicting me, my boat, and words of congratulations on my environmental mission, sang the national anthem. There was more handshaking and gift giving—more bags, a round cooking pot, a bunch of bananas, a handful of betel nuts.

At last Sir Peter extricated me and we escaped the crowds. He showed me to my room in a small annexe of the Madang Resort, just next to the dive shop behind a large metal gate. He explained that they had given me this room, usually reserved for the dive instructor, so I would be able to keep an eye on my boat. *Brocade* had by now been transported around the corner from the dock and was moored on long lines in the middle of a small lagoon, far enough from the banks to deter the curious from stepping aboard. I was grateful for their consideration. It seemed my every need had been anticipated and taken care of.

Throughout the day a steady procession of people came to see the boat. As I walked around the resort, yet more people shook my hand and congratulated me. It seemed hilarious that I had ever worried that there would be nobody to greet me in Madang. Had I really thought I was going to skulk quietly into town and then go and buy myself a solitary beer of celebration? Nothing could have been further from the truth.

I noted in my blog that night, after dinner with the governor:

It has been a day to remember, for sure. Spectacular. Thank you to everybody who has played a part—everybody here in Madang, the Governor, Sir Peter Barter, the staff at the Madang Resort, and of course my wonderful, indefatigable mother—my absent crewmate.

And thank you also for all the messages of congratulations that have been rolling in from all over the world. Thank you for your love, empathy, kindness and support during this third and final stage of my voyage. I feel very lucky that you are there for me through the highs and the lows, the trials and tribulations, and at last the final joyous celebrations at the successful conclusion of this 4-year, 250-day, 8,000-mile, 2.5 million oarstroke epic adventure. It's been special.

I had just become the first woman to row solo across the Pacific Ocean.

EPILOGUE

*"Being human always points, and is directed, to something,
or someone—other than oneself—be it a meaning to fulfill or
another human being to encounter. The more one forgets
himself—by giving himself to a cause or to another person to
love—the more human he is."*

— Viktor Frankl

My search for happiness and meaning took place on the Pacific Ocean, but I hope that we are all, in our own ways, searching for happiness and meaning, and where and how we conduct that search matters not one iota. This is what binds us, our shared mission as conscious and evolving human beings.

But do we search in vain? Has anybody, ever, convincingly claimed that they have found the meaning of life? Personally, I don't believe that there is such a thing—by which I mean that there is no intrinsic meaning to our existence. However, I do most strongly and strenuously believe that it is essential to happiness that we imbue our time here on Earth with meaning. Life does not create the meaning for us. We have to define it for ourselves. Note that I said *define*, not *find*. In my view, we don't *find* the meaning of life, any more than we *find* ourselves. We choose our beliefs about who we are and why we are here in order to reassure ourselves that we have significance, that we do not just get born, procreate (or not), and die.

It doesn't even matter whether we think we have found the answer or not. It is the fact that we are searching that matters. It is the search itself that gives meaning to our lives, lends our existence a narrative arc, makes us feel that we are on a quest, a journey, a trajectory. Without that sense of life's great adventure, it would be hard indeed to feel that life has meaning.

I saw my voyage across the Pacific as having three layers of significance. Superficially, it was an attempt to reach the other side. This was no doubt an intrepid and worthy endeavour, but to me it was the least important of the dimensions. To keep me motivated there had to be more to it than that.

The second layer was my environmental mission. Having belatedly discovered my environmental conscience, this was a powerful driving force. I passionately wanted to do all I could to spread the good green word.

Those two layers are external. But there had to be an internal driver as well. There may be some people in the world who can perform heroic feats out of pure altruism. I am not one of them. I needed to get something out of this too. And, in fact, I have got many, many things out of my experiences. I have felt part of something bigger than just myself and my trifling desires. I have been made happy by sharing my experiences with my blog readers, from office workers to stay-at-home parents, from the physically afflicted to enthusiastic athletes, from the environmentally passionate to the (hopefully no longer) environmentally oblivious. I have cherished the relationships that have developed along my way, across diverse cultures and backgrounds, in person and online.

Even though I strongly dislike exercise (yes, you can laugh, but it's true), I enjoy the feeling at the end of a day's rowing, of a challenging job well done, of having conquered my aversions and persevered when I wanted to give up. I am grateful for the way that the hardships of life at sea make me appreciate anew the comforts and conveniences of dry land that I previously took for granted. I love the sense of achievement that comes from trying new things—a new skill such as fixing a problem in the electrical system or exploring a new place. I relish having a clearly defined goal and working methodically towards it, knowing every day that I am getting a bit closer. I enjoy feeling resilient, mentally strong, and able to cope with whatever life and the ocean throw at me.

And most of all, it makes me happy to believe that my life has meaning. I do not have children, so my legacy was never going to be in the form of passing on my genes. I had to find a different way to touch lives, to make a difference, to feel that there was some point to being me. I have tried hard to be a good person and to leave the world a better place. To feel that I have in any small way succeeded is to me a prize beyond measure, the most wonderful wealth that I could ask for, a form of prosperity that I would wish for the whole world to experience and enjoy. This, surely, is the ultimate goal of our search for happiness and meaning.

ACKNOWLEDGMENTS

To all those who have helped me over the years and whom I have not thanked sufficiently, I would now like to make amends. I may not have shown it at the time, but as I row across the vast oceans, I look around my boat and see all the evidence of your love and support, and I feel you there with me. There have been times when I have doubted my own ability to continue, but when surrounded by the visible tokens of your commitment to my cause, I carry on—if not for me, then for you.

First and foremost, I would like to thank the stalwarts of Team Roz: Nicole Bilodeau, Ian Tuller, Aenor Sawyer, Doug Grandt, Jay Gosuico, Liz Fischer, Conrad Wade, Lee Bruce, Ricardo Diniz, and Rick Shema. And of course, my long-suffering but ever-wonderful mother, Rita Savage.

Over the course of the four years of my Pacific crossing, I spent more time in California than on any other piece of dry land and made many good friends in that beautiful state. For your time, kindness, wisdom, hospitality, advice, skills, and occasional money, I would like to thank Michael Klayko and all at Brocade, Marcus Eriksen and Anna Cummins of the 5 Gyres Institute, Angela Hey and John Mashey, Leo Laporte, Nova Lee, Carina Riordan and David Marsland at eBay, my friends at Google, Rich Crow, Bob Simmons and Kelly Luttrell, Karl Corey, Dr. Barbara Block, Bob and Meryl Selig, John Kay, Dennis Bonney, Gordy Nash, Ellen Leanse, Taylor Milsal, Jamis MacNiven, Richard and Barbara Pivnicka, JB Benna, Martha Kaufeldt, Karen Morss, Bill Chayes, Deb Dennis, Bebe Flynn, Steve Bein and the Adventurers Club of Los Angeles, Joni Harlem, Nancy Glenn, Elena Zhukova and Aleksey Bochkovsky, Sharon Levin, Josh Jenson, Lenny Lieberman, Phil Keoghan, Doug Woodring, Carol Mone and Roger Choplin, Ed Osgood, Steve Nelson, John Dawson, Dawn Pasinski, Minette Siegel, Roger Barnett and all at Shaklee, Joslyn Podesto, Connie Cook, Betsy Rosenberg, Chris Lynch, Mike Korchinsky, Niland Mortimer, David and Maureen Wilmot, Michael Sutton, David Helvarg and Blue Frontier Campaign, Eva Boris, David Faivus, Robert Kibble, John and Sarah De Heras, Melinda Griffith, Jean-Michel Cousteau, Paul Nordquist,

Diane Davis, Reuben Hechanova, Kristian Ruggieri, Shana Bagley, Mark Tishler, Douglas Lubes, Mark Featherstone, Nancy Scurka, Inka Petersen, Rob Rosen and all at Remote Satellite Systems, my friends at the San Francisco Ocean Film Festival, Captain Stephen Baxter and the rest of the U.S. Coast Guard crew at Humboldt.

I also spent several months enjoying Hawai'ian hospitality and feel fortunate to have met many wonderful people there: Henk Rogers and Blue Planet Foundation, Bobbie Jennings and all at the Waikiki Yacht Club, Jeff Apaka, Andy Bumatai, Liz Jackson, Ray Hollowell, "Scuba" Drew Wheeler, Barry Pickering, Mike Marsh, Cindy Hunter, Barry Pickering and the rest of the Blue Lady crew, Tom Pohaku Stone, Ryan Ozawa and Burt Lum of Bytemarks, Mike Rush, Gary Brookins, Liz Jackson, Albert and Elise Yellin, Evan Rapoport, Brian Dote, Traci and Hunter Downs and all at Archinoetics, Joel Paschal and Sea of Change, Scott Burgess, Marlene Depierre, Mariya Gold, Kevin Seid, Morgan Kavanaugh, Stuart Coleman, Stuart Scott, Phil Uhl, Blackie and all at Pacific Shipyards.

Elsewhere in the U.S. and Canada I made some very special friends, including Eric Sanford, Michelle Slade, John and Claire Reid, Bob and Jamie Craft, Jon Stryker and Slo Randjelovic, Kathleen Frith and the women of Pleiades, Daniel and Joanna Rose, Kerri Kolen, Jim Paulson, Tim Harincar, Joan Sherwood, Bill Spinks, Richard Cort, Tom Hernon, Lori Burken and Bottomsiders, Roxana Lopez and Wilderness Family Naturals, Sarah McDowell and Lärabar, David Saunders, Ann Luskey, Laurin Ensslin, Martin Tryon, Paul Minshall, Mark Einreinhof, Suzy Mack, John Herrick, Jim Salzman, Vic Jones, Laurey Masterton, Cindy Dover, Deb and Michael Follo, Stan Miller, Bob Pavia, Doug DeMark, Susan Bartlett, Roger Friesen, Kevin Doheny and Margo Pellegrino. I would also like to pay tribute to Timothy Ray, a promising young man who was a third-year doctoral student at Scripps Institution of Oceanography when he organized a speaking engagement there for me in 2010. Tragically, Tim died suddenly and unexpectedly in May 2011, leaving as his legacy our memories of his passion for, and commitment to, the oceans.

Thank you to my wonderful friends in Kiribati for taking such good care of me and my boat: David and Tessie Lambourne, John and Linda Anderson, President Anote Tong, Captain Superintendent Boro Lucic and all the cadets of the Marine Training Centre.

Amongst the many kind people I met in Papua New Guinea, several went above and beyond to help a solitary stranger from the other side of the world. Thanks especially to Sir Peter Barter, Jan and Eunie Messersmith, Lachlan Monsbourgh, Richard Coleman, Martin and Shirley Tsang, and Sir Arnold Amet.

Although I spent only a few precious weeks in my home country during the Pacific years, I am grateful to my friends there for not forgetting or forsaking me. Special thanks to Alan Murray, Anthony Swift, Alun Rees, Shane Winser and the Royal Geographical Society, Sue Losson, Charlotte Voehtz and Green People, Steve and Jane Shorney, Polly Higgins, Misty Oldland, Catt McLeod, Rodney Byram, Sam and Ella Allpass. Also to my magnificent team for the hike from Big Ben to Brussels en route to Copenhagen: Jane Hornsby, Laura Hazell, Alison Gannett, Mary Kadzielski, Nora McDevitt, and our European supporters Baldwin and Aey Hopmans, Yves Mathieu, and Frank Koelewijn. Thanks also to Søren and Rikke Gaard for inviting a stranger into their home for the duration of the COP15 conference.

Amongst my many friends in the conservation/environmental world, I'd like to particularly thank three wonderful people who have been great role models to me: Bill McKibben at 350.org, Dr. Sylvia Earle at Mission Blue, and Cynthia Gaik Suan at LEAP. Also Dianna Cohen and Daniella Russo and the rest of the team at the Plastic Pollution Coalition, Stiv Wilson at 5 Gyres, Conrad Humphreys and Teresa Page at the Blue Project, and Shaw Thacher.

And thank you to the authors whose books transported me from my tiny rowboat into other worlds via their audiobook versions, particularly: Kim Stanley Robinson, Jacqueline Winspear, Alexander McCall Smith, Diana Gabaldon, Richard Russo, and George R. R. Martin.

My heartfelt thanks to those who helped this book to see the light of day: my indefatigable agent Taryn Fagerness, the wonderful folks at Hay House in both the UK and U.S., and my editor Jessica Kelley.

Although we hadn't yet met (in this lifetime, anyway) during the Pacific years, this list of acknowledgments would not be complete without a mention of my beloved soul mate, Howard, who supported and encouraged me during the writing of this book. Thank you for the happiness and meaning—and the love and laughter—you have brought into my life.

And finally, my endless gratitude to all the thousands of people who have read my blog over the years. Thank you for your time, your caring, your support, and your kind messages of encouragement in bad times and good. Possibly I could have done it without you, but it wouldn't have meant anywhere near as much. I hope I have made, and will continue to make, you proud.

ABOUT THE AUTHOR

Roz Savage, Member of the Order of the British Empire, is a British ocean rower, environmental campaigner, author, and speaker. She holds four world records for ocean rowing, including first woman to row solo across the Atlantic, Pacific, and Indian Oceans. She has rowed more than 15,000 miles, taken around five million oar strokes, and spent cumulatively more than 500 days of her life at sea in a 23-foot rowboat. Her first book, *Rowing the Atlantic: Lessons Learned on the Open Ocean,* was published in 2009. She is a United Nations Climate Hero, a fellow of the Royal Geographical Society, a fellow of the Explorers Club of New York, and has been listed among the Top 20 Great British Adventurers by *The Telegraph.* She was named a 2011 Adventurer of the Year by *National Geographic;* and in 2012, she became a Yale World Fellow.

Website: www.rozsavage.com

Hay House Titles of Related Interest

YOU CAN HEAL YOUR LIFE, the movie, starring Louise L. Hay & Friends
(available as a 1-DVD program and an expanded 2-DVD set)
Watch the trailer at: www.LouiseHayMovie.com

THE SHIFT, the movie,
starring Dr. Wayne W. Dyer
(available as a 1-DVD program and an expanded 2-DVD set)
Watch the trailer at: www.DyerMovie.com

ACTIVATE YOUR GOODNESS:
Transforming the World Through Doing Good,
by Shari Arison

THE ASTONISHING POWER OF EMOTIONS:
Let Your Feelings Be Your Guide,
by Esther and Jerry Hicks (The Teachings of Abraham)

THE INSIDE-OUT REVOLUTION:
The Only Thing You Need to Know to Change Your Life Forever,
by Michael Neill

TUNE IN: Let Your Intuition Guide You to Fulfillment and Flow,
by Sonia Choquette

YOU CAN CREATE AN EXCEPTIONAL LIFE,
by Louise Hay and Cheryl Richardson

All of the above are available at your local bookstore,
or may be ordered by contacting Hay House (see next page).

We hope you enjoyed this Hay House book.
If you'd like to receive our online catalog featuring additional
information on Hay House books and products, or if you'd like to
find out more about the Hay Foundation, please contact:

Hay House, Inc., P.O. Box 5100, Carlsbad, CA 92018-5100
(760) 431-7695 or (800) 654-5126
(760) 431-6948 (fax) or (800) 650-5115 (fax)
www.hayhouse.com® • www.hayfoundation.org

Published and distributed in Australia by: Hay House Australia Pty. Ltd.,
18/36 Ralph St., Alexandria NSW 2015 • *Phone:* 612-9669-4299
Fax: 612-9669-4144 • www.hayhouse.com.au

Published and distributed in the United Kingdom by: Hay House UK, Ltd.,
Astley House, 33 Notting Hill Gate, London W11 3JQ • *Phone:* 44-20-3675-2450 •
Fax: 44-20-3675-2451 • www.hayhouse.co.uk

Published and distributed in the Republic of South Africa by:
Hay House SA (Pty), Ltd., P.O. Box 990, Witkoppen 2068
Phone/Fax: 27-11-467-8904 • www.hayhouse.co.za

Published in India by: Hay House Publishers India,
Muskaan Complex, Plot No. 3, B-2, Vasant Kunj, New Delhi 110 070
Phone: 91-11-4176-1620 • *Fax:* 91-11-4176-1630 • www.hayhouse.co.in

Distributed in Canada by: Raincoast, 9050 Shaughnessy St.,
Vancouver, B.C. V6P 6E5 • *Phone:* (604) 323-7100
Fax: (604) 323-2600 • www.raincoast.com

Take Your Soul on a Vacation
Visit www.HealYourLife.com® to regroup, recharge,
and reconnect with your own magnificence.
Featuring blogs, mind-body-spirit news,
and life-changing wisdom from Louise Hay and friends.

Visit www.HealYourLife.com today!

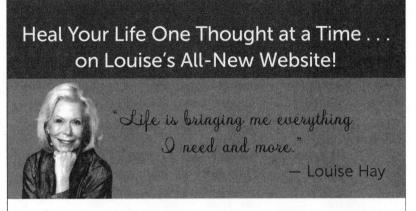